Visual Object Tracking with Deep Neural Networks

Edited by Pier Luigi Mazzeo, Srinivasan Ramakrishnan and Paolo Spagnolo

Published in London, United Kingdom

IntechOpen

Supporting open minds since 2005

Visual Object Tracking with Deep Neural Networks
http://dx.doi.org/10.5772/intechopen.80142
Edited by Pier Luigi Mazzeo, Srinivasan Ramakrishnan and Paolo Spagnolo

Contributors
Toshanlal Meenpal, Aarti Goyal, Moumita Mukherjee, Shahrel Azmin Suandi, Nuzrul Fahmi Nordin, Jia-Ching Wang, Viet-Hang Duong, Bui Manh Quan, Archana Sable, Soon Ki Jung, Mustansar Fiaz, Arif Mahmood, Muhammad Usman Ghani Khan, Gulraiz Khan, Zeeshan Tariq, Li Xiying, Zhou Zhihao, Ravi Sahu, Yogameena B, Nagavani C, Sangeetha A, Saravana Sri S

First published in London, United Kingdom, 2019 by IntechOpen
IntechOpen is the global imprint of INTECHOPEN LIMITED, registered in England and Wales, registration number: 11086078, 7th floor, 10 Lower Thames Street, London, EC3R 6AF, United Kingdom
Printed in Croatia

British Library Cataloguing-in-Publication Data
A catalogue record for this book is available from the British Library

Additional hard and PDF copies can be obtained from orders@intechopen.com

Visual Object Tracking with Deep Neural Networks
Edited by Pier Luigi Mazzeo, Srinivasan Ramakrishnan and Paolo Spagnolo
p. cm.
Print ISBN 978-1-78985-157-1
Online ISBN 978-1-78985-158-8
eBook (PDF) ISBN 978-1-78985-142-7

For EU product safety concerns:
IN TECH d.o.o., Prolaz Marije Krucifikse Kozulić 3, 51000 Rijeka, Croatia, info@intechopen.com or visit our website at intechopen.com.

Meet the editors

Pier Luigi Mazzeo obtained an MSc in Computer Science from the University of Salento, Lecce, Italy, in 2001. Since then, he has been working on several research topics regarding artificial intelligence and computer vision. Dr. Mazzeo joined the Italian National Research Council of Italy (CNR) as a researcher in 2002. He is currently involved in projects for algorithms for video object tracking, face detection and recognition, facial expression recognition, deep neural networks, and machine learning. He has authored and co-authored 80 publications, including 10 papers published in international journals and book chapters. He has also co-authored five national and international patents. Dr. Mazzeo acts as a reviewer for several international journals and for some book publishers. Since 2004, he has been regularly invited to take part in the scientific committees of national and international conferences.

Dr. Srinivasan Ramakrishnan has 20 years of teaching experience and one year of industry experience. He is a professor and the head of the Department of Information Technology at Dr. Mahalingam College of Engineering and Technology, Pollachi, India. He is an associate editor for *IEEE Access* and a reviewer for 25 international journals. He is also on the editorial board of seven international journals. Dr. Ramakrishnan is a guest editor for special issues in three international journals, including *Telecommunication Systems*. He has published 169 papers in international and national journals and conference proceedings. He has also published two books on cryptography and wireless sensor networks for CRC Press, six books on speech processing, pattern recognition, and fuzzy logic for IntechOpen, and a book on computational techniques for Lambert Academic Publishing.

Paolo Spagnolo received a five-year degree in Computer Science Engineering from the University of Salento, Lecce, Italy, in 2002. Since then, he has worked as a researcher at the Italian National Research Council. His research interests are in the field of artificial intelligence and computer vision. He is currently working on deep learning and its application in the field of automatic monitoring and surveillance of wide areas. He has authored and co-authored more than 100 publications in international journals, book chapters, and conference proceedings. He has also co-authored six national and international patents. He is co-editor of three international books. He has been involved in the organization of several international conferences and workshops. He also acts as a reviewer for several international journals.

Contents

Preface

Visual object tracking (VOT) and face recognition (FR) are both essential tasks in computer vision with various real-world applications, including human-computer interaction, autonomous vehicles, robotics, motion-based recognition, video indexing, surveillance and security. VOT and FT have remained active research topics due to both their opportunities and challenges. Significant efforts have been made by the research community in the past few decades, but VOT and FR have amazing potential still to be explored.

Major difficulties lie in different challenges, such as occlusions, clutter, illumination change, scale variations, low-resolution targets, target deformation, target re-identification, fast motion, motion blur, in-plane and out-of-plane rotations, and target tracking in presence of noise.

Traditional object tracking algorithms employed hand-crafted features like pixel intensity, color, and Histogram of Oriented Gradients (HOG) to represent the target in the object appearance model. Although hand-crafted features achieve satisfactory performance in constrained environments, they are not robust to severe appearance changes.

Recently, deep learning using a Convolutional Neural Network (CNN) has achieved a significant performance boost to various computer vision applications. VOT and FR have been affected by this popular trend in order to overcome tracking challenges and obtain better performance in respect to hand-crafted features.

This book presents the state-of-the-art and new algorithms, methods, and systems of these research fields by using deep learning. It is organized into nine chapters across three sections. Section I discusses object detection and tracking ideas and algorithms. Section II examines applications based on re-identification challenges. Section III presents applications based on FR research.

The editors thank the authors for their high-level contributions and their proactive collaboration in the realization of this book.

Pier Luigi Mazzeo and Paolo Spagnolo
National Research Council of Italy (CNR),
Institute of Applied Sciences and Intelligent Systems (ISASI),
Lecce

Srinivasan Ramakrishnan
Department of Information Technology at
Dr. Mahalingam College of Engineering and Technology,
Pollachi, India

Section 1

Detection and Tracking

Chapter 1

Deep Siamese Networks toward Robust Visual Tracking

Mustansar Fiaz, Arif Mahmood and Soon Ki Jung

Abstract

Recently, Siamese neural networks have been widely used in visual object tracking to leverage the template matching mechanism. Siamese network architecture contains two parallel streams to estimate the similarity between two inputs and has the ability to learn their discriminative features. Various deep Siamese-based tracking frameworks have been proposed to estimate the similarity between the target and the search region. In this chapter, we categorize deep Siamese networks into three categories by the position of the merging layers as late merge, intermediate merge and early merge architectures. In the late merge architecture, inputs are processed as two separate streams and merged at the end of the network, while in the intermediate merge architecture, inputs are initially processed separately and merged intermediate well before the final layer. Whereas in the early merge architecture, inputs are combined at the start of the network and a unified data stream is processed by a single convolutional neural network. We evaluate the performance of deep Siamese trackers based on the merge architectures and their output such as similarity score, response map, and bounding box in various tracking challenges. This chapter will give an overview of the recent development in deep Siamese trackers and provide insights for the new developments in the tracking field.

Keywords: Siamese networks, visual object tracking, deep learning, neural network, end-to-end learning

1. Introduction

In the past few decades, visual object tracking (VOT) has become a promising and attractive research field in computer vision area. It became popular among researchers due to its wide range of applications including autonomous vehicles [1, 2], surveillance and security [3, 4], traffic flow monitoring [5, 6], human computer interaction [7, 8] and many more. Popularity in the field is because of various tracking challenges and opportunities. In recent years, researchers have made remarkable endeavors and developed a number of state-of-the-art trackers to handle various tracking challenges. Despite the fact that significant progress has been made in the field but still trackers have not achieved consummate performance and VOT is still an open challenge yet to be fully addressed. Various challenges to be handled by VOT include fast motion, motion blur, occlusion, deformation, illumination variations, background clutter, in- or out-planer rotations, out-of-view, low resolution, and scale variations.

The objective of VOT is to identify a region of interest in video frames. VOT consists of four sequential components such as target initialization, target appearance modeling, motion estimation, and target localization. In target initialization, the region of interest is annotated using any of the representations including ellipse, centroid, object silhouette, object skeleton, object contour, or object bounding box. In generic object tracking, the position of the region of interest as the target is given in the first frame of a video and the tracking algorithm predicts the target location in the rest of the frames. The target appearance model represents a better target feature representation and a mathematical model to identify the region of interest using learning methodologies. While the target motion estimation module predicts the position of the target in sequential frames by either greedy search or maximum posterior prediction. The tracking problem is simplified as the constraints applied over the target appearance model and motion estimation. During tracking, both appearance and motion models are updated to capture the new target appearance and its behavior.

In this chapter, we focus on monocular, casual, model-free, short-term, and single-target trackers. The causality means that a tracker has the ability to estimate the target location in the current frame without prior information of the future frames. While model-free characteristic stands for supervised learning where target bounding box is given in the first frame of the video. Finally, short-term denotes that during tracking, a tracker is unable to re-detect the target once it is lost.

The performance of the trackers is highly affected by the feature representations. Features are broadly classified into hand-crafted (HC) and deep features. Traditional features are known as HC features such as histogram of oriented gradients (HOG), local binary patterns (LBP), color names and scale-invariant feature transform, etc. Nowadays, computer vision researchers are selecting deep features for better representation. Deep features are more capable to capture multi-level information and to encode the target appearance variant features compared to HC features. Deep features are extracted using different methods such as convolutional neural networks (CNN) [9], recurrent neural networks (RNN) [10], auto-encoder [11], residual networks [12], and generative adversarial networks (GAN) [13] for different computer vision applications.

In recent years, CNN-based methods have been adopted in various computer vision tasks and gained popularity due to improved performance in face verification [14], image classification [15], semantic segmentation [16], medical image segmentation [17], object detection [18], etc. An empirical and comprehensive study performed by Fiaz et al. [19] showed that deep trackers have shown an improved performance compared to HC feature-based trackers. The discriminative power of state-of-the-art deep trackers is explored by employing deep features. It is difficult to train a discriminative deep tracker efficiently due to data-hungry property. Various deep trackers are developed to handle scarce training data problem by employing shallow features extracted from pre-trained off-the-shelf models such as AlexNet [20], VGGNet [9], etc. Nevertheless, these approaches do not fully benefit from end-to-end learning. Deep trackers that apply stochastic gradient descent (SGD) methods are not real-time because they take a lot of time to fine-tune the multiple layers of the network.

In order to handle those restrictions, a simple advocate approach known as Siamese network is utilized to compute the similarity between the two input images. Siamese networks are trained offline to learn the similarity between two input images and are evaluated online without fine-tuning for new target estimation. In this chapter, we study different types of Siamese networks developed for tracking. We also present an experimental study to analyze the performance of the Siamese trackers over OTB2013 [21] and OTB2015 [22] benchmarks.

2. Related work

In the literature, there exist many comprehensive studies on VOT. Each study focuses on specific research aspects going on in the field. Fiaz et al. [19] classified the tracking algorithms into correlation and noncorrelation filter-based trackers. An extensive experimental study was performed over hand-crafted and deep feature trackers. Similarly, Li et al. [23] also studied the deep trackers and categorized deep trackers into three classes including network structure, network function, and network training. Leang et al. [24] discussed single target trackers while Zhang et al. [25] performed their study over the sparse trackers. Yang et al. [26] focused on the context information by considering auxiliary objects as the target context of the tracking object.

These studies have been performed by tireless efforts made by the research community and developed various state-of-the-art trackers. The tracking algorithms can be classified as tracking by detection, discriminative correlation filters, deep convolutional neural networks, and Siamese network-based trackers.

2.1 Tracking by detection-based trackers

In many tracking algorithms, classifiers are considered as the fundamental part to discriminate the target object from nontarget objects such as support vector machine (SVM), random decision forest, as well as various boosting-based classifiers. Classifiers are updated to integrate the new target appearance during online learning in various tracking by detection algorithms. For example, multiple instance learning framework proposed by Babenko et al. [27] employed gradient boosting to learn the classifiers. Hare et al. [28] utilized structured output to estimate the target location and employed SVM for online adaptive tracking. Zhang et al. [29] applied Bayes classifiers for online adaptation of the target over a multi-scale feature space built on a data-dependent basis.

2.2 Discriminative correlation filter-based trackers

The development of trackers based on correlation filters has boosted the tracking performance. Bolme et al. [30] proposed a fast tracker by minimizing the sum of squared error (SSE) between the actual output and the desired output in the frequency domain. Kernelized correlation filters (KCF) [31] utilized the multi-channel features using circulant matrices in the Fourier domain and used the Gaussian kernel function to discriminate a target from the background. The discriminative correlation filter trackers have their own limitations such as they require to fix model and patch sizes. A model may learn undesired information resulting in reduced performance. SRDCF [32] introduces a spatial regularization method in discriminative correlation trackers to reduce the effect of background information by penalizing it. SRDCFdecon proposed by Danelljan et al. [33] tackled the contaminated training samples to improve robustness. Li et al. [34] proposed STRCF that integrates the temporal regularization in SRDCF using a passive-aggressive algorithm to improve the tracking performance. CSRDCF [35] incorporates the channel and spatial reliability within correlation filters. CSRDCF integrates the spatial reliability using a spatial binary map at the target location, while the channel reliability by estimating the channel and detection reliability metrics.

2.3 Deep convolutional neural network-based trackers

Deep convolutional neural networks have presented an outstanding performance in many computer vision applications. Deep learning has limitations due to limited training data and high computational cost. However, much progress has been made and many state-of-the-art deep trackers have been proposed. Nam and Han employed CNN to develop a multi-domain adaptive deep tracker [36]. Nam et al. [37] integrated CNN in a tree structure to model the target appearance. A tree is constructed from multiple hierarchical CNN-based target appearances. Ma et al. [38] exploited the rich hierarchical deep features using correlation filters. Qi et al. [39] hedged the weak classifiers and obtained a strong classifier by captivating the benefit from multi-level deep features.

2.4 Template matching-based trackers

Tracking by matching is one of the most basic concepts in tracking where target pixels are directly compared with the input patches from the video. Briechle and Hanebeck [40] introduced the simplest template matching mechanism in tracking via a normalized cross-correlation. TLD-tracker [41] also employs normalized cross-correlation mechanism. Later on, many template matching trackers focused on distorted tracking objects. Wang et al. [42] performed matching using superpixels. Nguyen and Smeulders [43] used color invariants to discriminate targets from the background. Godec et al. [44] employed HOG features for probabilistic matching. Held et al. [45] used deep regression networks for matching. Bertinetto et al. [46] exploited fully convolutional features to compute the correlation between the target and the search patches.

In this section, we noticed that various tracking algorithms have been proposed to solve the tracking problem but still research area is active. We also observed that there exist different comprehensive surveys that focus on various tracking frameworks. On the contrary, we present a study on Siamese networks employed in tracking. We categorized the Siamese trackers into three categories. Moreover, we also evaluated the robustness of the different Siamese trackers.

3. Siamese networks for tracking

In correlation filter-based trackers, a response map is computed between a target template and a candidate patch in the Fourier domain. In object tracking, the center of the target is focused and a weight matrix w is trained such that it minimizes the squared error from the target y. The tracking problem can be defined as a regression problem which depicts a closed-form solution and is formulated as

$$\|Bw - y\|_2^2 + \lambda \|w\|_2^2, \tag{1}$$

where B is the search space feature vectors, λ is a regularization parameter, and $\|.\|2$ means the ℓ_2-norm of a vector. The solution for Eq. (1) is described as:

$$w = \left(B^T B + \lambda I\right)^{-1} B^T y. \tag{2}$$

Since Eq. (2) has high computational cost due to inverse matrix computation, thus cannot be used directly for tracking. Hence, the described problem can be resolved in the dual form as follows:

$$w = B^T \alpha, \tag{3}$$

where α denotes the discriminatory part. For tracking problems, the challenge is to optimize α in dual form solution in Eq. (3).

Another alternative approach is to learn a similarity function to compare the similarity between the template image and the candidate image. A Siamese network

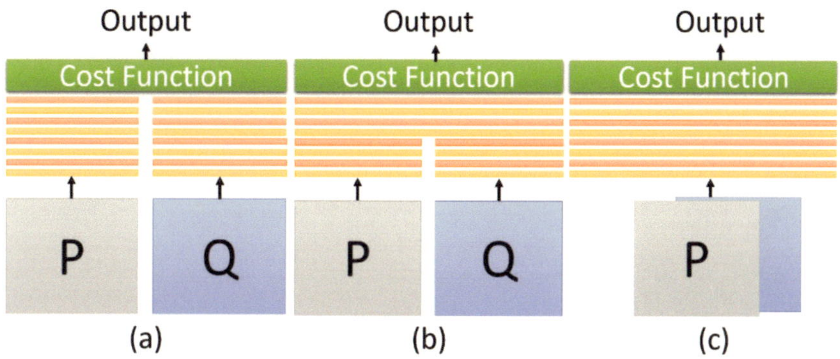

Figure 1.
Types of Siamese networks (a) Late merge, (b) Intermediate merge and (c) Early merge.

architecture is a Y-shaped network that takes two images as inputs and returns similarity as output. Siamese networks determine if the two input images have identical patterns or not. The concept of Siamese was initially introduced for signature verification and fingerprint recognition, and later adapted in many computer vision applications such as large scale video classification [47], stereo matching [48], face recognition and verification [49], and patch matching [50] etc. A series of state-of-the-art Siamese-based trackers have been proposed in the past few years. We observe that Siamese-based trackers utilize embedded features by employing CNN to compute the similarity. By analyzing the architecture of deep Siamese trackers, we classify them into three categories based on layer position of the merge; (i) late merge, (ii) intermediate merge, and (iii) early merge architectures as shown in **Figure 1**.

- Late merge: the input images are processed separately by two individual parallel networks and are merged at the last layer of the network (**Figure 1(a)**).

- Intermediate merge: the input images are processed separately in the initial part of the network and then merged well before the final layer (**Figure 1(b)**).

- Early merge: the input images are stacked before feeding to the network and then a unified input is fed forward to the network for inference (**Figure 1(c)**).

We also observe that Siamese-based trackers produce different types of output such as similarity score, response map, and bounding box. Siamese-based trackers with similarity score as output mean that they return the similarity as probability measure, whereas the response map means a two-dimensional similarity score map. The maximum value in the similarity map represents the location of maximum similarity between two patches and low value for the dissimilar region. Some Siamese-based trackers directly yield the bounding box location of the target.

3.1 Siamese late merge trackers

This subsection studies the tracker where the two input images are fed forward to two separate CNN models and are merged at the final layer to get the final response.

3.1.1 SINT

Siamese instance search tracker (SINT) is proposed by Tao et al. [51]. SINT learns an offline matching function and estimates the best-matched patch for incoming

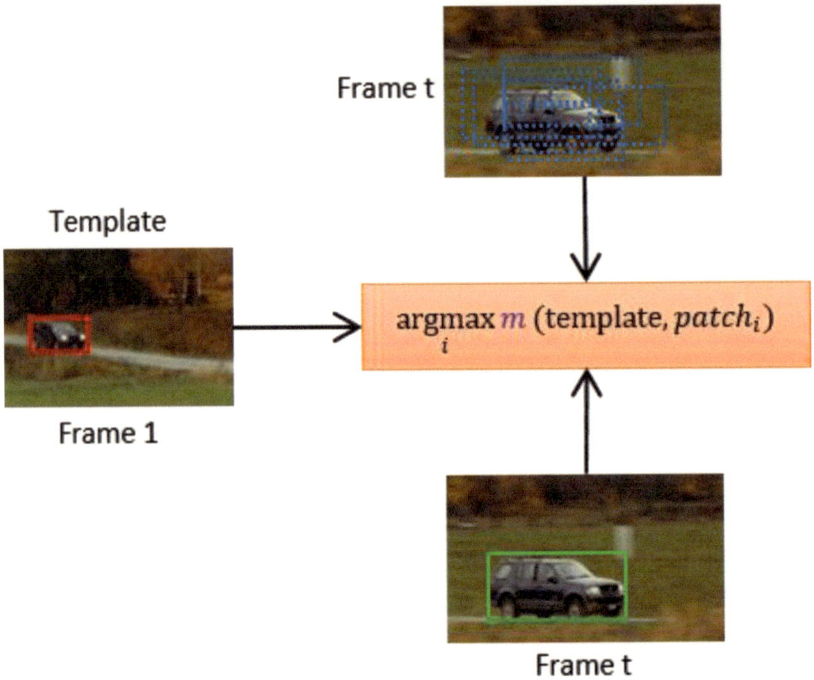

Figure 2.
SINT tracking framework [51].

frames in a video (**Figure 2**). The architecture of SINT consists of two streams including query stream and search stream. Each stream is composed of 5 convolutional layers, 3 region-of-interest pooling layers, and 1 fully connected layer. Both query and search streams are merged using a matching function known as contrastive loss function. The matching function is responsible to differentiate the background information from the target. The SINT is trained offline by giving template patch at query branch and candidate patches at the stream branch. During tracking, SINT does not update its weight parameters and template patch at query branch is matched with the candidate patches at the stream branch for each incoming frame. The SINT estimates the best-matched patch based on maximum score. A ridge-bounding box regression is employed to refine the bounding box.

3.1.2 SiameseFC

Siamese fully convolutional network (SiameseFC) proposed by Bertinetto et al. [46] addresses the general similarity learning between the target image and search image as shown in **Figure 3**. During training, SiameseFC exploits the deep features using embedding functions and learns the similarity between the two images. During tracking, SiameseFC takes two images and infers a response map. The new target position is estimated at the maximum value on the response map where input images have the maximum similarity.

3.1.3 CFNet

Valmadre et al. [52] proposed correlation filter network (CFNet) by adding two layers including correlation filter and crop layer within SiameseFC template branch which makes it more shallower but efficient. While SiameseFC learns the unconstrained features to estimate the similarity score, CFNet learns the discriminative features

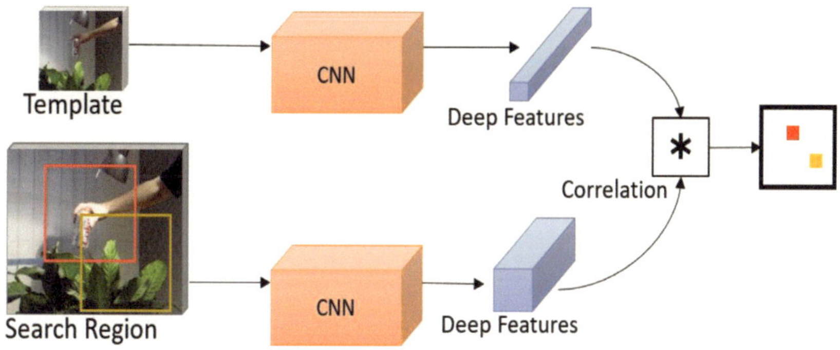

Figure 3.
SiameseFC architecture [46].

using correlation filter layer and solves the ridge regression problem via exploiting the negative samples in the search region. Similar to SiameseFC, CFNet is trained offline and weight parameters are fixed during tracking. CFNet produces a response map for template and search region with a high value representing the maximum similarity.

3.1.4 SIAMRPN

Li et al. [53] proposed a Siamese region proposal network (SIAMRPN) in order to improve the robustness compared to SiameseFC and CFNet. Both SiameseFC and CFNet do not employ bounding box regression and thus require multi-scale testing. SIAMRPN integrates region proposal network (RPN) within SiameseFC which makes it more elegant. The concept of RPN was introduced in Faster RCNN [18]. RPN has capability to extract more precise and efficient proposals due to the supervision of bounding box regression and binary classifier.

SIAMRPN consists of two components including Siamese network and RPN as shown in **Figure 4**. Siamese network is responsible for feature computation. Its template branch takes z as target patch and gives $\varphi(z)$ as output target features while detection branch requires x search image and returns $\varphi(x)$ as search region features. Whereas RPN is composed of a pairwise correlation module and a supervision module. The supervision module has two outputs consisting of a binary classifier and a bounding box regressor. If there are k anchors, the pairwise correlation module increases the channels for $\varphi(z)$ using convolution layers by 2k for classification denoted as $([\varphi(z)]_{cls})$ and 4k for regression represented as $([\varphi(z)]_{reg})$. The search region features $\varphi(x)$ are also divided into $[\varphi(x)]_{cls}$ and $[\varphi(x)]_{reg}$ branches using convolutional layers while the number of channels for $\varphi(x)$ is kept unchanged. A correlation operation is performed for both classification and regression branches by considering $\varphi(z)$ as correlation kernel in a group manner. It means that the channel number of a group $\varphi(z)$ is equal to the number of the channel $\varphi(x)$. The SIAMRPN is trained using Stochastic Gradient Descent (SGD) method to optimize the following loss function:

$$loss = L_{cls} + \lambda\, L_{reg}, \tag{4}$$

where L_{cls} represents the classification loss which is a cross entropy loss function and L_{reg} means bounding box regression loss, and λ is a balancing parameter.

3.2 Siamese intermediate merge trackers

This section describes the tracking models where the two input images are input separately to the network and are merged somewhere before the final layer of the CNN.

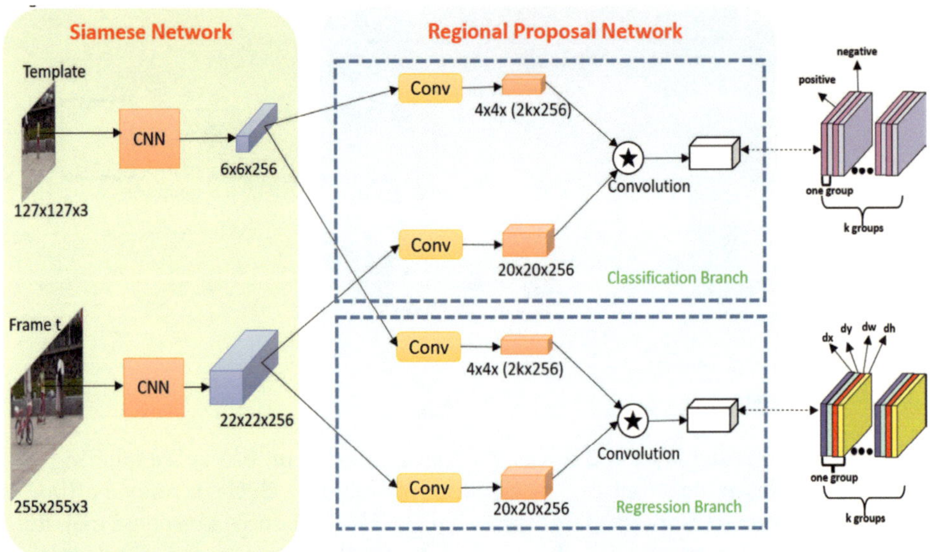

Figure 4.
SIAMRPN architecture [53].

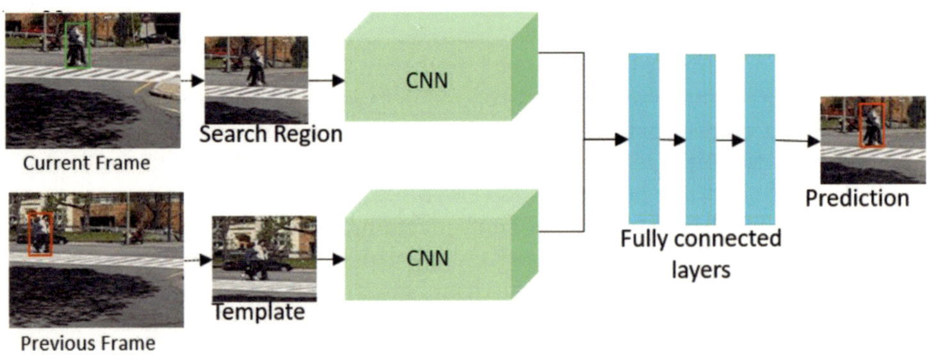

Figure 5.
GOTURN tracking framework [45].

3.2.1 GOTURN

Held et al. [45] proposed generic object tracking using regression network (GOTURN) and exploited the target appearance and motion relationships. GOTURN predicts the new target object for the current frame by taking the template image from the previous frame. Both input images are cropped with the background region for prediction as demonstrated in **Figure 5**. GOTRUN consists of two streams of 5 convolutional layers for both template and search images. The template and search streams are fused and feed-forwarded to three shared fully connected layers. During tracking, GOTURN directly regresses the target position and does not update the weight parameters to adapt the new target appearances.

3.2.2 YCNN

Chen and Tao [54] proposed the YCNN tracker to estimate the similarity between two input images. YCNN model consists of two separate 3 convolutional layers and two shared fully connected layers. The target object and search images are fed forward two separate 3 convolutional layers and then merged before forwarding to two shared fully connected layers. The output of YCNN is a response map. The network is trained end-to-end using Gaussian map as a label with the maximum value at the center. During tracking, the maximum position on the confidence map gives the new target position. The drift problem is handled by averaging the maximum five confidence values, while the scale problem is tackled by repeating the inference with different template sizes.

3.2.3 EAST

Huang et al. [55] proposed early stopping tracker (EAST) to exploit similarity between the two input images and learn the different policies by employing Reinforcement Learning (RL) to improve the accuracy while maintaining high speed. On the contrary to SiameseFC, EAST infers the new target position in single evaluation on original template size. The tracking problem is formulated as Markov decision process. The network agent is trained offline such that agent decides whether the target object has high confidence on early layers or continue to go deep by processing subsequent layers to obtain the maximum confidence for each frame. Agent makes a decision based on early stopping criterion for each layer.

3.3 Siamese early merge trackers

In this subsection, we study the tracking models where the input images are aggregated or stacked before feeding to the network.

3.3.1 CNNSI

Fiaz et al. [56] proposed CNN with structural input (CNNSI) to exploit the deep discriminative features to learn the similarity between the target and candidate patches as shown in **Figure 6**. The target and candidate images are stacked together and feed-forwarded to the network to get the similarity and dissimilarity scores. The CNNSI is trained offline end-to-end using SGD method to learn the similarity. During the tracking, target and candidate patches are stacked and fed to the network to get similarity and dissimilarity scores for all the candidate patches. The maximum similarity score yields the new target position. The bounding boxes are refined using

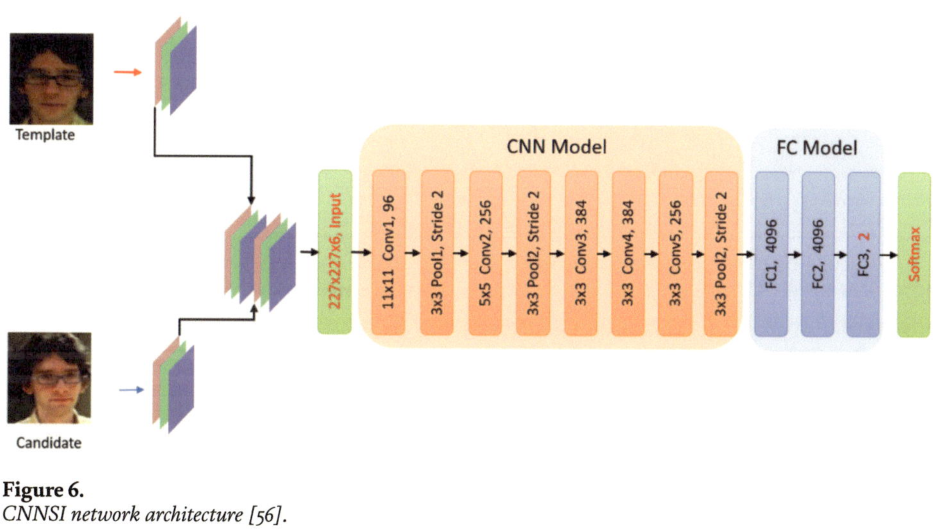

Figure 6.
CNNSI network architecture [56].

a bounding box regressor which is trained on the first frame of the sequence. Short-term and long-term updates are performed to integrate the new target appearance.

3.3.2 SiameseCNN

Taixé et al. [57] presented a Siamese CNN (SiameseCNN) for pedestrian tracking to exploit the pedestrian appearance and geometrical position. The proposed network requires a stack of two target images along with their optical flow and forwarded to three CNN layers and three fully connected layers. The network is trained using a gradient boosting classifier to predict the final trajectory of the pedestrian. For negative samples, contextual features along with relative geometry are provided to train the classifier. To infer the pedestrian, the gradient boosting classifier makes the final decision based on the maximum score.

4. Experimental analysis

This section discusses the experimental results and analysis over the OTB2013 [21] and OTB2015 [22] benchmarks. The OTB2013 consists of 50 different sequences having 11 challenges including fast motion (FM), background clutter (BC), motion blur (MB), low resolution (LR), scale variation (SV), in-plane rotation (IPR), out-plane rotation (OPR), deformation (DEF), occlusion (OCC), illumination variation (IV), and out-of-view (OV). OTB2015 contains 100 videos, which is an improved version of OTB2013 having all the challenges from OTB2013.

The Siamese trackers are evaluated using precision, success, and speed measures. One pass evaluation (OPE) is utilized to evaluate the robustness of the Siamese trackers. Performance of the trackers is illustrated using precision and success graphs. Euclidean distance is calculated between the ground-truth center and predicted centers to compute the precision as:

$$\varphi_{tp} = \sqrt{(x_t - x_p)^2 + (y_t - y_p)^2}, \tag{5}$$

where (x_t,y_t) and (x_p,y_p) shows the ground-truth center and predicted center in a frame respectively. A frame is measured as successful if the value of φ_{tp} is less than a threshold else not. The precision threshold value is set to 20 pixels. The target changes its size in a sequence and precision only considers the pixel difference of the center of the target. Thus precision does not a true picture of the target shape. Hence, a more robust success metric is employed for evaluation of trackers. An overlap score (OS) is calculated between the ground-truth and predicted bounding box to compute success as:

$$O_s = \frac{|b_t \cap b_p|}{|b_t \cup b_p|}, \tag{6}$$

where b_t represents the bounding box for ground-truth, b_p denotes the predicted bounding box, |.| shows the number of pixels, ∩ means intersection and ∪ shows the union operator. The O_s determines that a frame is successful or not. If O_s is less than a threshold then that frame is referred to as a successful frame and vice-versa. The overlap score for success varies between 0 and 1, and the threshold is set at 0.5. For precision and success, average precision and average success scores are reported by computing the mean of precision and OS for all the frames in a benchmark respectively. The speed of the Siamese trackers is reported in frames-per-second (FPS) by computing the mean of speed for all the frames in a benchmark.

For comparison of different Siamese architectures, we carefully selected Siamese trackers such that at least one tracker is selected from each category. The selected trackers are SINT [51], SiameseFC [46], CFNet [52], SIAMRPN [53], GOTURN [45], and CNNSI [56]. All results are reported from the original authors except, the GOTURN because the authors did not report results over the selected benchmarks.

4.1 Quantitative evaluation

In this subsection, we discuss the quantitative comparison of Siamese Trackers.

4.1.1 Overall performance

Figures 7 and **8** and **Table 1** show the precision and success of selected Siamese trackers over OTB2013 and OTB2015 respectively. The precision and success graphs show that SIAMRPN achieved outstanding performance compared to the other trackers. We also observe that the rank of the trackers does not change with respect to precision and success for both benchmarks. GOTURN does not perform well as compared to the other Siamese trackers.

4.1.2 Challenge-based evaluation

We also evaluated the performance of Siamese trackers for eleven different tracking challenges over OTB2015 benchmark. **Figures 9** and **10** and **Tables 2** and **3** show the performance of Siamese trackers using precision and success respectively. We observe that SIAMRPN attained better performance for all the tracking challenges

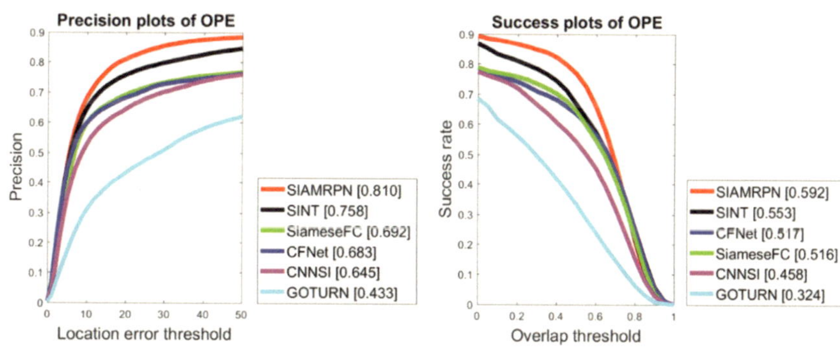

Figure 7.
Precision and success plots over OTB2013.

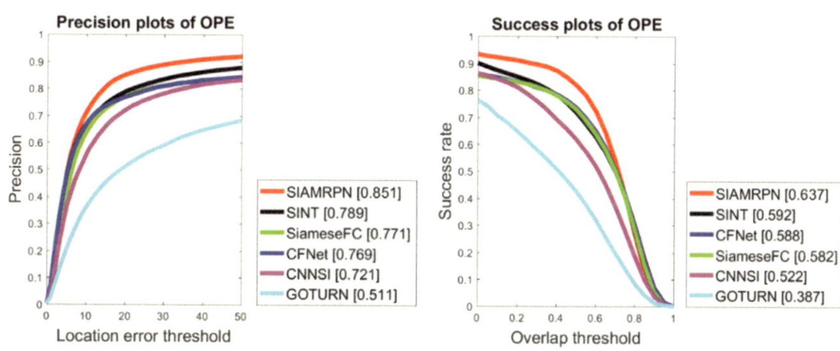

Figure 8.
Precision and success plots over OTB2015.

	Trackers	SIAMPRN	SINT	SiameseFC	CFNet	CNNSI	GOTURN
OTB2013	Precision	**81.0**	75.8	69.2	68.3	64.5	43.3
	Success	**59.2**	55.3	51.6	51.7	45.8	32.4
OTB2015	Precision	**85.1**	78.9	77.1	76.9	72.1	51.1
	Success	**63.7**	59.2	58.8	58.2	52.2	38.7
Speed (fps)		160	4	86	43	0.53	**165**

Table 1.
Comparison of Siamese trackers over OTB2013 and OTB2015 benchmarks.

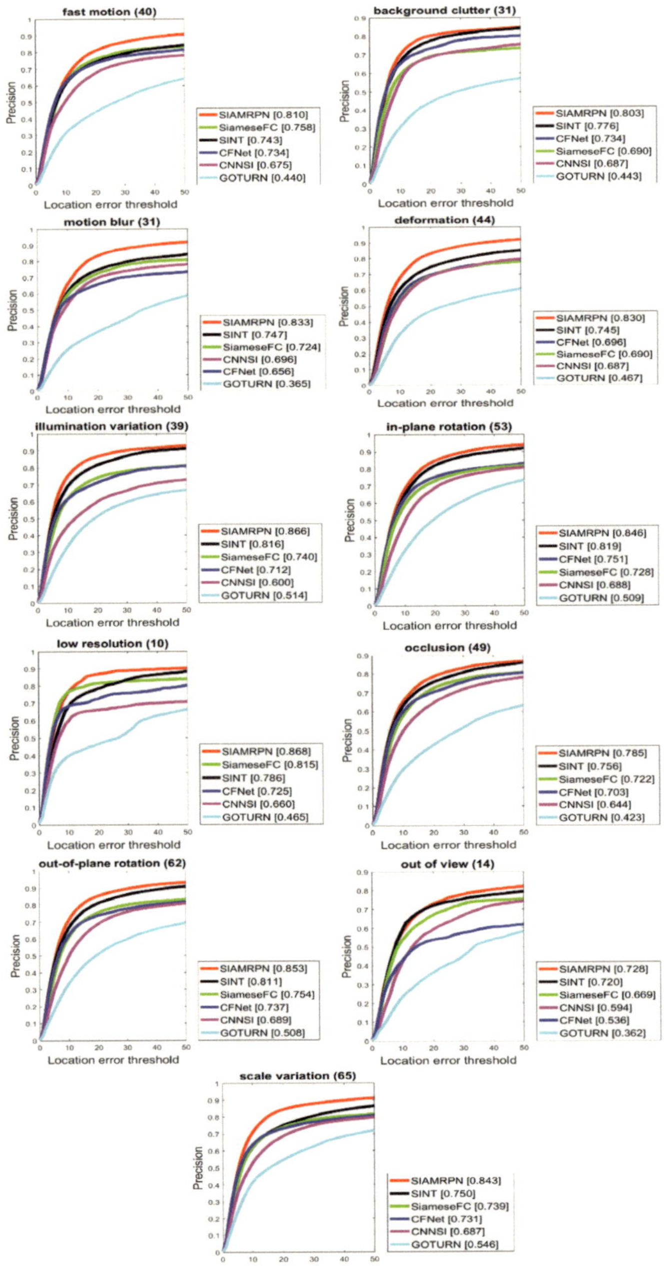

Figure 9.
Precision plots for eleven tracking challenges over OTB2015.

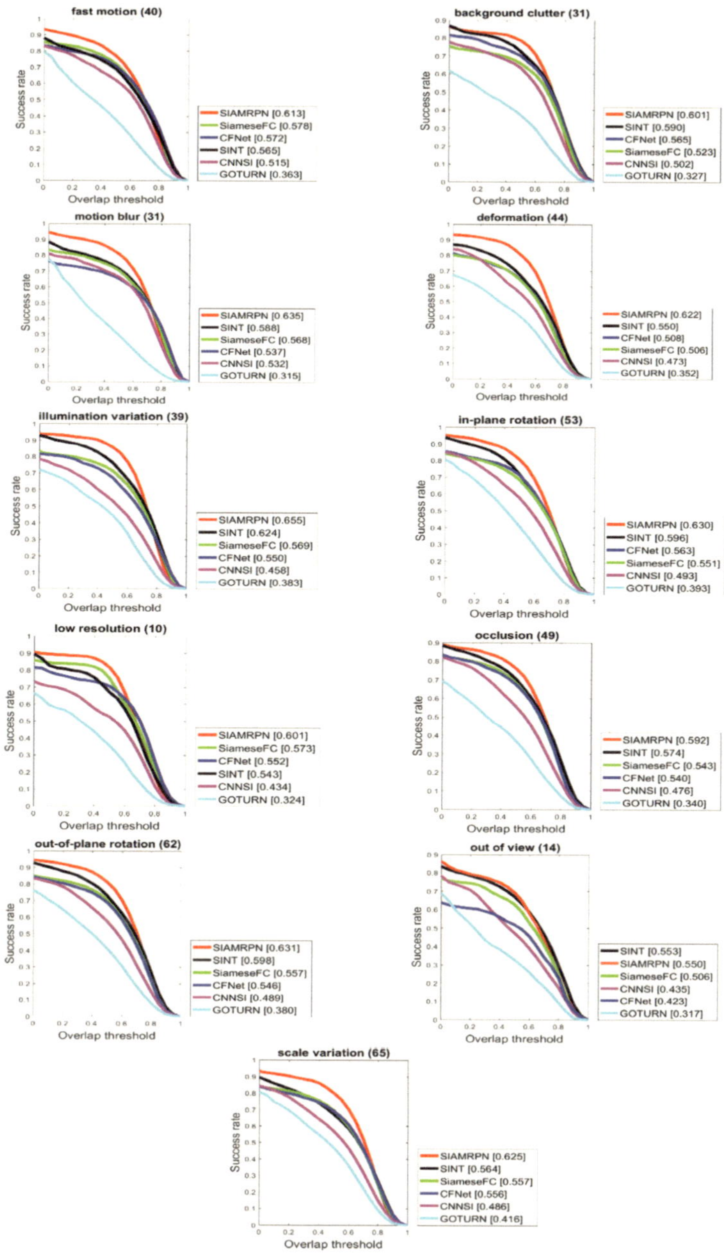

Figure 10.
Success plots for eleven tracking challenges over OTB2015.

using both precision and success. While GORTURN does not show good performance and ranked at the last. We noted that SiameseFC exhibited better performance after SIAMRPN for fast motion and low-resolution challenges while SINT ranked second best for the rest of the challenges handling those challenges more efficiently.

4.2 Qualitative evaluation

Qualitative study of Siamese-based trackers has performed over five different videos including *Bolt*, *ClifBar*, *FaceOcc1*, *Jogging-1*, and *CarScale* shown in **Figure 11**. The *Bolt* video depicts OCC, DEF, IPR and OPR challenges. Trackers such as SiameseFC, CFNet,

Trackers	SIAMRPN	SiameseFC	SINT	CFNet	CNNSI	GORTURN
FM	81.0	75.8	74.3	73.4	67.5	44.0
BC	80.3	69.0	77.6	73.4	68.7	44.3
MB	83.3	72.4	74.7	65.6	69.6	36.5
DEF	83.0	69.0	74.5	69.6	68.7	45.7
IV	86.8	74.0	81.6	71.2	60.0	51.4
IPR	84.6	72.8	81.9	75.1	68.8	50.9
LR	86.8	81.5	78.6	72.5	66.0	45.6
OCC	78.5	72.2	75.6	70.3	64.4	42.3
OPR	85.3	75.4	81.1	73.7	68.9	50.8
OV	72.8	66.9	72.0	53.6	59.4	36.2
SV	84.3	73.9	75.0	73.1	68.7	54.6

Table 2.
Precision of Siamese tracker over different challenges.

Trackers	SIAMRPN	SiameseFC	SINT	CFNet	CNNSI	GORTURN
FM	61.3	57.8	56.5	57.2	51.5	36.3
BC	60.1	52.3	59.0	56.5	50.2	32.7
MB	63.5	56.8	58.8	53.7	53.2	31.5
DEF	62.2	50.6	55.0	50.8	47.3	35.2
IV	65.5	56.9	62.4	55.0	45.8	38.3
IPR	63.0	55.1	59.6	56.3	49.3	39.3
LR	60.1	57.3	54.3	55.2	43.4	32.4
OCC	59.2	54.3	57.4	54.0	47.6	34.0
OPR	63.1	55.7	59.8	54.6	48.9	38.0
OV	55.0	50.6	55.3	42.3	43.5	31.7
SV	62.5	55.7	56.4	55.6	48.6	41.6

Table 3.
Success of Siamese tracker over different challenges.

and GOTURN failed to track the runner while SIAMRPN, SINT, and CNNSI have successfully tracked the runner. Meanwhile, the *ClifBar* sequence portrays SV, BC, MB, FM, IPR and OCC challenges and CNNSI only tracked the object efficiently while others failed. *FaceOcc1* and *Jogging-1* clearly show the occlusion challenge. We observe that all the trackers have tracked successfully face of the lady in *FaceOcc1* sequence where lady partially rotates a book in front of her face. While in *Jogging-1* sequence where occlusion is presented by a pole, all the Siamese trackers succeeded to track the lady except GOTURN. Another challenging sequence is *CarScale* which clearly shows that the size of the car is changing with the passage of time. We note that CFNet tracked the car efficiently while the rest of the trackers only tracked some region of the car.

4.3 Speed analysis

We also reported the speed of the trackers as frames per second (fps) as shown in **Figure 12**. We observe that GOTURN is computational cost effective and

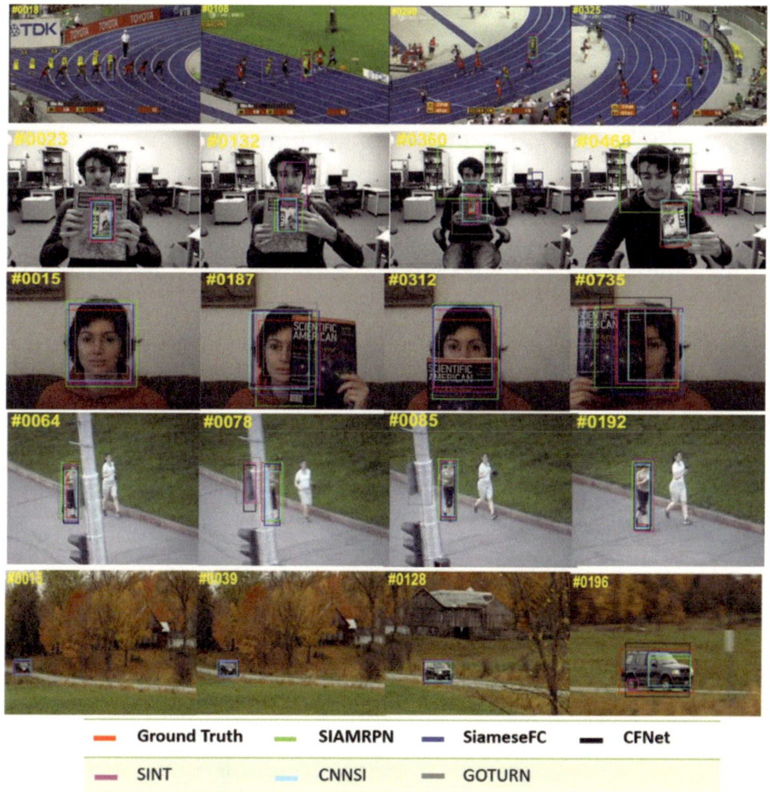

Figure 11.
Qualitative analysis of Siamese trackers over Bolt, ClifBar, FaceOcc1, Jogging-1, and CarScale sequences.

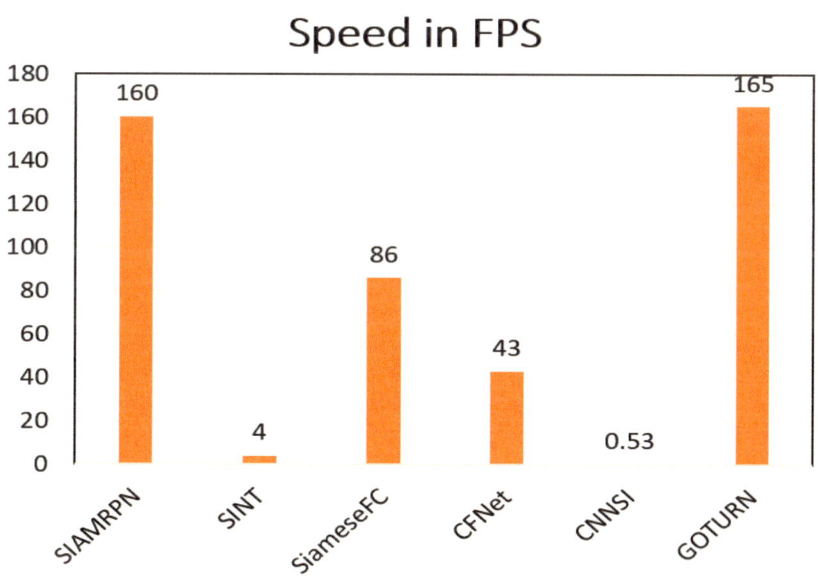

Figure 12.
Speed analysis of the trackers.

tracks objects at a speed of 165 fps. Similarly, SIAMPRN is also computational cost-efficient and can track at 160 fps. Although SiameseFC and CFNet have high computational cost compared to GOTURN and SIAMRPN but still manage to track at high speed. However, SINT (4 fps) and CNNSI (0.53 fps) have very low speed and consume a lot of computational costs.

5. Summary of Siamese networks comparison

We study three different types of Siamese network architectures employed in visual tracking application. We observe that all the Siamese trackers exploit the discriminative ability of deep CNN features. Experimental study revealed that late merge technique is better than others. **Table 4** shows the characteristics of the different architecture of Siamese networks.

	Late merge	**Intermediate merge**	**Early merge**
Definition	Inputs are combined at the final layer	Inputs are combined well before the final layer	Inputs are stacked before feeding network
Trackers	SiameseFC, CFNet, SINT, SIAMRPN	GOTURN, YCNN, EAST	CNNSI, SiameseCNN
Output (bounding box/ score map/ scores)	All	All	Scores
Features exploitation	Exploits the input images separately which are more discriminative	Initially exploits the input images features and then fused features are exploited which reduces the discriminative ability	Inputs are merged and then processed which reduces the discriminative ability of deep CNN features
Performance (precision and success)	Efficient	Moderate	Moderate
Speed	Fast	Fast	Slow

Table 4.
Characteristics of Siamese trackers.

6. Conclusions and future directions

In this chapter we study Siamese networks and their different variants for the task of visual object tracking. Siamese networks are classified into three categories based on their architecture including late merge, intermediate merge, and early merge. We observe that late merge Siamese trackers have shown better performance compared to the other trackers. Our study concludes that SIAMRPN has shown outstanding performance and ranked the best among the selected Siamese trackers. The tracking performance of the Siamese trackers can be improved by integrating both the spatial and temporal information. We observe that almost all the Siamese Networks do not perform the online model update. It would be a great challenge to update the model during the tracking while maintaining the robustness of the Siamese trackers. Other deep features such as RNN, Residual Net and GAN can be exploited within the Siamese networks to improve the tracking performance. Zero-shot and one-shot learning are getting popular due to the limited data issue. Integration of zero-shot and one-shot with Siamese trackers is yet to be explored in the visual object tracking field.

Acknowledgements

This research was supported by Development project of leading technology for future vehicle of the business of Daegu metropolitan city (No. 20190405).

Author details

Mustansar Fiaz[1], Arif Mahmood[2] and Soon Ki Jung[1*]

1 Kyungpook National University, Daegu, Republic of Korea

2 Information Technology University, Lahore, Pakistan

*Address all correspondence to: skjung@knu.ac.kr

References

[1] Laurense VA, Goh JY, Gerdes JC, editors. Path-tracking for autonomous vehicles at the limit of friction. In: 2017 American Control Conference (ACC); IEEE. 2017

[2] Brown M, Funke J, Erlien S, Gerdes JC. Safe driving envelopes for path tracking in autonomous vehicles. Control Engineering Practice. 2017;**61**:307-316

[3] Ali A, Jalil A, Niu J, Zhao X, Rathore S, Ahmed J, et al. Visual object tracking—Classical and contemporary approaches. Frontiers of Computer Science. 2016;**10**(1):167-188

[4] Liu G, Liu S, Muhammad K, Sangaiah AK, Doctor F. Object tracking in vary lighting conditions for fog based intelligent surveillance of public spaces. IEEE Access. 2018;**6**:29283-29296

[5] Tian B, Yao Q, Gu Y, Wang K, Li Y, editors. Video processing techniques for traffic flow monitoring: A survey. In: 2011 14th International IEEE Conference on Intelligent Transportation Systems (ITSC); IEEE. 2011

[6] Datondji SRE, Dupuis Y, Subirats P, Vasseur P. A survey of vision-based traffic monitoring of road intersections. IEEE Transactions on Intelligent Transportation Systems. 2016;**17**(10):2681-2698

[7] Rautaray SS, Agrawal A. Vision based hand gesture recognition for human computer interaction: A survey. Artificial Intelligence Review. 2015;**43**(1):1-54

[8] Maqueda AI, del-Blanco CR, Jaureguizar F, García N. Human-computer interaction based on visual hand-gesture recognition using volumetric spatiograms of local binary patterns. Computer Vision and Image Understanding. 2015;**141**:126-137

[9] Simonyan K, Zisserman A. Very deep convolutional networks for large-scale image recognition. arXiv preprint arXiv: 14091556; 2014

[10] Schuster M, Paliwal KK. Bidirectional recurrent neural networks. IEEE Transactions on Signal Processing. 1997;**45**(11):2673-2681

[11] Kodirov E, Xiang T, Gong S, editors. Semantic autoencoder for zero-shot learning. In: Proceedings of the IEEE Conference on Computer Vision and Pattern Recognition. 2017

[12] He K, Zhang X, Ren S, Sun J, editors. Deep residual learning for image recognition. In: Proceedings of the IEEE Conference on Computer Vision and Pattern Recognition. 2016

[13] Goodfellow I, Pouget-Abadie J, Mirza M, Xu B, Warde-Farley D, Ozair S, et al., editors. Generative adversarial nets. In: Advances in Neural Information Processing Systems. 2014

[14] Chen J-C, Patel VM, Chellappa R, editors. Unconstrained face verification using deep CNN features. In: 2016 IEEE Winter Conference on Applications of Computer Vision (WACV); IEEE. 2016

[15] Wang J, Yang Y, Mao J, Huang Z, Huang C, Xu W, editors. CNN-RNN: A unified framework for multi-label image classification. In: Proceedings of the IEEE Conference on Computer Vision and Pattern Recognition. 2016

[16] Girshick R, Donahue J, Darrell T, Malik J, editors. Rich feature hierarchies for accurate object detection and semantic segmentation. In: Proceedings of the IEEE Conference on Computer Vision and Pattern Recognition. 2014

[17] Moeskops P, Wolterink JM, van der Velden BH, Gilhuijs KG, Leiner T, Viergever MA, et al., editors. Deep

learning for multi-task medical image segmentation in multiple modalities. In: International Conference on Medical Image Computing and Computer-Assisted Intervention; Springer. 2016

[18] Ren S, He K, Girshick R, Sun J, editors. Faster r-CNN: Towards real-time object detection with region proposal networks. In: Advances in Neural Information Processing Systems. 2015

[19] Fiaz M, Mahmood A, Javed S, Jung SK. Handcrafted and Deep trackers: Recent Visual Tracking Trends and Approaches. ACM Computing Surveys; 2019

[20] Krizhevsky A, Sutskever I, Hinton GE, editors. Imagenet classification with deep convolutional neural networks. In: Advances in Neural Information Processing Systems. 2012

[21] Wu Y, Lim J, Yang M-H, editors. Online object tracking: A benchmark. In: Proceedings of the IEEE Conference on Computer Vision and Pattern Recognition. 2013

[22] Wu Y, Lim J, Yang M-H. Object tracking benchmark. IEEE Transactions on Pattern Analysis and Machine Intelligence. 2015;**37**(9):1834-1848

[23] Li P, Wang D, Wang L, Lu H. Deep visual tracking: Review and experimental comparison. Pattern Recognition. 2018;**76**:323-338

[24] Leang I, Herbin S, Girard B, Droulez J. On-line fusion of trackers for single-object tracking. Pattern Recognition. 2018;**74**:459-473

[25] Zhang S, Yao H, Sun X, Lu X. Sparse coding based visual tracking: Review and experimental comparison. Pattern Recognition. 2013;**46**(7):1772-1788

[26] Yang M, Wu Y, Hua G. Context-aware visual tracking. IEEE Transactions on Pattern Analysis and Machine Intelligence. 2009;**31**(7):1195-1209

[27] Babenko B, Yang M-H, Belongie S. Robust object tracking with online multiple instance learning. IEEE Transactions on Pattern Analysis and Machine Intelligence. 2011;**33**(8):1619-1632

[28] Hare S, Golodetz S, Saffari A, Vineet V, Cheng M-M, Hicks SL, et al. Struck: Structured output tracking with kernels. IEEE Transactions on Pattern Analysis and Machine Intelligence. 2016;**38**(10):2096-2109

[29] Zhang K, Zhang L, Yang M-H, editors. Real-time compressive tracking. In: European Conference on Computer Vision; Springer. 2012

[30] Bolme DS, Beveridge JR, Draper BA, Lui YM, editors. Visual object tracking using adaptive correlation filters. In: 2010 IEEE Computer Society Conference on Computer Vision and Pattern Recognition; IEEE. 2010

[31] Henriques JF, Caseiro R, Martins P, Batista J. High-speed tracking with kernelized correlation filters. IEEE Transactions on Pattern Analysis and Machine Intelligence. 2015;**37**(3):583-596

[32] Danelljan M, Hager G, Shahbaz Khan F. Learning spatially regularized correlation filters for visual tracking. In: Felsberg M, editor. Proceedings of the IEEE International Conference on Computer Vision. 2015

[33] Danelljan M, Hager G, Shahbaz Khan F, Felsberg M, editors. Adaptive decontamination of the training set: A unified formulation for discriminative visual tracking. In: Proceedings of the IEEE Conference on Computer Vision and Pattern Recognition. 2016

[34] Li F, Tian C, Zuo W, Zhang L, Yang M-H, editors. Learning spatial-temporal

regularized correlation filters for visual tracking. In: Proceedings of the IEEE Conference on Computer Vision and Pattern Recognition. 2018

[35] Lukezic A, Vojir T, Čehovin Zajc L, Matas J, Kristan M, editors. Discriminative correlation filter with channel and spatial reliability. In: Proceedings of the IEEE Conference on Computer Vision and Pattern Recognition. 2017

[36] Nam H, Han B, editors. Learning multi-domain convolutional neural networks for visual tracking. In: Proceedings of the IEEE Conference on Computer Vision and Pattern Recognition. 2016

[37] Nam H, Baek M, Han B. Modeling and propagating cnns in a tree structure for visual tracking. arXiv preprint arXiv: 160807242; 2016

[38] Ma C, Huang J-B, Yang X. Hierarchical convolutional features for visual tracking. In: Yang M-H, editor. Proceedings of the IEEE International Conference on Computer Vision. 2015

[39] Qi Y, Zhang S, Qin L, Yao H, Huang Q, Lim J, et al., editors. Hedged deep tracking. In: Proceedings of the IEEE Conference on Computer Vision and Pattern Recognition. 2016

[40] Briechle K, Hanebeck UD, editors. Template matching using fast normalized cross correlation. In: Optical Pattern Recognition XII; International Society for Optics and Photonics. 2001

[41] Kalal Z, Mikolajczyk K, Matas J. Tracking-learning-detection. IEEE Transactions on Pattern Analysis and Machine Intelligence. 2012;**34**(7):1409-1422

[42] Wang S, Lu H, Yang F, Yang M-H, editors. Superpixel tracking. In: 2011 International Conference on Computer Vision; IEEE. 2011

[43] Nguyen HT, Smeulders AW. Robust tracking using foreground-background texture discrimination. International Journal of Computer Vision. 2006;**69**(3):277-293

[44] Godec M, Roth PM, Bischof H. Hough-based tracking of non-rigid objects. Computer Vision and Image Understanding. 2013;**117**(10): 1245-1256

[45] Held D, Thrun S, Savarese S, editors. Learning to track at 100 fps with deep regression networks. In: European Conference on Computer Vision; Springer. 2016

[46] Bertinetto L, Valmadre J, Henriques JF, Vedaldi A, Torr PH, editors. Fully-convolutional siamese networks for object tracking. In: European Conference on Computer Vision; Springer. 2016

[47] Karpathy A, Toderici G, Shetty S, Leung T, Sukthankar R, Fei-Fei L, editors. Large-scale video classification with convolutional neural networks. In: Proceedings of the IEEE Conference on Computer Vision and Pattern Recognition. 2014

[48] Zbontar J, LeCun Y, editors. Computing the stereo matching cost with a convolutional neural network. In: Proceedings of the IEEE Conference on Computer Vision and Pattern Recognition. 2015

[49] Schroff F, Kalenichenko D, Philbin J, editors. Facenet: A unified embedding for face recognition and clustering. In: Proceedings of the IEEE Conference on Computer Vision and Pattern Recognition. 2015

[50] Zagoruyko S, Komodakis N, editors. Learning to compare image patches via convolutional neural networks. In: Proceedings of the IEEE Conference on Computer Vision and Pattern Recognition. 2015

[51] Tao R, Gavves E, Smeulders AW, editors. Siamese instance search for tracking. In: Proceedings of the IEEE Conference on Computer Vision and Pattern Recognition. 2016

[52] Valmadre J, Bertinetto L, Henriques J, Vedaldi A, Torr PH, editors. End-to-end representation learning for correlation filter based tracking. In: Proceedings of the IEEE Conference on Computer Vision and Pattern Recognition. 2017

[53] Li B, Yan J, Wu W, Zhu Z, Hu X, editors. High performance visual tracking with siamese region proposal network. In: Proceedings of the IEEE Conference on Computer Vision and Pattern Recognition. 2018

[54] Chen K, Tao W. Once for all: A two-flow convolutional neural network for visual tracking. IEEE Transactions on Circuits and Systems for Video Technology. 2018;**28**(12):3377-3386

[55] Huang C, Lucey S. Learning policies for adaptive tracking with deep feature cascades. In: Ramanan D, editor. Proceedings of the IEEE International Conference on Computer Vision. 2017

[56] Fiaz M, Mahmood A, Jung SK. Convolutional neural network with structural input for visual object tracking. In: ACM Symposium on Applied Computing. 2019

[57] Leal-Taixé L, Canton-Ferrer C, Schindler K, editors. Learning by tracking: Siamese CNN for robust target association. In: Proceedings of the IEEE Conference on Computer Vision and Pattern Recognition Workshops. 2016

Chapter 2

Multi-Person Tracking Based on Faster R-CNN and Deep Appearance Features

Gulraiz Khan, Zeeshan Tariq and Muhammad Usman Ghani Khan

Abstract

Mostly computer vision problems related to crowd analytics are highly dependent upon multi-object tracking (MOT) systems. There are two major steps involved in the design of MOT system: object detection and association. In the first step, desired objects are detected in every frame of video stream. Detection quality directly influences the performance of tracking. The second step involves the correspondence of detected objects in current frame with the previous to obtain their trajectories. High accuracy in object detection system results in less number of missing detection and finally produces less fragmented tracks. Better object association increases the affinity between objects in different frames. This paper presents a novel algorithm for improved object detection followed by enhanced object tracking. Object detection accuracy has been increased by employing deep learning-based Faster region convolutional neural network (Faster R-CNN) algorithm. Object association is carried out by using appearance and improved motion features. Evaluation results show that we have enhanced the performance of current state-of-the-art work by reducing identity switches and fragmentation.

Keywords: face-based tracking, target tracking, object detection, tracking

1. Introduction

We witness the truthfulness of the saying of Greek philosopher Aristotle "Man is by nature a social animal" in our daily life, as we see thousands of humans walk on roads, terminals, shopping malls, and other public places on a daily basis. They intentionally or unintentionally keep interacting with each other. They also make decision on where to go and how to reach their destinations. So their movement is not always straight away. It changes based on external environmental factors. Study and analysis of human dynamics play an important role in public security, public space management, architecture, and design. These tasks are highly dependent upon proper multi-person tracking (MPT) and trajectory extraction procedure. So this thing motivated us to contribute in the development of such system which performs these tasks with real-time speed and high accuracy.

Before moving further we have to know what is meant by multi-object tracking (MOT). The multiple object tracking is the process of localizing multiple moving objects over time using a camera as input or capturing device. A unique identity is assigned to every detected object. This identity remains specific for that object up to the certain time period. Based upon these identities, we draw motion trajectories of objects that are being tracked. We can also make an analysis of the behavior of objects. **Figure 1** depicts the steps involved in multi-object tracking. Here to be noted that multi-object tracking is different from multi-object detection. Multi-object detection is sub-part of multi-object tracking. In short object detection is the process of locating object of interests in a single frame, while MOT is associated with detecting multiple objects of interests across a series of frames. In tracking the object detected in next frame should be able to relate same object detected in previous frame.

MOT has a variety of uses, some of which are human-computer interaction, surveillance and security, video communication and compression, augmented reality, traffic control, medical imaging, and video editing. Apart from these mentioned uses, there are some certain reasons which describe why tracking is useful.

- First of all, if there are too many objects detected in a video frame, then tracking will make it possible to establish the identity of certain objects across all the frames.

- Second, if there is the case that object detection has failed to detect object, then it may be still possible to track those objects because tracking system extracts and stores the location and appearance features of detected objects from the previous frame.

- Third, tracking methods could perform very efficiently because they perform a local search in place of a global. So, we can achieve a good performance in terms of high frame rate for our proposed hybrid system. The proposed system performs object detection for every nth frame and tracks the target object in intermediate frames based on their position in the frame and appearance features.

The proposed work has many applications in different fields, surveillance, entertainment, gaming, and autonomous vehicles, as shown in **Figure 2**. This system also has applications in crowded scene that enables the analysis of each individual moving opposite to the group movement. Visual surveillance usually requires the detailed human activity of each individual separately. Detecting activity for each person separately demands people to be tracked. Precise information of a person can be obtained by using previous trajectories of each subject. The analysis of drawn trajectories for each area can be helpful to find whether a person has been in forbidden area or not and performing what type of activities (running, walking, and fighting). Combining the tracking information of two or more characters can precisely elaborate the interaction between them.

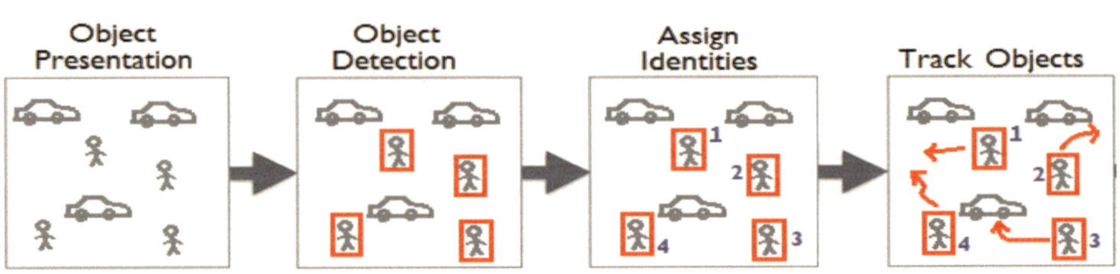

Figure 1.
Flow of steps involved in multi-object tracking.

Figure 2.
Applications of multi-object tracking system.

Multi-human tracking is also useful for multiplayer interactive games. Two humans playing fighting game can be easily tracked using MOT. Similarly, in autonomous vehicle industry, self-driving cars can employ tracking system to follow some specific vehicle. Based on the tracked vehicle, autonomous vehicles can take decisions.

We can track an object continuously after the first-time detection. But a tracking algorithm may sometimes lose track of the objects they are tracking. For instance, when the movement of the target object is too high, a tracking algorithm may not be able to maintain the track of the object. So the solution is to use detection and tracking algorithms together.

In recent years, there has been a lot of focus on MOT because of advancements in object detection techniques, which increased the robustness of tracking algorithms. So, stat-of-the-art techniques are way better than tradition ones. Most of traditional techniques do not perform well in real-time environments. For example, there are some batch-based movement tracking methodologies [1, 2] in which complete batch is required for tracking the human. Some others are probability-based systems for finding the track of the subject [3–5]. These methods require a complete batch of visual frames for processing and tracking the target object. But in real-time scenarios, there is a continuous stream of frames which are being fed to the system, and their number increases by time duration. So it is impossible to convert into batch and perform tracking on real-time bases.

1.1 Challenges in tracking systems

Recent advancements in object detections have made MOT more realistic. Multiple object tracking requires precise tracking of multiple objects based on apparent identity and relative position. MOT paradigm demands entire video batch at the same time and applies global optimization for finding the associations. Individuals in live stream need to be tracked based on history of each individual in the stream. The strong basic emphasis of this work is on the time efficiency and less number of identity switches.

The first and foremost topic of concern in the development of tracking system is time efficiency. Due to limitations of batch-based tracking algorithms, there are certain challenges to implement these systems in real-time scenarios. A plethora of work has been done to compete related challenges to make multi-person tracking and trajectory drawing real time and robust. A lot of efforts are being made to move tracking system from batch based to real time.

The second and important area of interest includes finding the solution of the problem of identity switches. Identity switch means how many times the particular object changes its identity number across all the frames or in a specific time duration. Identity switches mostly occur due to missed detection of object in between frames. The other reason is occlusion between different objects which causes identity switches.

The third one is fragmentation issue. Fragmentation occurs when identity switch does not occur but detection of object is missing in some frames, and due to this a fragmented trajectory is generated, meaning tracking breaks where human is not detected.

As we have understood that the problem of identity switches is due to missing detections. So there are two possible solutions for this problem. Solution one is to reduce or eliminate the number of missing object detection in frames. This can be done by improving the object detection algorithm. We have proposed a solution for this problem, which uses the deep learning-based algorithm to detect a person by detecting their shoulder, head, or complete body.

But the problem of identity switches will still persist due to occlusion mechanism. Here comes the second solution, which is to make use of appearance and localization features of objects. As every object have a different location in the frame and different appearance relative to each other, we can build a tracking algorithm which will track multiple objects in a series of frames based on these features. Face recognition can also be used to reduce the number of identity switches. Based upon appearance and motion features, we can relate a trajectory fragmentation of one object with the other fragmentation of that object and can complete the trajectory path. The complete process is shown in **Figure 3**.

One of the recent available tracking systems is simple online and real-time tracking (SORT) [6] that tried to overcome these challenges. It is a simple framework to track persons in real time. SORT utilizes the Kalman filter features on input frames. Hungarian algorithm is employed to find the association in visual tracks. Their proposed system is only applicable for human tracking in different appearance scenes. This system still involves identity switch problem.

Another tracking system, simple online and real-time tracking with a deep association metric (Deep SORT) [7], utilized apparent features extracted from deep convolution neural network (CNN) for tracking the individuals. Deep SORT generates a cost matrix based on motion information and appearance features to avoid missing tracking because of occlusion or missed detection of persons. Their system includes convolution neural network for a person's apparent features trained on person reidentification dataset. Deep SORT has a high rate of missed detection for elevated view, crowded view, and distant view because detected humans are obtained from pre-trained models of object detection.

In this paper, we proposed a novel technique for individual human detection and tracking. We provide a unique real-time tracking using motion information and appearance information. Our system employs convolution neural network to provide the visual appearance features for tracking the individual. The CNN for visual

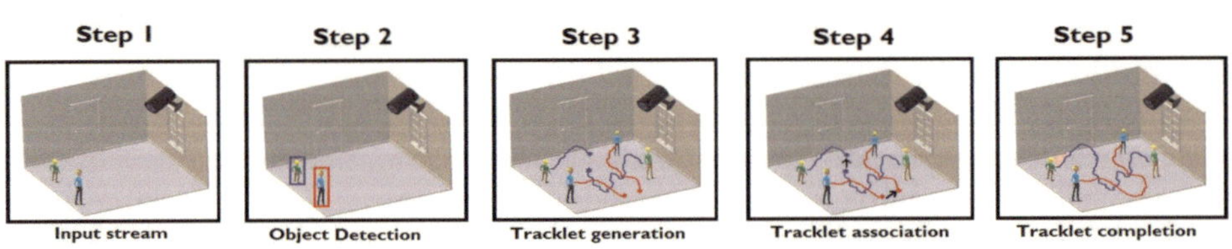

Figure 3.
Fragmentation removal steps.

appearance is trained on person reidentification dataset [8]. Appearance features allow us to improve the tracking results by making it robust for occlusion and detection after multiple frames.

1.2 Major contribution

The proposed system improved the overall detection and tracking problem in MOT problem. Furthermore, we have also improved the detection of human by re-training the Faster region convolutional neural network (Faster R-CNN) on human body parts. Provided better hardware resources, the proposed system outperforms the existing state-of-the-art systems in terms of accuracy and performance. Major contributions of our system are manifold.

- Improved detection by Faster R-CNN trained on human pedestrian dataset from different views.
- We also improved the feature set for tracking the subjects that includes color features, area, mutual distance, and HSV histograms for each region of interest.
- The system behaves better than both SORT and Deep SORT in real-time scenarios for pedestrian tracking.

The rest of the paper is divided into different sections. Section 2 provides the detailed background of previous methodologies for MOT systems. Methodology is described in Section 3 along with complete architecture. Section 4 throws light on experimentation. The last section concludes the proposed system for human tracking in a different environment.

2. Background

With the improvement in multi-object detection, research community has started focusing on tracking of every single object in different environments. The complete MOT problem can be considered as an association problem in which the basic objective is to associate the detected objects. Tracking is carried out after object detection using some object detector. In this section, we will focus on the background of the following systems:

- Object detection algorithms as humans need to be detected before person tracking
- Face recognition systems for target tracking based on recognized faces
- Tracking algorithms for reviewing already available tracking algorithms

2.1 Object detection in past years

In the early 1990s, object detection was carried out using template matching based algorithms [9], where a template of the specific object is slid over the input image to find the best possible match in the input image. In the late 1990s, the focus was shifted toward the geometric appearance-based object detection [10, 11]. In these methods, the basic focus was on height, width, angles, and other geometric properties.

In the 2000s, object detection paradigm was transferred to low-level features based on some statistical classifiers such as local binary pattern (LBP) [12], histogram of oriented gradient [13], scale-invariant feature transform [14], and covariance [15]. Feature extraction-based object detection and classification involved training of machine based on extracted features.

For many years in computer vision field, handcrafted traditional features were used for object detection. But, with the progress in deep learning after accomplishing the remarkable performance in 2012 image classification challenge [16], convolution neural networks are being used for this purpose. After the success of object classification in [16], researchers transferred their attentions toward object detection and classification. Deep convolution neural networks work exceptionally good for extraction of local and global features in terms of edges, texture, and appearance.

In recent years, the research community has moved in the direction of region-based networks for object detection. This type of object detection is being used in different applications like video description [17]. In region-based algorithms for object detection, convolution features are extracted over proposed regions followed by categorization of the region into a specific class.

With the attractive performance of AlexNet [16], Girshick et al. [18] proposed the idea of object detection using convolution neural network. They employed selective search for proposing the areas where the potential objects can be found [19]. They called their object detection network as region convolution neural network (R-CNN). The basic flow of region convolution neural network (R-CNN) can be described as follows:

- Regions are proposed for each object in the input image using selective search [19].

- Proposed regions are resized to same consistent size for classification of the proposal into predefined classes based on extracted CNN features of regions.

- Linear SVM classifier replaced the softmax layer for training the system on fixed length CNN features.

- Finally, a bounding box regressor is utilized for perfect localization of object.

Although the proposed R-CNN was a major breakthrough in the field of object detection, it has some significant weaknesses:

- Training processes is quite slow because R-CNN has different separate stages to train.

- Regions are proposed by selective search that is itself a slow process.

- Training the separate SVM classifier is expensive as CNN features are extracted for each individual region that makes the training of SVM even more challenging.

- Object detection is slow because CNN features are extracted for individual proposal for each testing image.

To overcome the feature extraction issue for each proposal, Kaiming He et al. [20] proposed spatial pyramid pooling (SPP). The basic idea was that the convolution layers accept the input of any size; fully connected layers force input to be fixed size for making matrix multiplication possible. They used SPP layer after last convolution layer for obtaining the fix-sized features to feed in fully connected layer. Using SPPNet R-CNN performance improved comprehensively. SPPNet extracts convolution features on input image only once for proposals of different sizes. This network improves the performance of testing, but it does not improve the performance of training the R-CNN. Furthermore, weights of convolution layers before SPP layer cannot be changed which limits the fine-tuning process.

The main contributor of R-CNN, Girshik et al. [21], proposed Fast-ECNN to address some problems of R-CNN and SPPNet. Fast R-CNN employs the idea of computation sharing of convolution for different proposed regions. It adds region of interest (ROI)-pooling layer after the last convolution layer for generating fix-sized features of individual proposals. The fix-sized features from ROI-pooling layers are fed to the stack of fully connected layers that further split down into two branch networks: one acts as the object classification network and the other for bounding box regression. They claimed that the overall performance of training step of R-CNN is enhanced by three times and ten times for testing.

Although Fast R-CNN improved the performance of R-CNN notably, it still uses selective search as a region proposal network (RPN). Region proposal step consumes the time comprehensively that acts as the bottleneck in Fast R-CNN. Modern advancements in object localization using deep neural network [22] motivated Ren et al. [23] to employ CNN for replacing slow process of region proposal using selective search. They proposed efficient RPN for proposing proposals for objects. In Faster R-CNN, RPN and Fast R-CNN share the convolution layers for region proposal and region classification, respectively. Faster R-CNN is a purely convolution neural network without any handcrafted features that employ fully convolution neural network (FCN) for region proposal. They claimed that Faster R-CNN can work at 5fps for testing phase.

Redmon et al. [24] proposed You Only Look Once (YOLO) for object detection. They completely dropped the region proposal step; YOLO splits the complete image into grids and predicts the detection on the bases of candidate regions. YOLO divides the complete image into $S \times S$ grids. Each grid has a class probability C, B as the bounding box locations and a probability for each box. Removing the RPN step enhances the performance of the detection; YOLO can detect the objects while running in real time with about 45 fps.

2.2 Face recognition over past years

In current era, biometric identification systems are required more than ever because of the improved security requirement in the globe. There have been a lot of efforts by researchers for face recognition technology (FRT). The basic division of FRT can be the traditional handcrafted feature-based identification and deep learning-based identification.

2.2.1 Handcrafted feature-based identification

Eigenface [25] and Fisherface [26] were commonly used approaches in the last decade for face identification. Eigenfaces reduced the feature points for measuring maximum change in face features using minimum set of features. For reducing the features, they used principal component analysis (PCA). Linear face can be recognized based on linear structure of the face using Eigenfaces. In contrast with the Eigenfaces, Fisherfaces are a supervised learning-based face identification method based on traditional texture features. Fisherfaces employ linear discriminator analysis for finding the uniquely describing data points. Both of these methodologies extract features in terms of Euclidean distance to identify the face.

Researchers have also used LBP for facial recognition [27, 28]. Hadid et al. [27] exploited LBP features for face recognition. They worked on face detection and recognition. Face detection was achieved by training a support vector machine of second degree on extracted features. Face recognition was achieved using LBP-based texture descriptor. Machine was trained on these descriptors for face recognition.

2.2.2 Deep learning-based identification

Advancement in convolution neural networks has achieved remarkable performance by increasing accuracy and efficiency. The very basic assumption in deep neural networks is to feed as much data as possible for getting better results. Requirement of huge data makes deep learning-based approaches data hungry.

Lu et al. [29] implemented a residual network (ResNet)-based model for face recognition. They divided their complete network into three networks: one backbone network called trunk network and two other networks called branch networks that emit from trunk network. The central network is trained once for learning the deep features for face identification. The central network is generated using residual blocks. Resolution-specific coupled mapping is employed in branch network for training. Input image and comparison image from gallery are transformed to same representation for comparing. Based on distance the decision is made about identified face.

Schroff et al. [30] developed a deep neural network based on convolution neural network and then named it as FaceNet. Their proposed system extracts the feature space in terms of Euclidean space. They optimized the feature mapping of facial structure using deep convolution neural network. Their proposed system, FaceNet, generates a feature vector of 128 dimensions that is optimized using triplet loss. Their proposed triplet loss comprises three face images: two from the same pair and one from a separate individual. The loss function tries to separate the same individual faces from different individual faces. Their triplet loss function is trained to minimize the distance between the same identity faces and maximize the distance between different identities. Inception model with little modification is employed in FaceNet for extracting convolution features. They tested their system on LFW dataset [31].

A research group from Facebook, Taigman et al. [32], developed a state-of-the-art system for face alignment and face recognition, named as DeepFace. They used deep convolution neural network having nine convolution layers for extracting facial features. Facial landmarks are used in their system for face alignment. The facial landmarks are estimated using support vector regressor (SVR). Extracted features from nine-layered network are passed to Softmax layer for classification. They employed cross-entropy to reduce the loss of correct labels. They also proposed a huge face recognition dataset named as Social Face Dataset [32]. They used their dataset for training the system for face identification.

2.3 Multi-object tracking

Multiple researchers have focused on movement and spatial features for tracking the multiple objects [33, 34]. Some of the researchers have focused on appearance features for capturing the associations between different detections [2, 35].

There are some traditional methods that make prediction on frame-by-frame basis. These traditional approaches involve multiple hypothesis tracking (MHT) [36] and joint probability data association filter (JPDAF) [37]. Both of these old methodologies require a lot of computation for tracking the detected objects. The complexity of these methodologies increases exponentially with increasing the number of trackable objects that makes them really slow to be used for online applications in complex environment. In JPDAF hypothesis of single state is generated based on relation between individual measurement and association likelihood. In MHT, a complete set of hypotheses is taken into consideration for tracking followed by post pruning for tractability.

Rezatofighi et al. [1] made an effort to improve the JPDAF performance by providing approximation of JPDA. They exploited recent advancement in solving m-best solution for an integer program. The main advantage of this system is to make JPDA less complex and more tractable. They redefined the method for calculating individual JPDAF assignment in terms of a solution to a linear program. Another group of researchers Kim et al. [2] used appearance-based features for tracking the target. They improved the MHT by pruning the graph of MHT for achieving state-of-the-art performance. They employed regularized least squares for increasing the efficiency of the MHT methodology.

These two improvements perform quite well as compared to the legacy implementations, but these two methods still have much delay in the decision-making step which makes these methods inappropriate for real-time applications. These methods require large computational resources with increasing the individual density.

Some researchers worked on graph theory for tracking human. Kayumbi et al. [38] proposed an algorithm to find football players' trajectories based on distributed sensing algorithm in multi-camera view. Their algorithm starts with mapping of camera view plane to virtual top-view of the ground plane. Finally, they exploited graph theory for tracking each individual in the ground plane.

Some online tracking methods utilize appearance features of individuals for tracking [39, 40]. These models extract apparent look features of individuals. Both of the systems provide accurate appearance descriptors for providing guidance to data association. First system incorporates temporal appearance of individuals along with the spatial appearance features. Their appearance model is learned by applying incremental evaluation after tuning the parameters in each iteration. In the second system, Markov decision process (MDP) is employed to map the age of the detected object in terms of Markov chain. MDP decides the tracks based on current status and history of the target.

Recently, some of the researchers worked on simple online tracking and tried to make tracking real time in live stream [6, 7]. These systems are named as simple online and real-time tracking and simple online and real-time tracking with a deep association metric, respectively. Both of these systems are two successive versions of the same methodology. In both systems Kalman filter is employed to find the movement features of the target. These systems used intersection over union, central position, height, width, and velocity as the core features for tracking. In Deep SORT, convolution features for targets appearance are also used along with motion features to reduce the missing tracks after occlusions and missed detections in multiple frames. Despite the real-time performance, these systems miss tracks after the changed posture and missed detection in a large number of frames.

Our proposed system reduces the limitation of missed detection of the human body, and it also reduces the track missed by incorporating extra features and better human detection system.

3. Methodology and framework

Multi-object tracking (MOT) in real time with good accuracy has been a challenge from decades. Many systems have been developed for this task during the last few decades, using tradition computer vision techniques. But due to rebirth of deep learning, object tracking has been robust. As object detection is the backbone of object tracking systems and deep learning techniques are good at object detection problem with real-time speed and accuracy, it is a better choice to use deep learning algorithm for detection purpose.

We have solved the MOT problem using state-of-the-art techniques. The proposed method is explained by the key components of human detection, position prediction of objects in future frames, tracklet associations, and managing the life span of identities for tracked objects. The mostly used state-of-the-art object detection algorithm is YOLO [24] which is fast enough to detect multiple objects in real time, but it has the problem of missed detections which leads to fragmentation and identity switch problems. So we conduct proper survey to choose the best detection algorithm for the problem. We have divided this methodology into sub-components for detection, track handling, and association as follows:

- Faster R-CNN for human detection
- Kalman filter
- CNN for appearance features
- Hungarian algorithm for tracking nearby rectangles
- Additional features like area, relative distance, color, nearest color, and HSV

The basic modules of the proposed system are described in the following sections.

3.1 Person detection using Faster R-CNN

As mentioned above, with the advancement in deep learning-based algorithms, real-world object detection has been a lot easier. So we have employed Faster Region Convolutional Neural Network (Faster R-CNN) detection network [23].

There are two stages of Faster R-CNN. In the first stage, region proposal network (RPN) generates the anchors on the regions present in the image where there might be a high possibility of the presence of an object. This process is further divided into three steps:

1. First step involves the process of feature extraction by using convolution neural network. Convolution feature maps are generated at the end of last layer.

2. In second step, a sliding window approach is used on these feature maps to generate anchor boxes. These anchor boxes are further refined in the next step to indicate the presence of objects.

3. Finally, in the third step, generated anchors are refined using a smaller network which calculates the loss function to select top anchors containing objects.

For region proposal network, prerequisite step is extraction of convolution features that are extracted using backbone network.

3.1.1 Residual Network-30 (backbone network)

As object detection problem is dependent upon feature extraction process to produce good quality proposals. So we used ResNet-based model containing 30 layers named as ResNet-30. ResNet or residual networks are special type of convolution neural networks which have residual connections in between layers. The benefit of these residual connections is that the network is able to learn local, global, and intermediate features in parallel, making it more efficient as compared to simple CNN. Residual connections also help in avoiding vanishing gradients problem, which is a major issue in networks containing high number of layers. So, ResNet-30 is able to learn more patterns than simple CNN by grasping more information. There are two types of short connections used in ResNet in different scenarios as described below:

1. In the first case, when the inputs and outputs are of the same dimensions, shortcuts (x) can be used directly. As illustrated in Eq. 1

$$l = F(x, W_i) + x \tag{1}$$

2. In the second case, we have changed dimensions, and the identity mapping is performed by padding extra zero entries to make dimension suitable. Another option is to use the projection shortcut to match the dimension (done by 1×1 conv) using Eq. 2:

$$l = F(x, W_i) + W_j x \tag{2}$$

where W is the weight matrix, x is the feature vector from previous layer, and F is the convolution function. Pictorial representation for residual block is given in **Figure 4**.

3.1.2 Anchor generation

Now to propose the regions in image which contains the high probability of presence of objects, the sliding window approach is used. A sliding window moves across the feature maps to generate anchors. The sliding window has the size of

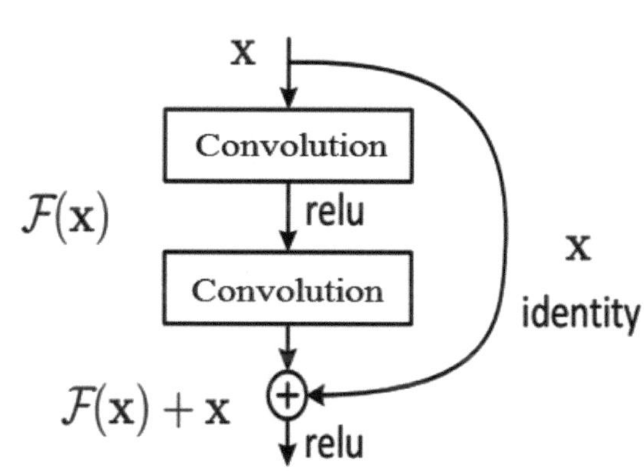

Figure 4.
Basic building block of residual learning.

$n \times n$. In our case $n = 3$; this means a 3×3 window is used. A set of nine anchors is generated for each pixel, having the same center (x, y) for all anchors. All nine anchors have three multiple aspect ratios and three varieties in scales. **Figure 5** represents the nine anchors having the same center point. Anchors with the same color have the same aspect ratio but different scaling. An intersection of union (IoU) approach is used to determine how much of these anchors overlapped with ground-truth bounding boxes. A threshold value is set based on IoU. Mostly anchors are discarded and some are selected using threshold. Anchors having IoU value >0.7 are considered as object-containing regions and anchors with value <0.3 considered as background. Eq. 3 represents the formula to find the probability of object based upon IoU value.

$$IoU = \frac{Anchor \cap Gt}{Anchor \cup Gt} \begin{cases} > & 0.7 & = & Object \\ < & 0.3 & = & NotObject \end{cases} \tag{3}$$

3.1.3 Loss function

The selected anchors are further finė-tuned using the loss function at the end of region proposal network. A shallow network is used for this purpose which performs two tasks: classification and regression. The classification performed here is binary classification which classifies anchors in one of two classes. The first class is object and the second is background.

The output of regressor determines the position of predicted bounding box in terms of four parameters (x, y, w, h), where x and y indicate the center point of anchor, w stands for width, and h represents the height of anchor box. The formula of loss function which calculates the loss for both regression and classification is given in Eq. 4:

$$L(p_i, r_i) = \frac{1}{N_{cls}} \sum_i G_{cls}(p_i, p_i^*) + \lambda \frac{1}{N_{reg}} \sum_i P_i^* G_{reg}(r_i, r_i^*) \tag{4}$$

RPN is trained to propose regions of interest (ROIs) on feature maps which are obtained from input image. These RoIs are enclosed in bounding boxes. RPN outputs different scales of bounding boxes, on feature maps. These bounding boxes contain high probability of presence of objects.

Now comes the second stage of Faster R-CNN, which is a classification of ROIs obtained from RPN network. To bring the ROIs in feedable format for the classifier, a ROI-pooling method is used which uses the pooling mechanism to shape all RoIs in the same scales. Its purpose is to perform max pooling on inputs of nonuniform sizes to obtain fix-sized feature maps for each RoI.

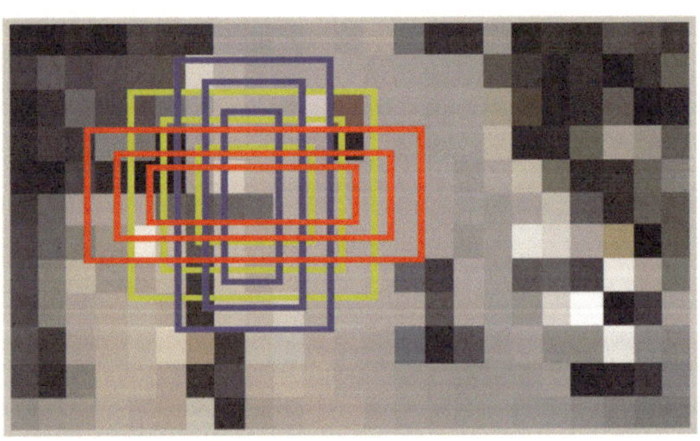

Figure 5.
Nine different proposed anchors for each single point.

3.1.4 ROI classification and regression

Now same-sized feature maps or RoIs obtained from RoI-pooling are further proceeded for classification and regression purpose. This step runs two stages in parallel. Bounding box classification and regression loss are calculated based on the optimization of the loss function. Classification head results in the class score for each individual category, and regression head resizes the bounding box values (x, y, w, h) to cover complete object. Overall performance and accuracy of Faster R-CNN is better than all the traditional object detectors. A diagram for Faster R-CNN is given in **Figure 6**.

We have trained Faster R-CNN on 4000 annotated images of human heads, shoulders, and complete bodies which improved detection accuracy efficiently having only few numbers of miss rate.

3.2 Track handling and state estimation of future frames

Kalman filter is used in its standard form as proposed in [41]. We have defined tracking scenario on the multidimensional state space $(x, y, \gamma, h, s, t, u, v)$ that consists of the bounding box center location (x, y), with height h, their respective velocities (s, t, u, v) in image coordinates, and aspect ratio γ. We keep on calculating the total count of frames for every individual track T, starting from previous correct association S_T. When Kalman filter predicts opposite features then this counter is incremented. When the track is assigned with a previous list, then the counter is reset to 0. In those tracks that are newly detected and cannot be assigned to any of the current list, then new track prediction is initiated. For the first three frames, these tracks are classified as tentative. If the association of a measurement at every time step t is found, the tracks are kept for further processing and otherwise deleted.

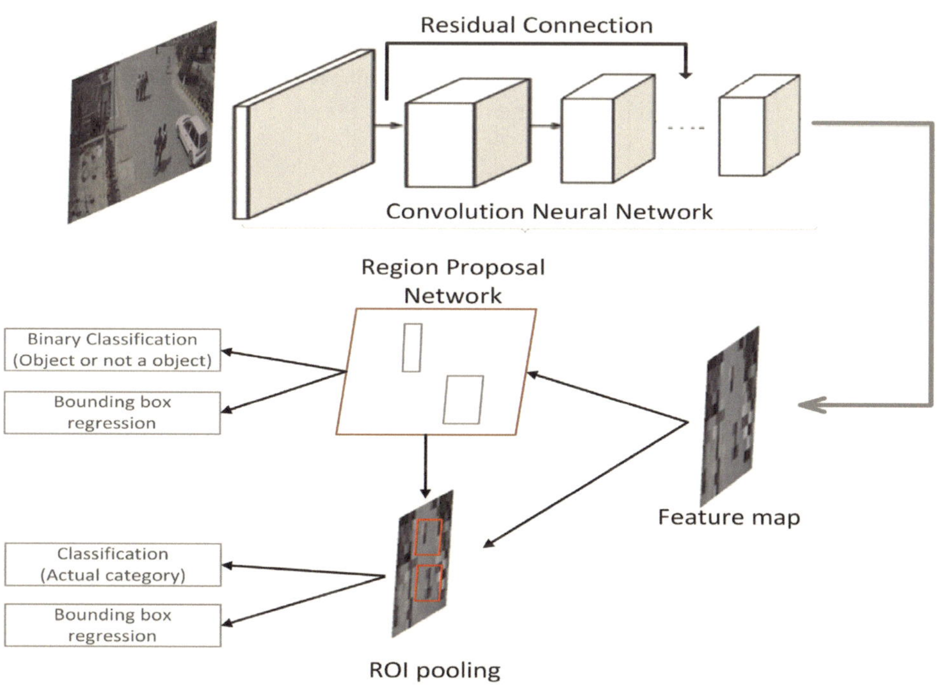

Figure 6.
Complete framework diagram of Faster R-CNN.

3.2.1 Association of newly predicted states and current states

A traditional approach to find association between the current Kalman states and newly arrived detections is to use the Hungarian algorithm. We integrated spatial displacement and apparent features by creating two different metrics. For motion information, we used Mahalanobis distance between current list of states and newly arrived states. The Mahalanobis distance removes state estimation uncertainty by measuring deviations between detection and mean track location. Further, false associations can be excluded by thresholding at a 90% confidence interval computed from the inverse x^2 distribution. We have set the value of threshold t as 9 for the decision based on Mahalanobis distance.

Mahalanobis distance matrix provides robust association metric when the overall motion transition is not high and the Kalman filter framework supply only a vague approximation of the object position. Specifically, rapid movement of capturing device can lead to displacements, making it uninformed metric for tracking in the presence of occlusions. Therefore, we integrate a second metric for tracking the pedestrians; we have utilized a pre-trained convolution network to extract the bounding box appearance features. The complete architecture of the proposed convolution neural network is shown in **Table 1**.

In combination, both techniques support each other by handling different aspects of association problem. In particular, the Mahalanobis distance matrix is employed to extract information about object positions based on movement of the objects for a short period. Along with the distance matrix, we have employed convolution for appearance feature descriptor; the CNN considers appearance information for those long-term occluded detection that are not possible to be captured through motion features. Moreover, we have used some additional features like area of human, relative distance between tracked humans, color or nearest color of object, and HSV to handle occlusions quite efficiently.

Area of human can accommodate the occlusion problem quite well because the area mostly remains the same during the whole tracking, for example, if a person is short, they will remain short before and after occlusion which makes it easy to reidentify a person after a long-time occlusion. Similarly, if someone is sitting on a wheel chair, their area will be the same throughout the time of tracking.

Name	Filter size	Stride	Output size
Conv 1	3 × 3	1	32 × 128 × 64
Conv 2	3 × 3	1	32 × 128 × 64
Max pool 1	3 × 3	2	32 × 64 × 32
Residual block 1	3 × 3	1	32 × 64 × 32
Residual block 2	3 × 3	1	32 × 64 × 32
Residual block 3	3 × 3	2	64 × 32 × 16
Residual block 4	3 × 3	1	64 × 32 × 16
Residual block 5	3 × 3	2	128 × 16 × 8
Residual block 6	3 × 3	1	128 × 16 × 8
Dense layer 1		—	128
Batch norm		—	128

Table 1.
Complete architecture for appearance feature extractor network.

Relative distance is another important appearance feature to keep track updated. Let us assume if the targeted person is moving in a group with few other people, their relative distance can be used to keep track of target even after the long-term occlusion.

Color or nearest color can be helpful to reidentify after occlusion because humans mostly keep the same clothes within a session. Similarly, if the nearest color is predicted, the person can be reidentified even after a sudden change of lighting or contrast.

HSV and RGB histograms are employed for comparing the histogram based on object appearances. We compare the histogram appearance model in both color spaces using cumulative brightness transfer function (CBTF) as mapping function between the two fields of views, which helps us handle occlusions in a better way.

3.3 Tracking options

In this system we have provided multiple options for enabling the tracking. Major tracking options include (1) face recognition-based tracking and (2) target tracking.

3.3.1 Face recognition-based tracking

As the object tracking system trained by us also detects faces, so we take benefit of this approach and make use of these detected faces in our tracking system. We used the face recognition proposed by Lu et al. [29] to recognize the detected faces. When any new face enters in frame, then the system extracts and stores these features by assigning a specific ID for later use. These feature maps and IDs are used in the future to associate the face detected with saved faces. That's how data association accuracy increased and helped in better tracking. But the limitation of this system is that it works only in case-detected face that is visible enough. This system works within 15 to 20 feet distance from camera. It also depends upon camera resolution; as the resolution is high, the better feature will be extracted.

3.3.2 Target tracking

Developed system can also perform specifically selected object tracking task. We have to basically select the object which we want to track by clicking on the detected object. This system enables us to perform analysis of only desired object by hiding the tracking details of other objects. The system is a practical implementation of human-computer interaction facilitated by the user. The overall tracking of pedestrians is improved based on robust detection of human using multiple views and body parts (head, shoulder, and complete body). Furthermore, the problem of identity switches and fragmentation is addressed by appearance features and increased spatial features (area, relative distance, color, and histograms).

4. Evaluation

Training of proposed detection system is performed on self-generated dataset, and for tracking purpose, we employed standard tracking dataset for evaluating the overall system.

4.1 Environment setup

To setup environment, we used GeForce GTX 1080 Ti GPU with Ubuntu OS installed in the system. We chose Python programming language to perform the experimentation steps. System is built by using Tensor Flow framework. We evaluated five different models of ResNet integrated with Faster R-CNN architecture on self-generated dataset, and the results are further discussed in Section 4.4.

4.2 Self-generated dataset

For training the detection system, we have utilized self-generated dataset having 4000 image of human in different postures. Each image in the dataset contains on average five different subjects with limited repetition in other images. The dataset has images from different environment conditions (rain, snow, and shadow) and in different lighting conditions (day and night). Some of the images are collected over the Internet, and some are generated within university premises using surveillance cameras. The dataset is comprehensive in terms of human densities, view angle, posture, and scale. The dataset covers different scenes: streets, bazars, buildings, malls, parks, roads, and stadium. **Figure** 7 shows some images from self-generated dataset.

We have annotated human body parts in different categories. The visible human body can be categorized into three classes based on occlusion and density of the crowd. These classes include the head, shoulder, and complete body. Based on the visible category, we have annotated the images. The details of each annotated category in the dataset are shown in **Table 2**.

4.3 MOT benchmark dataset

For evaluating our proposed tracking system, we have employed multiple object tracking (MOTChallenge) benchmark dataset [42] that contains a variety of

Figure 7.
Sample images from self-generated dataset.

Category	Instances	Number of images
Head	4325	987
Shoulder	3130	2031
Complete body	12,690	3411

Table 2.
Each category division in proposed dataset.

sequences with dynamic camera and static camera. In this dataset, they have combined 22 different available datasets. Some sample images from MOTChellange dataset are shown in **Figure 8**.

They have provided a 10-minute video of individuals with 61,440 rectangles of human detection. This dataset is composed of 14 different sequences with proper annotations by expert annotators. They also annotated different objects like chair and car for better representation of the occlusions. Three different aspects of MOTChallenge are described below:

1. Dynamic or static stream: A camera while capturing can have multiple states, placed on a stroller, in a car or a person holding the camera that makes it dynamic and static.

2. Viewpoint variation: Video camera can be elevated, at same height as pedestrian, or at low position.

3. Weather conditions: The weather condition of the captured stream is also provided with sequences to get the idea of lighting, shadows and blurring of the pedestrians.

4.4 Results

We integrated and tested multiple ResNet backbone network architectures in Faster R-CNN-based object detection. We evaluated the networks based on detection accuracy and performance. After proper evaluation, we found that ResNet-30

Figure 8.
Samples from MOT dataset. Top, training images; bottom, test sequences.

Model (residual networks)	Layers	Top-1 error	Top-5 errors (avg.)	Runtime (ms)
ResNet-34	34	25.27	8.51	52.09
ResNet-50	50	23.93	7.82	104.13
ResNet-101	101	22.81	7.11	158.35
ResNet-152	52	22.52	6.63	219.06
ResNet-30 (proposed)	30	26.02	8.04	48.93

Table 3.
Comparison table of different ResNet architectures as backbone network for object detection.

		MOTA	MOTP	MT	ML	ID	FM	FP	FN	Runtime
KDNT [43]	Batch based	68.2	79.4	41.0%	19.0%	933	1093	11,479	45,605	0.7 Hz
LMP p [44]	Batch based	71.0	80.2	46.9%	21.9%	434	587	7880	44,564	0.5 Hz
MCMOT HDM [45]	Batch based	62.4	78.3	31.5%	24.2%	1394	1318	9855	57,257	35 Hz
NOMTwSDP16 [46]	Batch based	62.2	79.6	32.5%	31.1%	406	642	5119	63,352	3 Hz
EAMTT [47]	Real time	52.5	78.8	19.0%	34.9%	910	1321	4407	81,223	12 Hz
POI [43]	Real time	66.1	79.5	34.0%	20.8%	805	3093	5061	55,914	10 Hz
SORT [6]	Real time	59.8	79.6	25.4%	22.7%	1423	1835	8698	63,245	60 Hz
Deep SORT [7]	Real time	61.4	79.1	32.8%	18.2%	781	2008	12,852	56,668	40 Hz
Proposed system	Real time	75.2	81.3	33.2	17.5	825	1225	4123	52,524	42 Hz

Table 4.
Evaluation table.

performed better in our case as our major concern is minimum runtime with maintaining the accuracy. Response time of our system is 25 frames per second. So, we decided to use ResNet-30 in designed system for better speed and accuracy. The evaluation matrix for different tested models is given in **Table 3**.

As **Table 3** depicts, the runtime for ResNet-30 is lower than other ResNet models, and Top-5 error rate is not significantly low. Based on this evaluation, ResNet-30 was our ultimate choice for backbone architecture of Faster R-CNN.

Table 4 provides the evaluation results of our complete tracking system on MOT dataset. This evaluation provides results of our designed system on seven challenging test sequences, on human eye level and elevated view of camera scenes. The tracking system highly relies on detection mechanism to perform better detection followed by better tracking; we used Faster R-CNN trained on our self-collected dataset. We rerun Deep SORT on the same evaluation dataset for fair comparison.

We set threshold of 0.7 for detection confidence score. We further fine-tuned the other parameters of network to produce better model. Following metrics are used for comparison purpose:

- Multi-object tracking accuracy (MOTA): It provides complete accuracy of system incorporating with false negatives, identity switches, and false positives.

- Multi-object tracking precision (MOTP): It gives complete tracking precision for bounding boxes overlapping between predicted location and ground-truth value.

- Mostly tracked (MT): It is the percentage of ground-truth tracks that do not change their labels at least during 80% of their life span.

- Mostly lost (ML): It provides the percentage of actual tracks that are being tracked by the system at most 20% of their life span.

- Identity switches (ID): It defines the total reported identity changes of ground-truth tracks.

- Fragmentation (FM): It provides the detail of how many times the track is interrupted by missed detection of person.

The results of our evaluation are shown in **Table 4**. The numbers of identity switches have been reduced due to our alteration in detection network. As compared to Deep SORT [7], MOTA is increased from 61.4 to 75.2.

5. Conclusion

The goal of this work was to implement a fast and competitive MOT system. We presented a multiple object tracker that combines a deep learning-based object detection network named as Faster R-CNN with the tracking algorithm. The proposed system performed tracking by detecting multiple objects followed by assigning each object a unique ID and generating their tracklets. In the case of fragmentation in tracklet of any object, the system uses tracklet association mechanism to generate a complete trajectory. Tracking is performed based upon appearance and motion features of objects. When in any frame object detection network fails to detect objects, these features are used to track object again with the same ID. Kalman filter and Hungarian algorithm both collectively used to predict the position of object in the frame. Other features like area, color, relative distance, nearest color, and HSV histograms are also used to increase the tracking accuracy. Overall the system performed very well, and it has shown improvement in MOTA, MOTP, ML, and FP fields as shown in comparison in **Table 4**. But considering environmental constraints and hardware limitations, our system has some pros and cons. We have listed some strengths and weaknesses as follows.

5.1 Pros

- Efficient in terms of response time because of less number of layer of residual network

- Have minimum number of missing detections because of improved object detection process

- Less fragmentation in drawn trajectories because of continuous detection of persons in consecutive frames

- Introduction of visual and motion feature-based tracking for reducing identity switches
- Trajectory completion in the case of fragmentation

5.2 Cons

- It requires GPU-based hardware for enabling real-time tracking.
- For highly dense crowd identity, switches may occur because of similar features of the head for each person.
- Performance reduces in dark environmental condition.

Acknowledgements

This work is carried out at UET Lahore under Intelligent Criminology Lab, National Center of Artificial Intelligence.

Author details

Gulraiz Khan[1], Zeeshan Tariq[1] and Muhammad Usman Ghani Khan[2*]

1 Al-Khawarizmi Institute of Computer Science, UET Lahore, Pakistan

2 Department of Computer Science and Engineering, UET Lahore, Pakistan

*Address all correspondence to: usman.ghani@kics.edu.pk

References

[1] Rezatofighi AM, Zhang Z, Shi Q, Dick A, Reid I. Joint probabilistic data association revisited. In: Proceedings of the IEEE International Conference on Computer Vision. 2015. pp. 3047-3055

[2] Kim C, Li F, Ciptadi A, Rehg JM. Multiple hypothesis tracking revisited. In: Proceedings of the IEEE International Conference on Computer Vision. 2015. pp. 4696-4704

[3] Yang B, Nevatia R. Multi-target tracking by online learning of non-linear motion patterns and robust appearance models. In: 2012 IEEE Conference on Computer Vision and Pattern Recognition (CVPR); IEEE. 2012. pp. 1918-1925

[4] Andriyenko A, Schindler K, Roth S. Discrete-continuous optimization for multi-target tracking. In: 2012 IEEE Conference on Computer Vision and Pattern Recognition (CVPR); IEEE. 2012. pp. 1926-1933

[5] Milan A, Schindler K, Roth S. Detection-and trajectory-level exclusion in multiple object tracking. In: Proceedings of the IEEE Conference on Computer Vision and Pattern Recognition. 2013. pp. 3682-3689

[6] Bewley A, Ge Z, Ott L, Ramos F, Upcroft B. Simple online and realtime tracking. In: 2016 IEEE International Conference on Image Processing (ICIP); IEEE. 2016. pp. 3464-3468

[7] Wojke N, Bewley A, Paulus D. Simple online and realtime tracking with a deep association metric. In: 2017 IEEE International Conference on Image Processing (ICIP); IEEE. 2017. pp. 3645-3649

[8] Zheng L, Bie Z, Sun Y, Wang J, Su C, Wang S, et al. Mars: A video benchmark for large-scale person re-identification. In: European Conference on Computer Vision; Springer. 2016. pp. 868-884

[9] Jain AK, Zhong Y, Lakshmanan S. Object matching using deformable templates. IEEE Transactions on Pattern Analysis and Machine Intelligence. 1996;**18**(3):267-278

[10] Mundy JL. Object recognition in the geometric era: A retrospective. In: Toward Category-Level Object Recognition. Springer; 2006. pp. 3-28

[11] Ponce J, Hebert M, Schmid C, Zisserman A. Toward Category-Level Object Recognition. Vol. 4170. Springer; 2007

[12] Ojala T, Pietikainen M, Maenpaa T. Multiresolution gray-scale and rotation invariant texture classification with local binary patterns. IEEE Transactions on Pattern Analysis and Machine Intelligence. 2002;**24**(7):971-987

[13] Dalal N, Triggs B. Histograms of oriented gradients for human detection. In: IEEE Computer Society Conference on Computer Vision and Pattern Recognition, 2005. CVPR 2005; volume 1; IEEE. 2005. pp. 886-893

[14] Lowe DG. Distinctive image features from scale-invariant key points. International Journal of Computer Vision. 2004;**60**(2):91-110

[15] Tuzel O, Porikli F, Meer P. Region covariance: A fast descriptor for detection and classification. In: European Conference on Computer Vision; Springer. 2006. pp. 589-600

[16] Krizhevsky A, Sutskever I, Hinton GE. Imagenet classification with deep convolutional neural networks. In: Advances in Neural Information Processing Systems. 2012. pp. 1097-1105

[17] Khan G, Ghani MU, Siddiqi A, Seo S, Baik SW, Mehmood I, et al. Egocentric visual scene description based on human-object interaction and

deep spatial relations among objects. Multimedia Tools and Applications. 2018:1-22

[18] Girshick R, Donahue J, Darrell T, Malik J. Rich feature hierarchies for accurate object detection and semantic segmentation. In: Proceedings of the IEEE Conference on Computer Vision and Pattern Recognition. 2014. pp. 580-587

[19] Uijlings JRR, Van De Sande KEA, Gevers T, Smeulders AWM. Selective search for object recognition. International Journal of Computer Vision. 2013;**104**(2):154-171

[20] He K, Zhang X, Ren S, Sun J. Spatial pyramid pooling in deep convolutional networks for visual recognition. In: European Conference on Computer Vision; Springer. 2014. pp. 346-361

[21] Girshick R. Fast R-CNN. In: Proceedings of the IEEE International Conference on Computer Vision. 2015. pp. 1440-1448

[22] Zhou B, Khosla A, Lapedriza A, Oliva A, Torralba A. Learning deep features for discriminative localization. In: Proceedings of the IEEE Conference on Computer Vision and Pattern Recognition. 2016. pp. 2921-2929

[23] Ren S, He K, Girshick R, Sun J. Faster R-CNN: Towards realtime object detection with region proposal networks. In: Advances in Neural Information Processing Systems. 2015. pp. 91-99

[24] Redmon J, Divvala S, Girshick R, Farhadi A. You only look once: Unified, real-time object detection. In: Proceedings of the IEEE Conference on Computer Vision and Pattern Recognition. 2016. pp. 779-788

[25] Turk MA, Pentland AP. Face recognition using eigenfaces. In: IEEE Computer Society Conference on Computer Vision and Pattern Recognition, 1991. Proceedings CVPR'91; IEEE. 1991. pp. 586-591

[26] Kwak K-C, Pedrycz W. Face recognition using a fuzzy fisherface classifier. Pattern Recognition. 2005; **38**(10):1717-1732

[27] Ahonen T, Hadid A, Pietikainen M. Face description with local binary patterns: Application to face recognition. IEEE Transactions on Pattern Analysis and Machine Intelligence. 2006;**28**(12):2037-2041

[28] Hadid A, Pietikainen M, Ahonen T. A discriminative feature space for detecting and recognizing faces. In: Proceedings of the 2004 IEEE Computer Society Conference on Computer Vision and Pattern Recognition, 2004. CVPR 2004; volume 2; IEEE. 2004

[29] Lu Z, Jiang X, Kot ACC. Deep coupled resnet for low-resolution face recognition. IEEE Signal Processing Letters. 2018

[30] Schroff F, Kalenichenko D, Philbin J. Facenet: A unified embedding for face recognition and clustering. In: Proceedings of the IEEE Conference on Computer Vision and Pattern Recognition. 2015. pp. 815-823

[31] Huang GB, Mattar M, Berg T, Learned-Miller E. Labeled faces in the wild: A database for studying face recognition in unconstrained environments. In: Workshop on Faces in 'Real-Life' Images: Detection, Alignment, and Recognition. 2008

[32] Taigman Y, Yang M, Ranzato MA, Wolf L. Deepface: Closing the gap to human-level performance in face verification. In: Proceedings of the IEEE Conference on Computer Vision and Pattern Recognition; 2014. pp. 1701–1708

[33] Dicle C, Camps OI, Sznaier M. The way they move: Tracking multiple targets with similar appearance. In: Proceedings of the IEEE International Conference on Computer Vision. 2013. pp. 2304-2311

[34] Yoon JH, Yang M-H, Lim J, Yoon K-J. Bayesian multiobject tracking using motion context from multiple objects. In: 2015 IEEE Winter Conference on Applications of Computer Vision (WACV); IEEE. 2015. pp. 33-40

[35] Bewley A, Ott L, Ramos F, Upcroft B. Alextrac: Affinity learning by exploring temporal reinforcement within association chains. In: 2016 IEEE International Conference on Robotics and Automation (ICRA); IEEE. 2016. pp. 2212-2218

[36] Reid D et al. An algorithm for tracking multiple targets. IEEE Transactions on Automatic Control. 1979;**24**(6):843-854

[37] Fortmann T, Bar-Shalom Y, Scheffe M. Sonar tracking of multiple targets using joint probabilistic data association. IEEE Journal of Oceanic Engineering. 1983;**8**(3):173-184

[38] Kayumbi G, Mazzeo PL, Spagnolo P, Taj M, Cavallaro A. Distributed visual sensing for virtual top-view trajectory generation in football videos. In: Proceedings of the 2008 International Conference on Content-Based Image and Video Retrieval; ACM. 2008. pp. 535-542

[39] Yang M, Jia Y. Temporal dynamic appearance modeling for online multi-person tracking. Computer Vision and Image Understanding. 2016;**153**:16-28

[40] Xiang Y, Alahi A, Savarese S. Learning to track: Online multi-object tracking by decision making. In: Proceedings of the IEEE International Conference on Computer Vision. 2015. pp. 4705-4713

[41] Kalman RE. A new approach to linear filtering and prediction problems. Journal of Basic Engineering. 1960; **82**(1):35-45

[42] Leal-Taixé L, Milan A, Reid I, Roth S, Schindler K. Motchallenge 2015: Towards a benchmark for multi-target tracking. 2015; arXiv preprint arXiv: 1504.01942

[43] Yu F, Li W, Li Q, Liu Y, Shi X, Yan J. Poi: Multiple object tracking with high performance detection and appearance feature. In: European Conference on Computer Vision; Springer. 2016. pp. 36-42

[44] Keuper M, Tang S, Zhongjie Y, Andres B, Brox T, Schiele B. A multi-cut formulation for joint segmentation and tracking of multiple objects. arXiv preprint arXiv:1607.06317; 2016

[45] Lee B, Erdenee E, Jin S, Nam MY, Jung YG, Rhee PK. Multi-class multi-object tracking using changing point detection. In: European Conference on Computer Vision; Springer. 2016. pp. 68-83

[46] Choi W. Near-online multi-target tracking with aggregated local flow descriptor. In: Proceedings of the IEEE International Conference on Computer Vision. 2015. pp. 3029-3037

[47] Sanchez-Matilla R, Poiesi F, Cavallaro A. Online multi-target tracking with strong and weak detections. In: European Conference on Computer Vision; Springer. 2016. pp. 84-99

Chapter 3

Detecting and Counting Small Animal Species Using Drone Imagery by Applying Deep Learning

Ravi Sahu

Abstract

This work represents deep learning approach for detecting lizards on the summer grass background. It is the main part of general use case formulation—"how many animals are located now on this substitute habitat. Determine in which parts they prefer to stay". For this purpose, the U-Net architecture neural network was implemented. Dilated convolution layer was added to usual U-Net. Smoothly blending filter was applied to result probability patches for connecting them in one big probability map without sewed edges. Designed flexible architecture allows to train neural network for pixel-wise semantic segmentation with accuracy value 0.9863 on the tiny dataset.

Keywords: machine learning, deep learning, semantic segmentation, U-Net, Keras, blending filter

1. Introduction

In 2018, the strictly protected sand lizards were relocated from several construction sites to this formerly military-used area. If possible, even more animals should be relocated here in the following years. Special habitat elements were created for this area. The fenced area is grazed, so that there is no need for mowing.

The conservation status is controlled by monitoring the population. For this purpose the animals have to be counted rotationally.

Machine learning (and deep learning in particular) focused on using modern mathematics and programming tools to figure out numerical presentation of abstract and stochastic source data. In the past few years, deep learning helped moving the computer vision to production by extending possibilities and improving result accuracy.

Before starting the model synthesis for the task of lizard localization on the ground, we have collected objective features (issues):

- The object is very small. To be able to distinguish from leaves and branches, drone camera should detect a back drawing of lizard and its legs.

- Distribution of lizards on the ground is very small. After reviewing 1800 sample, images of two to three lizards were found.
- Nature has created lizards very similar to the leaves around them (natural camouflage effect).
- Partially displayed. Except two to three lizards which were found in source dataset, some potential objects were found too. It could be lizards hidden under branches, leaves, and grass.
- Different sunlight angle and brightness.
- Motion blurring.

Some of these issues could be delegated to drone-shooting side, but most parts should be solved by machine learning.

2. Data

Running ahead we could say that it is a classical binary classification problem where the prediction result will be measured in continuous space.

In the notation of binary classification problem, there are two classes: positive—part of image where lizards exist; and negative—all except lizards.

To narrow the negative class presentation, and make it representative for our task, negative samples for this class were taken from the source image dataset. In such a way, we specify all features on the ground except lizards as a negative class (**Figure 1**).

The positive class was represented by extremely small number of lizards from the initial dataset.

We reviewed manually 1800 images from the drone dataset, and only two to three lizards had been found. It appeared that we have not enough positive images for training. To solve this problem and move forward, we reused lizards' images

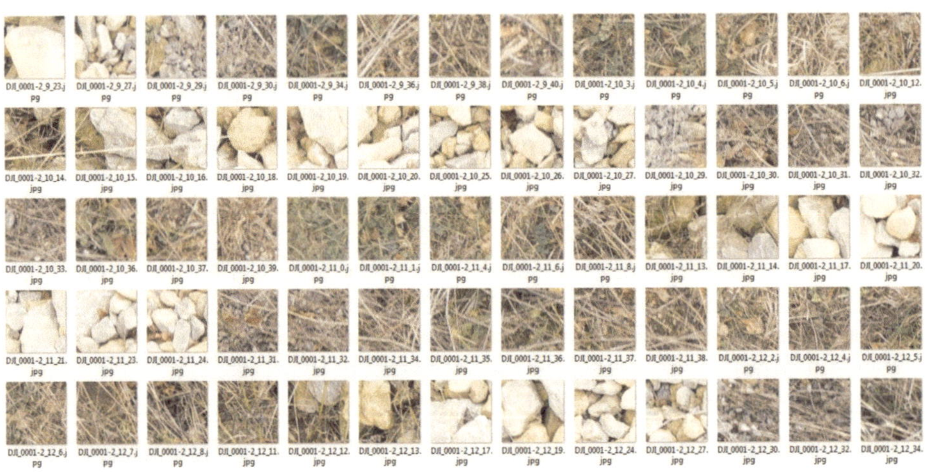

Figure 1.
Example of negative sample images.

Figure 2.
Example of positive sample images.

from the Internet. About 1000 lizard images were taken from "ImageNet" dataset. After obvious filtering, about 600 images remained. We left green lizards which were shot from the top view (similar to drone view dataset) (**Figure 2**).

For labeling masks for positive image samples, we used simple and standalone manual annotation software "VGG Image Annotator (VIA)" [1].

At the end of data presentation, we should note about the great approach of growing the source dataset. The examples available for learning were limited so the classification problem added a layer of complexity. So this is a challenging machine learning problem, but it is also a realistic one: in a lot of real-world use cases, even small-scale data collection can be extremely expensive or sometimes near-impossible. Being able to make the most out of very little data is a key skill of a competent data scientist.

In order to make the most of our few training examples, we "augment" them via a number of random transformations, so that our model would never see twice the exact same picture. This helps prevent overfitting and helps the model generalize better:

- Flip vertical/horizontal
- Rotation
- Translation
- Zooming
- Color desaturation

3. Training scheme

Two-steps training scheme separates "rough training" and "subtle training". Each step is supported by fourfold cross-validation to obtain the best representative results. Well parameterized model allows using the same model with different parameters (**Figure 3**):

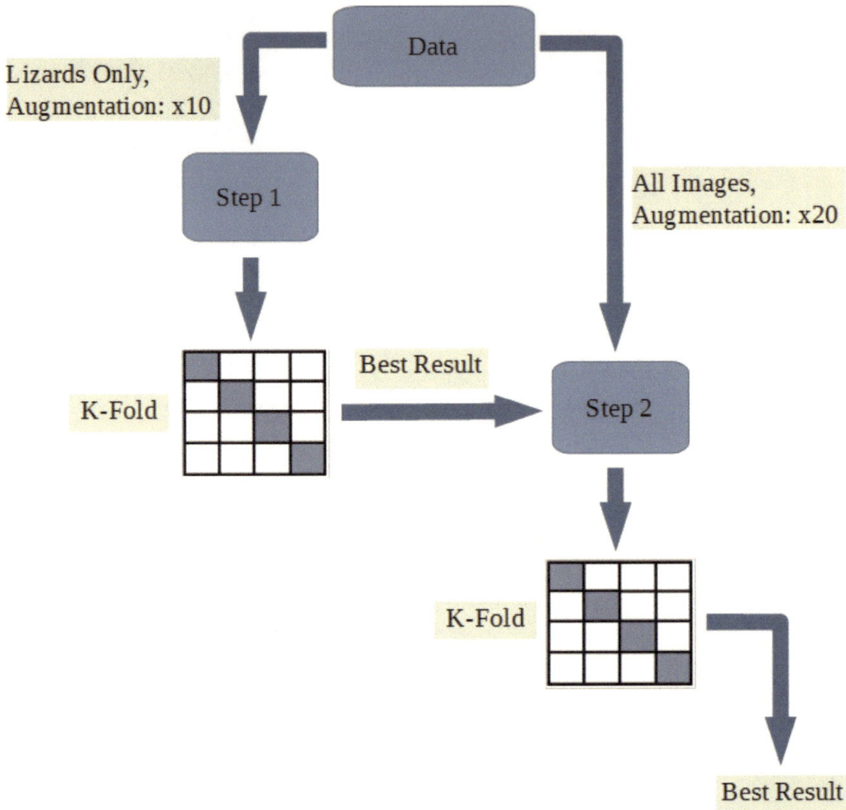

Figure 3.
Multistage scheme of the training process.

Step 1 (rough training)
Aims:

- Avoid class imbalance during initial training
- Attention to local minima

Methods:

- Training on samples which contains positive objects only (lizards)
- Rough regularization to avoid overfit
- Augmentation increase dataset size by $\times 10$
- Optimizer: Adam (learning rate: 0.001)

Step 2 (subtle training)
Aims:

- Training to obtain the best possible result
- Attention to global minima

Methods:

- Training on all samples (as lizards as background)
- Tiny regularization
- Augmentation increase dataset size by ×20
- Optimizer: Nadam (learning rate: default)

4. Data generator

Parameterized data generator allows to control the data filing used for training and for testing. Augmentation allows to drastically increase the dataset size by image transforming. Content filter allows filling the control of the percent of positive (lizards) pixels in each image used for training (**Figure 4**):

- Image augmentation parameters
    - Rotation up to 360 degrees
    - Width/height shifting up to 20%
    - Shear up to 20 degrees
    - Zoom +/− up to 20%
    - Random horizontal/vertical flip
    - Fill mode: "reflect"
- Content data filter controls class-imbalance in source dataset
- K-fold splitter provides datasets for separate training and implement cross-validation

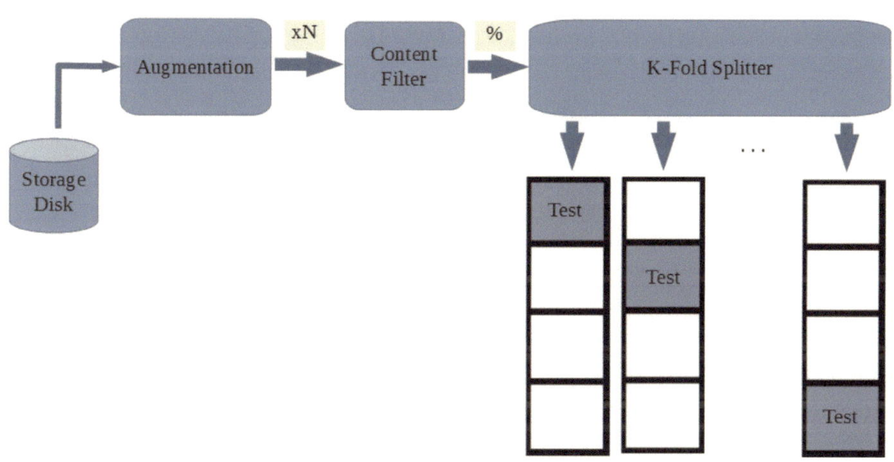

Figure 4.
Scheme of data generator.

5. Model

We did not reuse the existing solution like YOLO [2] or MASK-RCNN [3] because benefits of these networks focused on relatively big objects with at least 10–20% covered by a whole image. In case with lizards, we have only 0.08% coverage of the object on the image.

Instead, the model architecture was based on the well-known pixel-wise image segmentation approach "U-Net" [4] and extended by adding atrous/dilated convolution layers [5] to the low-resolution part of the neural network.

The model was implemented in Keras [6]—a high-level neural network API, written in Python and capable of running on TensorFlow, CNTK, or Theano.

Input layer "input_1" gets three-channel (RGB) image in range 0–255.

Pre-processing layer "lambda_1" converts input 255-ranged values to 0–1 range.

As the usual U-Net neural network, it has encoder and decoder parts, connected each other via residual connections.

Encoder block contains a pair of convolution layers with regularization block in the middle and max pooling layer in output (**Figure 5**).

We found that encoder block requires only dropout regularization.

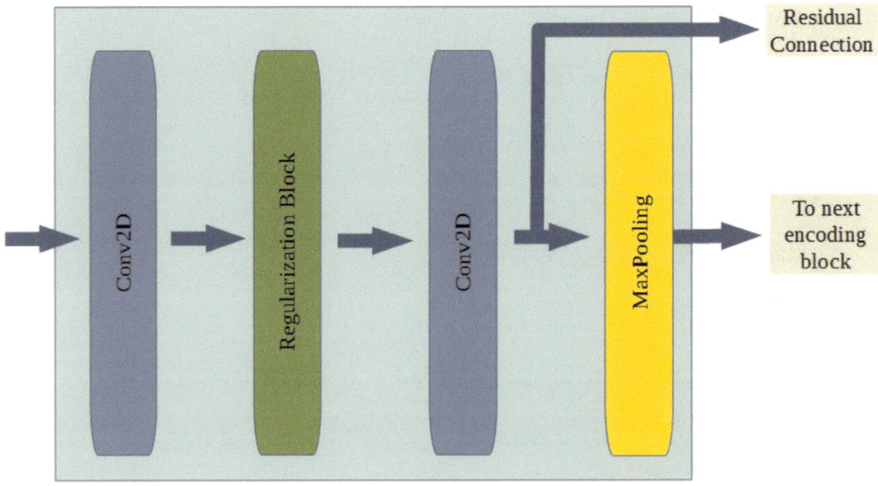

Figure 5.
Encoding block.

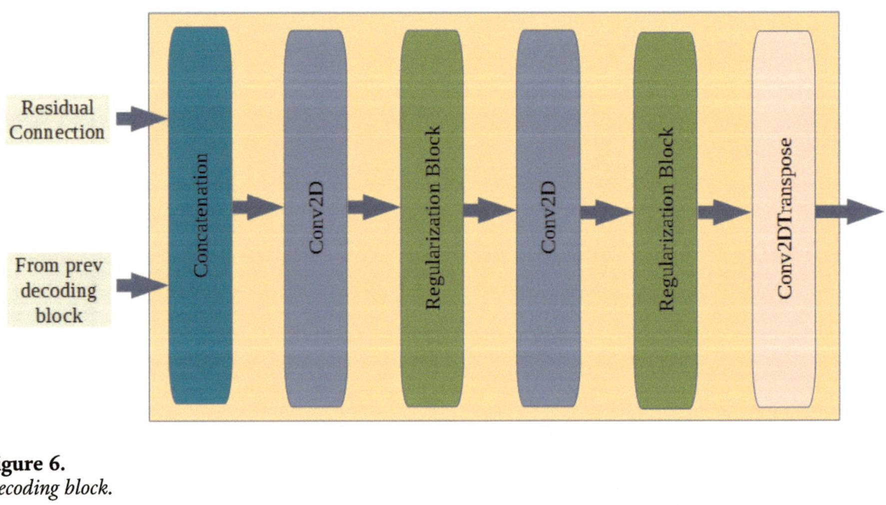

Figure 6.
Decoding block.

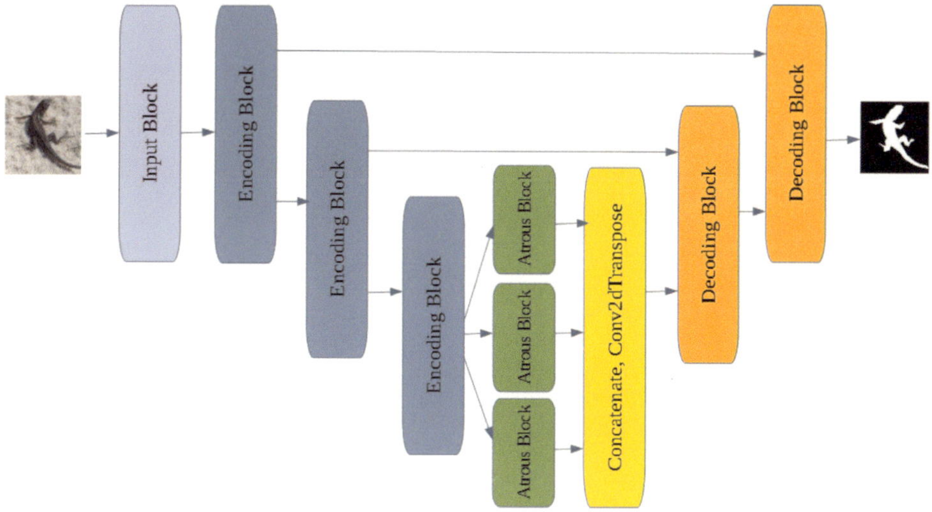

Figure 7.
Final scheme of neural network model.

Decoder block contains a pair of convolution layers with regularization block in the middle as well as encoder block, but instead of max pooling output layer, it uses Conv2DTranspose layer and input layer concatenation to connect the result of the previous block with residual connection (**Figure 6**).

We found out the best regularization for decoder block is mix dropout with batch normalization.

To extend basic U-Net, we added three dilated convolution blocks with dilation rates 4, 8, and 12 between encoder and decoder parts of the NN.

The final block scheme of used neural network is displayed in **Figure** 7.

Model details:

- Encoder/decoder convolution layers
  - Initializes: He normal
  - Padding: Same
  - Kernel size: 3
  - Activation function: Rectified linear unit (ReLU)
- Dilated convolution layers
  - Initializes: He normal
  - Padding: Same
  - Kernel size: 1
  - Activation function: Rectified linear unit (ReLU)
  - Dilation rates: 4, 8, 12

- Max Pooling
  - Pooling size: 2
- Conv2DTranspose layers (except output layer)
  - Initializes: He normal
  - Padding: Same
  - Kernel size: 3
  - Activation function: Rectified linear unit (ReLU)
  - Strides: 2
- Conv2DTranspose layers (output layer)
  - Initializes: Glorot/Xavier normal
  - Padding: Same
  - Kernel size: 3
  - Activation function: Sigmoid
  - Filters: 1
- Loss function: BinCrossE-Log(Jaccard index)

It is obvious for the binary classification task to use logistic sigmoid function [7] as activation function in output layer which represents the probability of relation between each pixel to positive class.

Loss function of the neural network was binary cross entropy [8] extended by Jaccard index [9].

Winners of Kaggle competitions, who used U-Net for proving their approach said:

"It is well known that in order to get better results your evaluation metric and your loss function need to be as similar as possible. The problem here however is that Jaccard index is not differentiable. One can generalize it for probability prediction, which on one hand, in the limit of the very confident predictions, turns into normal Jaccard and on the other hand is differentiable—allowing the usage of it in the algorithms that are optimized with gradient descent" [10].

6. Post-processing

In fact, the U-Net takes an image patch and makes predictions on those small local windows, without data near the border of the patches, so there might first be a high error on the predictions made near the boundary of the window, in plus of the fact that predictions may be just concatenated, so it looks even more jagged (**Figure 8**).

To get with this problem, we reused well-designed solution prepared to deal with it—"blending predicted patches smoothly is a must to please the human eye."

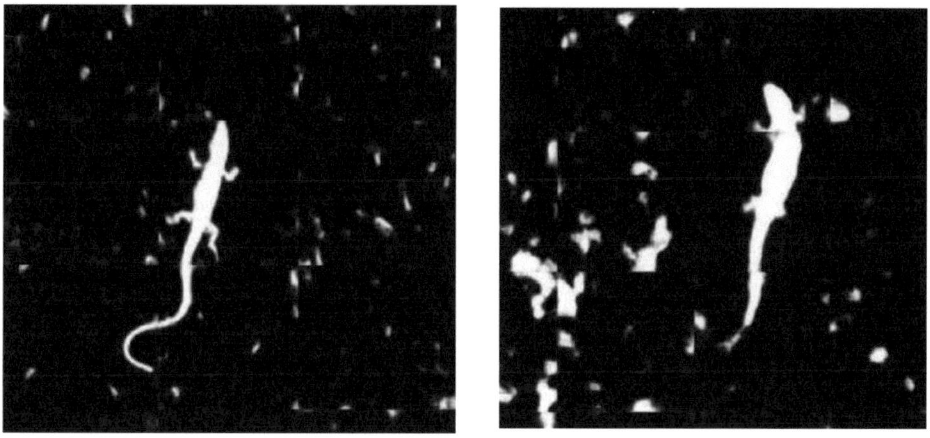

Figure 8.
Connected patches without any blending.

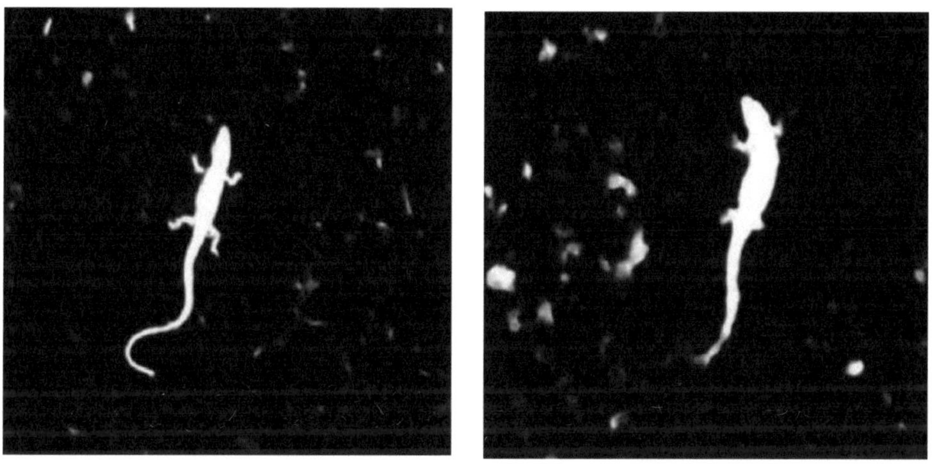

Figure 9.
Connected patches with applied blending.

(https://github.com/Vooban/Smoothly-Blend-Image-Patches)
To get smoothed results, the following steps are applied to each patch:

- Use the four possible 90 degrees rotations, as well as a mirrored version of those rotations, so as to augment the images eightfold for prediction before blending the predictions together

- 2D interpolation between overlapping patches when doing the final predictions

After applying the post-processing filter, we obtain the following probability map for the same samples (**Figure 9**).

7. Logs

We used online service https://www.comet.ml for monitoring the training process. Following are the results of training network with different hyperparameters values (**Figures 10–11**).

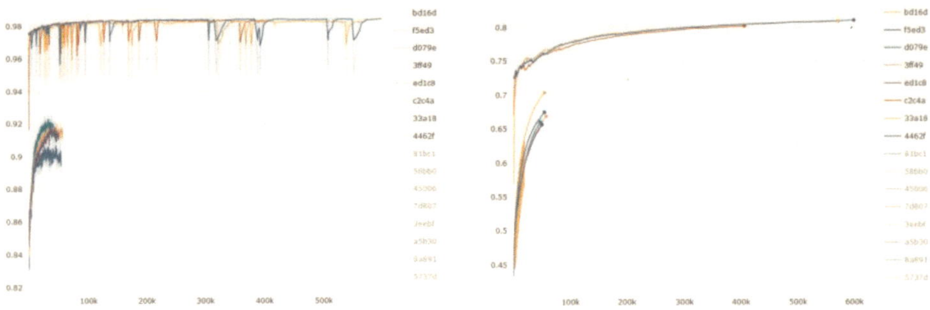

Figure 10.
The model's training history which does not use bias in convolution layers and does not use additional batch normalization in atrous blocks.

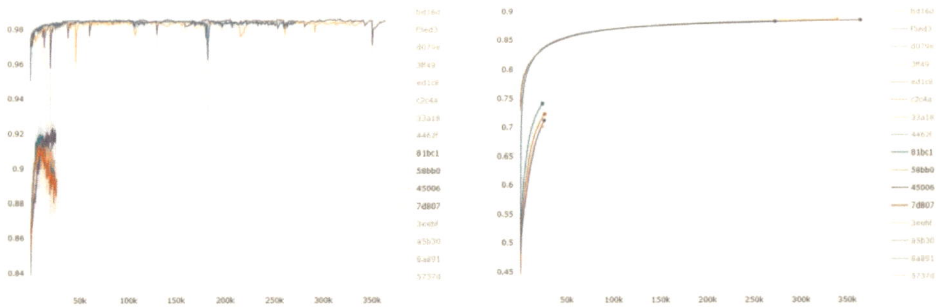

Figure 11.
The model's training history which uses bias in convolution layers and does not use additional batch normalization in atrous blocks.

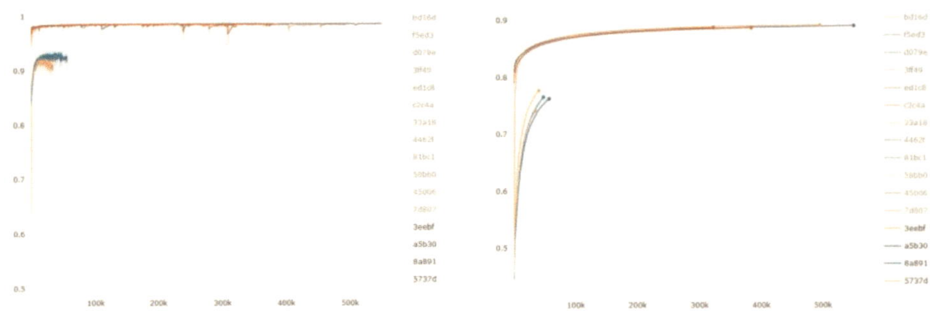

Figure 12.
Model's training history which does not use bias in convolution layers and use additional batch normalization in atrous blocks.

7.1 Model does not use bias in convolution layers and does not use additional batch normalization in atrous blocks

Best validation accuracy: 0.9841.
Best Jaccard index: 0.8098.

7.2 Model use bias in convolution layers and do not use additional batch normalization in atrous blocks

Best validation accuracy: 0.9844.
Best Jaccard index: 0.8857.

7.3 Model does not use bias in convolution layers and use additional batch normalization in atrous blocks

Best validation accuracy: 0.9863.
Best Jaccard index: 0.8913.

8. Results

Below are the set of result images taken from a drone with highlighted objects predicted as lizards.

The color of the highlighted rectangles has a range from blue to red with respect to the probability of the predicted object. Blue rectangles highlighted predictions with low probability. Red rectangles highlighted predictions with high probability (**Figures 13–15**).

Figure 13.
Example of detection. Gray lizard detected with high probability. There are gaps between rocks that could have quite high probability too.

Figure 14.
Example of detection. Green lizard detected with high probability. Branches have less but detected probabilities.

Figure 15.
Example of detection. One gray (between rocks) and one white (on the rock) lizard detected with high probability. Branches have less but detected probabilities.

9. Conclusion

The design and the architecture of the developed application allowed us to build a flexible model of the neural network and find the best configuration of hyperparameters.

As was found with the help of using CometML service, the best case of hyperparameters is:

"Model does not use bias in convolution layers and use additional batch normalization in atrous blocks."

Best validation accuracy: 0.9863.

Best Jaccard index: 0.8913.

The following is a list of implemented features:

- Disk-caching allows to use unlimited size of datasets and avoid memory overflow problem.

- Used GPU memory amount control allows using several trainings on the same GPU.

- Attention to reproducing trainings allows to compare different results.

- Source data augmentation allows training on the tiny-size dataset.

- K-fold cross-validation allows training more deeper and obtain better results.

- Parametrized training allows stacking training solutions.

- Structured solutions allows to build multistep training.

- Post-processing allows to obtain smoothly blended probability for the whole image and, as a result, better prediction quality for big image resolution.

DOI: http://dx.doi.org/10.5772/intechopen.88437

Author details

Ravi Sahu
Strayos, St. Louis, MO, USA

*Address all correspondence to: ravi@strayos.com

References

[1] Dutta A. Visual Geometry Group. Oxford University. Available from: http://www.robots.ox.ac.uk/~vgg/software/via/

[2] Redmon J, Divvala SK, Girshick RB, Farhadi A. You Only Look Once: Unified, Real-Time Object Detection. Available from: https://arxiv.org/abs/1506.02640

[3] He K, Gkioxari G, Dollár P, Girshick G. Mask {R-CNN}. Available from: https://arxiv.org/abs/1703.06870

[4] Ronneberger O, Fischer P, Brox T. U-Net: Convolutional Networks for Biomedical Image Segmentation. Available from: https://arxiv.org/abs/1505.04597

[5] Chen L-C, Papandreou G, Schroff F, Adam H. Rethinking Atrous Convolution for Semantic Image Segmentation. Available from: https://arxiv.org/abs/1706.05587

[6] Chollet F. Available from: https://keras.io/

[7] https://www.sciencedirect.com/topics/computer-science/sigmoid-function

[8] http://neuralnetworksanddeeplearning.com/chap3.html

[9] https://www.sciencedirect.com/topics/computer-science/jaccard-coefficient

[10] Iglovikov V, Mushinskiy S. Kaggle: Dstl Satellite Imagery Competition, 3rd Place Winners' Interview: Vladimir & Sergey. Available from: http://blog.kaggle.com/2017/05/09/dstl-satellite-imagery-competition-3rd-place-winners-interview-vladimir-sergey/

Section 2

Re-Identification

Chapter 4

Deep-Facial Feature-Based Person Reidentification for Authentication in Surveillance Applications

Yogameena Balasubramanian, Nagavani Chandrasekaran, Sangeetha Asokan and Saravana Sri Subramanian

Abstract

Person reidentification (Re-ID) has been a problem recently faced in computer vision. Most of the existing methods focus on body features which are captured in the scene with high-end surveillance system. However, it is unhelpful for authentication. The technology came up empty in surveillance scenario such as in London's subway bomb blast, and Bangalore ATM brutal attack cases, even though the suspected images exist in official databases. Hence, the prime objective of this chapter is to develop an efficient facial feature-based person reidentification framework for controlled scenario to authenticate a person. Initially, faces are detected by faster region-based convolutional neural network (Faster R-CNN). Subsequently, landmark points are obtained using supervised descent method (SDM) algorithm, and the face is recognized, by the joint Bayesian model. Each image is given an ID in the training database. Based on their similarity with the query image, it is ranked with the Re-ID index. The proposed framework overcomes the challenges such as pose variations, low resolution, and partial occlusions (mask and goggles). The experimental results (accuracy) on benchmark dataset demonstrate the effectiveness of the proposed method which is inferred from the observation of receiver operating characteristic (ROC) curve and cumulative matching characteristics (CMC) curve.

Keywords: video surveillance, person reidentification, facial feature-based reidentification, Faster R-CNN, SDM

1. Introduction

Nowadays, a large network of cameras is predominantly used in public places like airports, railway stations, bus stands, and office buildings. These networks of cameras provide enormous video data, which are monitored manually and may be utilized only when the need arises to ascertain the fact. Fascinatingly, an automated analysis of such huge video data can improve the quality of surveillance by processing the video faster. Above all, it is more useful for high-level surveillance tasks like suspicious activity detection or undesirable event prediction for timely alerts. Especially, the person Re-ID task is one of the current attentions in computer vision research. Establishing the correspondence between the image sequences of a person, across multiple camera views or in same camera at different time intervals, is known as person Re-ID. Simply, it implies that a person, seen previously, is identified in his/her next appearance using a unique descriptor of the person. Humans do it all the time without much effort. Our eyes and brains are trained to detect, localize, identify, and later reidentify the objects and people in the real world. Humans are able to extract such a descriptor based on the person's face, height and structure, attire, hair color, hair style, walking pattern, etc. However, a person's face is the most unique and reliable feature that human uses to identify the people [1]. Therefore, facial feature-based Re-ID is used to verify and recognize either the person seen in the camera is the same person spotted earlier in the same camera at a different time. Especially, it is applicable in controlled environment where the face database is available.

1.1 Facial feature-based person reidentification

In earlier days, it was stated that "reidentification cannot be done by face due to immature camera capturing technology" [2]. Nowadays due to remarkable growth of VLSI-based fabrication techniques, a person's face-capturing ability of camera has increased even in low illumination condition [3]. Therefore, facial feature Re-ID booms, and it is a well-authenticated one. Facial feature-based reidentification is a process of identifying a person using his/her face under consistent labeling across multiple cameras or even with the same camera to reestablish different tracks. Since the face is a biometric feature that cannot be replicated easily, it is used for human reidentification [4]. Also the face is the most natural and unique hallmark widely used as a person's identifier [5]. In reality, reidentification cannot be applied to find similarity among people after several days due to likely alterations in their visual appearance like attire, gait, etc. Li et al. [6] say that the face is also helpful in person reidentification and deserves attention. Li et al. [7] says the feature extracted from neck and above is an important clue for person reidentification. Biometric recognition features like the face, iris, and fingerprint can overcome these constraints by working on highly discriminative and stable features. Unlike the iris and fingerprint, to identify and recognize a person's "face" are successfully captured in the scene with improved camera technology. Beyond face recognition techniques, face reidentification techniques improve the system's metric learning and provide the best assurance to person's presence in the captured environment [8]. This proposed framework focuses on facial feature-based Re-ID for indoor surveillance such as IT sectors, government agencies, and ATM centers. The emergence of the facial feature-based person Re-ID task can be attributed to the increasing demand of public safety and the widespread huge camera networks in theme parks, university campuses, streets, IT sectors, etc. However, it is extremely expensive to rely solely on brute-force human labor to accurately and efficiently spot a person-of-interest or to track a person across cameras [9, 10]. Automation of the facial feature-based person Re-ID is quite difficult to be accomplished without human intervention. It is still a challenging topic, due to the fact that the appearance of the same face looks dramatically different in controlled or uncontrolled environments with pose variations, different expressions, illumination conditions, low resolutions, and partial occlusions specifically, in the abovementioned scenarios.

The rest of the chapter is organized as follows. In Section 2, prior research works on person reidentification including non-facial feature-based and facial feature-based Re-ID are summarized. Section 3 includes problem formulation, objective, and the key contribution toward this work. Section 4 elucidates the detailed description of the proposed Re-ID framework. Section 5 presents the experimental results and discussion on face detection and Re-ID with challenging face detection benchmark datasets and TCE dataset. The step-by-step process of the proposed facial feature-based Re-ID framework's result for TCE dataset is also explored in Section 5. Finally, conclusions and the future research scope are presented in Sections 6 and 7, respectively.

1.2 Motivation

Three incidents in surveillance scenario motivate the research work toward person Re-ID. The first, being the London's subway bomb blast on July 7, 2005, where 52 persons were killed and 784 persons injured. It took thousands of investigators and several weeks to parse the city's CCTV footage after the attacks. The second, being the Boston Marathon bombing on April 15, 2013, where 3 persons were killed and 264 persons injured. Investigators had gone through hundreds of hours of video, looking for people "doing things that are different from what everybody else is doing." The work was painstaking and mind-numbing. One agent watched the same segment of video 400 times [11]. The third incident was the Bangalore ATM brutal attack on November 19, 2013, where one woman was seriously injured. The police commissioner of Bangalore expressed that in spite of all their sincere efforts, no arrest was made in the ATM attack case. However, they could identify the assailant only through CCTV footage. In all these three cases, the technology came up empty, even though the suspected images especially faces exist in official databases.

1.3 Applications

Facial feature-based person reidentification has various applications. It is applied in tracking a particular person across multiple nonoverlapping cameras and detecting the trajectory of a person for surveillance, forensic, and security applications. Further, in government offices and IT parks, the access card-based entry system can be replaced by facial feature-based Re-ID system to improve security and authentication.

1.4 Challenges

Facial feature-based person Re-ID as a task has many challenges such as varying poses, low resolution, illumination variations, different expressions, different hairstyles, wearing goggles, and occlusions. These challenges create intricacy in face detection and verification. In this chapter, the major challenges such as pose variations, partial occlusions, and wearing goggles are focused.

2. Related works

The person reidentification research started along with multi-camera tracking in the year 2005 [12]. Several important Re-ID directions have been addressed since then; some of them are based on camera setting, sample set, appearance-based, nonappearance-based, and body model as shown in **Figure 1**. Comparison of recent facial feature-based reidentification techniques are shown in **Table 1**.

Apart from facial feature-based person reidentification algorithms which suffer from noisy samples with background clutter and partial occlusion, it is problematic to differentiate an individual. Very few deep learning algorithms on "facial

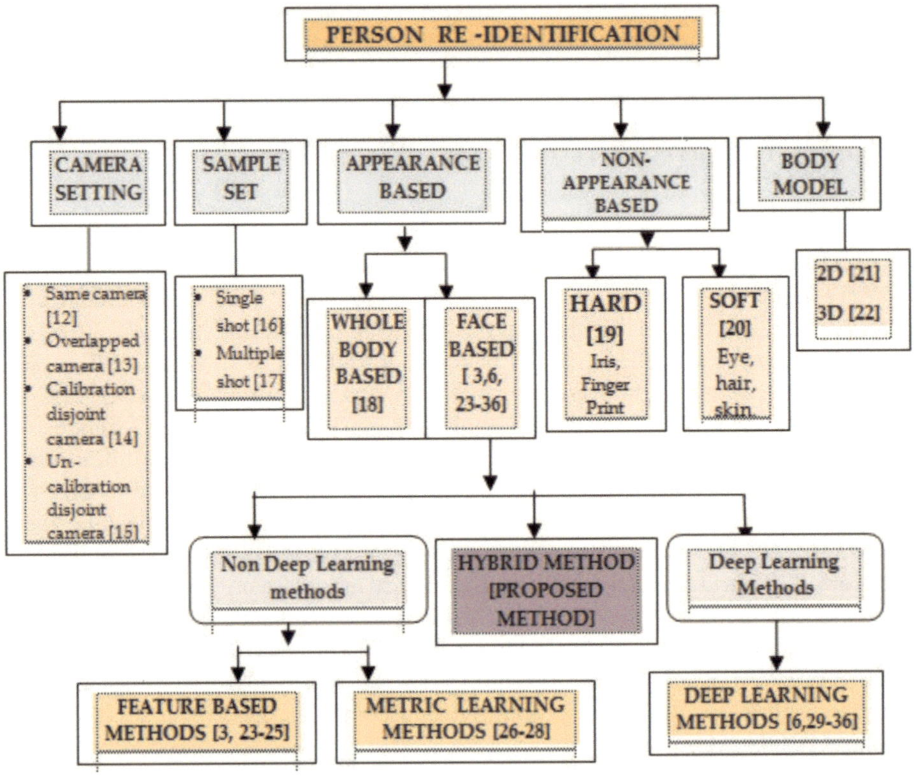

Figure 1.
Categorization of person reidentification algorithms [3, 6, 12–36].

feature-based" person reidentification are found in literature. However, deep learning features are heavily dependent on large-scale labeling of samples, they deal only with frontal and profile faces, and they fail under various illumination conditions, pose variations, and partial occlusions.

2.1 Observation and inference

From the existing related works, it can be concluded that very few works focus on deep learning methods for facial feature-based person reidentification. These works do not concentrate on the real-world challenges such as low image resolution, pose variations, and partial occlusions. Nevertheless, when we consider a controlled environment, such as authenticated laboratories and IT parks, face recognition-based person reidentification is possible which is vague currently. From the above discussion and analysis, a deeply trained facial feature-based person Re-ID framework is proposed which includes face detection by Faster R-CNN, joint Bayesian face-verification approach, and face reidentification. The scope of this chapter incorporates the challenges in the real-world environment like pose variation, low resolution, illumination changes, partial occlusion, and even goggle-wearing conditions.

3. Problem formulation

Existing works, related to the person Re-ID, deal only with the gait-based Re-ID for a short period, and very few works focus on long period reidentification of an individual. Research has been in progress toward long-term Re-ID (i.e., video is

TITLE	NON DEEP LEARNING METHODS	MERITS AND DEMERITS	TITLE	DEEP LEARNING METHODS	MERITS AND DEMERITS
	FEATURE BASED		[30]	Face Net	Online triplet method-face aligned matching Fails for crowded scenario.
[24]	HAAR+LBP(LAB) CS-LBP, XCS-LBP	Fast and Accurate face detection. When detection rate slightly increases, false positive also increases.	[31]	Deep transfer metric learning	Cross dataset verification Does not work in crowded scenario.
[25]	Active shape Model(ASM), Extended Active shape model	Ability to recognize 2D & 3D face images. This statistical model, deformed while fitting the target image.	[32]	Deep Face	Strong Abilities of independent learning & feature extraction. Complex and long process
[26]	Adaptive Ensemble	Efficient ranking system. Only highest KL divergence samples are preserved in memory for future adaptations.	[6]	Thermal face Net	Ability to detect spoofing attacks. Deal only thermal frontal images and not suitable for profile faces.
[3]	3D face recognition	Good success rate. Restricted only to KINECT bounded environment.	[33]	Hyper plane-VGG Net	Efficient for profile faces and pose variations. Fails with partial occluded faces.
	METRIC LEARNING BASED		[34]	Deep self paced Learning	Learning stable discriminative features Ranking performance is poor.
[27]	LMNN	Learn with Multiple features Do not recognize occluded Faces	[35]	Siamese DNN	Efficient for low illumination images Fails under pose variations.
[28]	ITML & LUPI	Learn an additional metric for privileged information. Learning Metrics are complex.	[36]	GAN	Best for pose variation and large viewpoint variation Huge training samples are required to improve the accuracy, which is challenging in case of surveillance dataset.
[29]	Multimodal distance metric learning methods	Efficient learning metrics Demands large computational time.	[37]	Multi-stream features distance fusion method	Excellent Extraction using body partition network Fails under partial occlusions.

Table 1.
Comparison of recent face reidentification techniques [3, 6, 24–37].

recorded for a month using a single camera), but at the same time, it is the need of the hour problem for authentication as well as for public safety. Here, facial feature-based Re-ID is the authenticated one, and other feature-based Re-ID is the suspicious one. Hence, there is a need to develop facial feature-based Re-ID using deep learning algorithm which handles low resolution, illumination variation, pose variation, and partial occlusion.

3.1 Objective

The main objective of the proposed framework is to develop facial feature-based person reidentification algorithm, using deep learning technology that works well for long-term Re-ID even in low illumination, pose variation, partial occlusion condition (Goggles, Mask, etc.) for a controlled environment.

3.2 Contribution face-based: hybrid Re-ID method

The existing person reidentification is entirely based on global appearances or gait features. The prevailing algorithms have been developed so far to reidentify a person, based on his/her facial features that identify a person and do not address the experimentation on the challenging conditions such as low resolution, varying illumination, pose variations, and partial occlusion. This chapter proposes a hybrid combination of deep learning method Faster R-CNN for face detection and uses traditional method like joint Bayesian with SDM approach for reidentification which takes the advantages of both methods.

Moreover, another key contribution is the strong experimentation with benchmark datasets and TCE dataset captured under varying illumination conditions, with pose variations, various resolutions, and partial occlusion such as mask (green, blue, black shawl), specs, and goggles.

4. Methodology

The proposed facial feature-based person reidentification framework for surveillance applications in a controlled environment is portrayed in **Figure 2**.

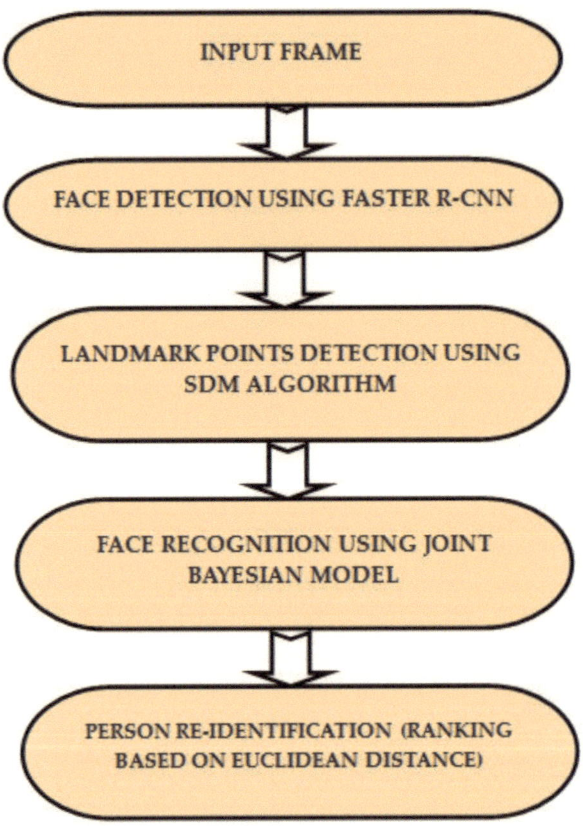

Figure 2.
Overview of the proposed deep-facial feature-based person Re-ID framework.

Here, the face detection module is implemented, by means of the deep learning-based approach (Faster R-CNN), where several convolutional and pooling layers are employed to extract deep features. Face recognition is performed, using the joint Bayesian model. Finally, the ranking is done, based on the similarity measure between the query image and the images in the database to provide a Re-ID. Finally, the ranking is done, based on the similarity measure between the query image and the images in the database to provide a Re-ID.

4.1 Overview of deep learning algorithms for face detection

After the remarkable success of a deep CNN in image classification on the ImageNet Large Scale Visual Recognition Challenge (ILSVRC) 2012, Ross Girshick and his peers concluded that for a given complicated image, CNNs can be used to identify different objects and their boundaries in the image. Ross et al. [38] introduced a region-based CNN (R-CNN) for object detection. The pipeline consists of two stages. First, R-CNN creates bounding boxes, or region proposals, using a process called selective search. The selective search process identifies the object selecting the image area through the windows of different sizes, and for each size, it tries to group together the adjacent pixels by texture, color, or intensity. Once the proposals are created, R-CNN warps the region to a standard square size (e.g., 227×227) and passes it through to a modified version of AlexNet. On the final layer of the CNN, R-CNN adds a classifier that simply classifies whether this is an object, and if so, identifies the type of the object. The final step of R-CNN is to tighten the bounding box to fit the true dimension of the object. This is done, by using a simple linear regressor on the region proposal. The significance of the R-CNN is that it brings high accuracy by CNNs on classification tasks for the object detection problem. Its success is largely due to the act of transferring the supervised pretrained object representation for image classification. The R-CNN used different models to extract CNN-based image features, classify, and tighten bounding boxes. This makes the pipeline extremely hard to train these models. Ross Girshick, the first author of R-CNN, solved these problems, leading to the second algorithm—the Fast R-CNN [39]. Fast R-CNN uses a technique known as RoI Pool (region of interest pooling), which shares the forward pass of a CNN for an image across its subregions. For each region, the CNN features are obtained by selecting a respective region from the CNN's feature map. In addition, the Fast R-CNN jointly trains the CNN, classifier, and bounding box regressor in a single model. The R-CNN used different models to extract CNN-based image features, classify, and tighten bounding boxes, whereas Fast R-CNN used a single network to compute all these three. **Figure 3a** shows sample face detection results along with the confidence score using R-CNN. Even with all these advancements, there was still one remaining clog in the Fast R-CNN process, the region proposer. In the Fast R-CNN, these were done, using a slow process selective search, which was found to be the hindrance of the overall process. In [40], Ross Girshick and his team found a way to solve this problem and named it Faster R-CNN. The Faster R-CNN works to combat the complex training pipeline that both R-CNN and Fast R-CNN get exhibited. The slowest part in the Fast R-CNN was the selective search.

4.2 Face detection using Faster R-CNN

This chapter trains the Faster R-CNN on the existing benchmark datasets and in our TCE dataset for face detection. The input frames are resized based on the ratio 1024/max (w, h) in order to fit it in the GPU memory, where w and h are the width and height of the image, respectively. The Faster R-CNN is designed to

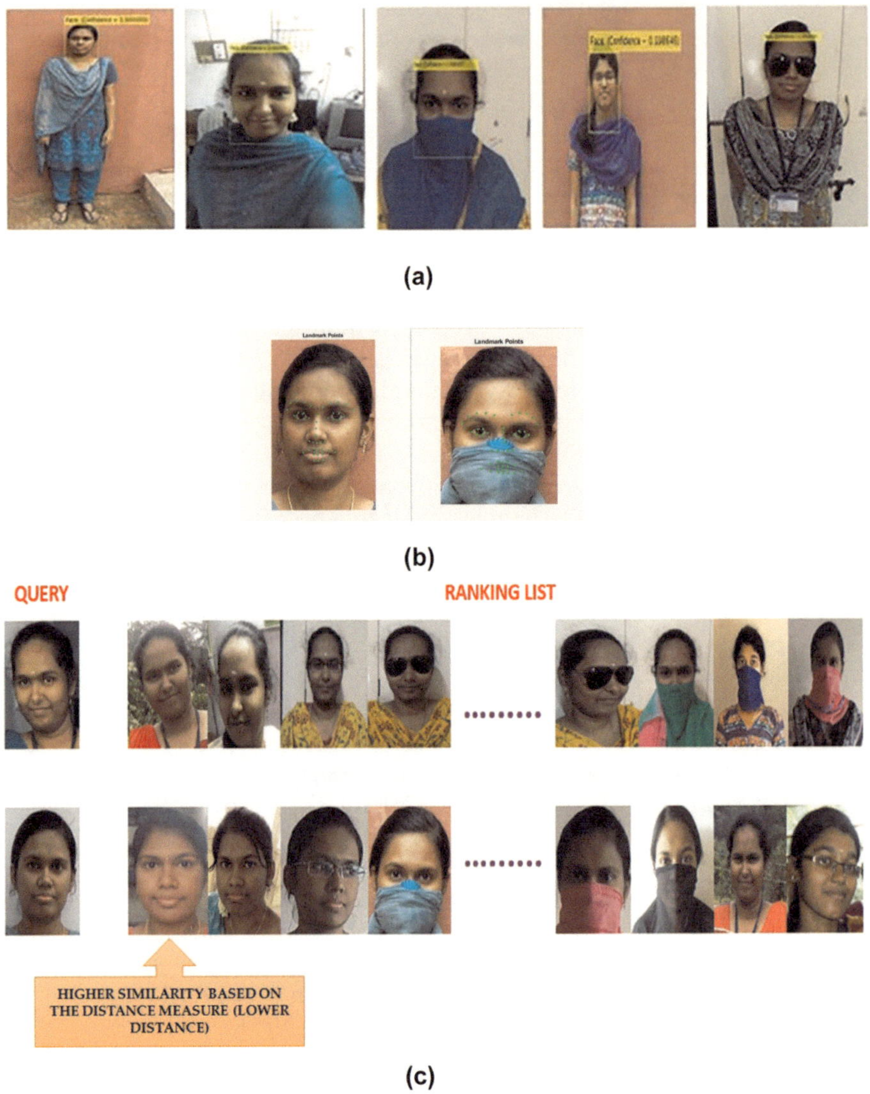

Figure 3.
(a) Face detection result using R-CNN for TCE dataset, (b) detected landmark points using SDM algorithm, and (c) ranking list of the TCE gallery set with similarity.

extract the visual features hierarchically, from local low-level features to global high-level ones, by using convolution and pooling operations. Region proposal network (RPN) is used to generate region proposals for faces in an image. In the RPN, the convolution layers of a pretrained network are succeeded by a 3×3 convolutional layer. This corresponds to map a large spatial window or receptive field (e.g., 227×227 for AlexNet) in the input image to a low-dimensional feature vector at a center stride. Two 1×1 convolutional layers are then added for classification and regression branches for all spatial windows. Here, the regions are positive if the sample is >0.5 (denoted as $L = 1$), when the region has an intersection over union (IOU) overlap with the ground truth and the regions are negative if sample is <0.35 (denoted as $L = 0$). The remaining regions are ignored [41].

Softmax loss function given by Eq. (1) is used for training the face detection task:

$$Loss = -(1-L).\log(1-p) - L.\log(p) \tag{1}$$

In the aforementioned equation, p is the probability of occurrence of the candidate region, which is a required facial feature. The probability values p and $1-p$ are obtained from the final fully connected CNN layer for the detection task.

4.3 Face recognition using SDM and joint Bayesian approach

After detecting the face and extracting the facial feature, the next task is recognition of face, i.e., the given face is verified with the class of faces (face verification) and certified with face identity (face identification). Face verification means verifying whether the given two faces belong to the same person or not. Face identification means an identity number is assigned to the probe person face with respect to the gallery. The conventional face recognition pipeline uses the facial features for face alignment and face verification. To detect facial landmark points SDM is used. SDM learns in a supervised manner generic descent directions and is able to overcome many drawbacks of second-order optimization schemes, such as non-differentiability and expensive computation of the Jacobians and Hessians. Moreover, it is extremely fast and accurate. This method improves the minimization of analytic functions that overcomes the problem of facial feature detection and tracking. SDM solves nonlinear least squares (NLS) and accurate in facial feature detection and tracking in challenging databases. SDM algorithm [42] detects facial landmarks as shown in **Figure 3b**. By detecting the landmarks, face images are globally aligned by similarity transformation. Further based on the extracted features, the face is recognized by joint Bayesian model [43]. The joint probability of two faces of the same or different persons is calculated, by using joint Bayesian model. The feature representation of a face is given as a combination of inter- and intrapersonal variations, or $f = \sum(\mu, \varepsilon)$, where both μ and ε are estimated from the training data and represented in terms of Gaussian distributions. Face recognition is achieved through log-likelihood ratio test, as given in Eq. (2):

$$\text{Log}\ \frac{p(f1,f2|H_{\text{inter}})}{p(f1,f2|H_{\text{intra}})} \tag{2}$$

Here, the numerator and denominator are the joint probabilities of two faces ($f1$ and $f2$), when given the inter- or intrapersonal variation hypothesis (), respectively.

4.4 Euclidean distance-based reidentification process

Let us consider a probe person image p and a gallery set $G = \{g_i \mid i = 1, 2...n\}$, where n is the size of the gallery. Through computing their L2 (Euclidean) distances (p, g_i), the query result can be obtained as $R_p(G) = \{g_1^0, g_2^0, ...g_n^0\}$ where g_i^0 represents i-th image in the rank list and the distances between ? and g_i^0 satisfy $d(p, g_1^0) < d(p, g_2^0) < .... < d(p, g_n^0)$. Here a score $S(p, g_i^0)$ is used to define the similarity between p and g_i^0, and it is equal to the rank index of g_i^0. Based on the similarity score, a smaller distance indicates that the two images are more similar. Finally, all gallery images are ranked in ascendant order, by matching their L2 distances with the probe image to find out, which top n images can perform the corrected matches. **Figure 3c** shows the order in which the gallery images are ranked based on their similarity with the query image. The first image on the left corner has a higher similarity or a lower distance.

5. Experimental results

5.1 Dataset description

The HALLWAY, the WIDER FACE, FDDB, SPEVI (surveillance performance evaluation initiative) datasets are the benchmark datasets, used for face detection in this experiment. The HALLWAY dataset is used to evaluate person-to-person interaction recognition module. The WIDER FACE dataset is an effective training source for face detection. The WIDER FACE dataset is 10 times larger than existing dataset. The FDDB is designed for studying the problem of unconstrained face detection. It contains annotations for 5171 faces in a set of 2845 images taken from wild dataset. The SPEVI dataset is used for testing and evaluating target tracking algorithms for surveillance-related applications. Apart from these benchmark datasets, real-time TCE dataset is also used in this experiment. Sample frames of various benchmark datasets and TCE dataset is depicted in **Figure 4**. It consists of face images of various persons, captured under varying illumination conditions, with pose variations, various resolutions, and partial occlusion such as mask (green, blue, black shawl), specs, and black goggles. In TCE dataset, each row in figure corresponds to the same person, but the variations exist due to the difference in pose, viewpoint, illumination, image quality, and occlusion. Their corresponding specifications are given in **Table 2**.

5.2 Evaluation using benchmark and TCE dataset

This chapter considers a single-size training mode. **Figure 5a–c** brings out the sample detection results on the WIDER FACE, FDDB, and HALLWAY dataset, where the red color bounding boxes are ground-truth annotations and the yellow color bounding boxes are the detection results, using Faster R-CNN. Finally, more

Figure 4.
Sample frames with challenging conditions (a) HALLWAY, (b) and (c) WIDER FACE, (d) FDDB, (e) SPEVI, and (f) TCE dataset.

DATASETS	IMAGE/ VIDEO	SCENARIO	FRAME SIZE	NUMBER OF FACES	FRAME FORMAT
Hallway	Video(17 FPS)	Indoor	320*240	Interaction faces	.avi
WIDER FACE (Press Conference)	Image	Indoor & Outdoor	576*1024 to 1544*1024	393,703 labeled faces	.jpg
WIDER FACE (handshaking)	Image	Indoor and Outdoor	295*1024 to 1249*1024	90	.jpg
FDDB	Image	Indoor and Outdoor	450*320 (approx.)	5,171 Faces	.jpg
SPEVI 1	Image	Indoor	21*53 to 176*326	3081 faces	.jpg
TCE	Image	Indoor	576*576	300 faces	.jpg

Table 2.
Specifications of various benchmark datasets and TCE dataset.

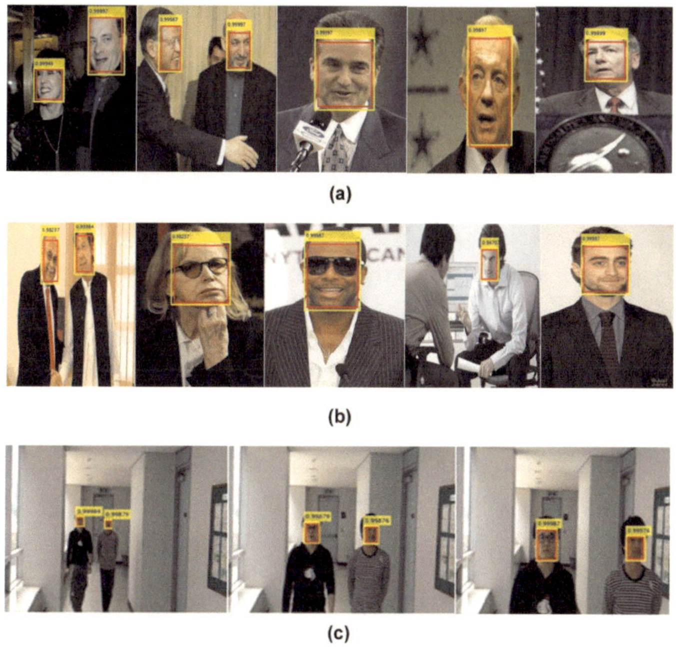

Figure 5.
Sample detection results on the various dataset, where red color bounding boxes are ground-truth annotations and yellow color bounding boxes are detection results using Faster R-CNN sample detection results using Faster R-CNN, (a) WIDER FACE dataset, (b) FDDB dataset, and (c) HALLWAY dataset.

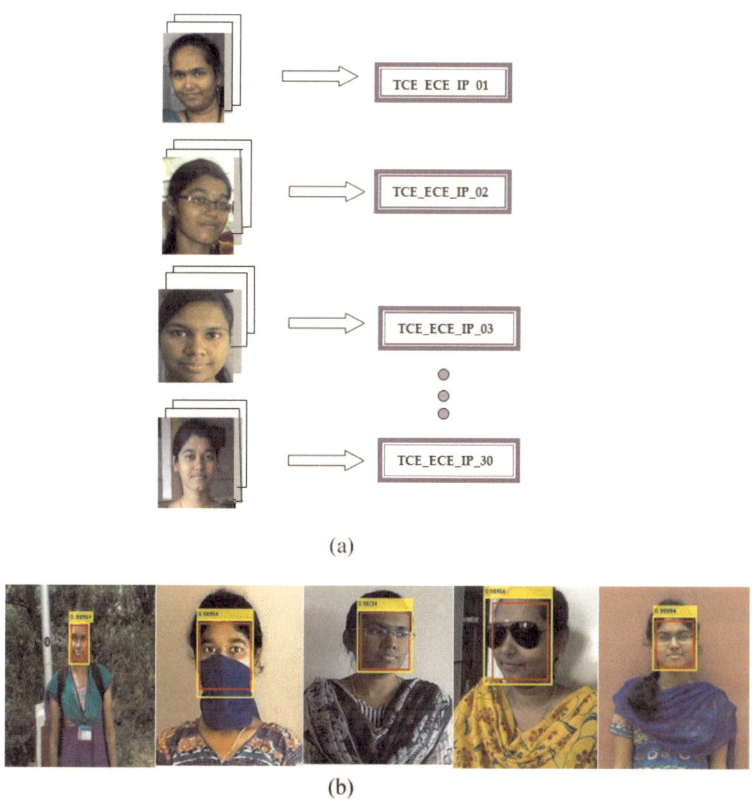

Figure 6.
(a) TCE dataset gallery—persons with ID and (b) sample detection results using Faster R-CNN-TCE dataset.

number of faces are trained and learned, and the experiments prove that Faster R-CNN achieves highly triggering results against the other state-of-the-art face detection methods.

Apart from the above benchmark datasets, our approach is evaluated on TCE dataset. It is captured to test all the challenges in one single dataset which is absent as benchmark. The gallery of the TCE dataset consists of the images of 30 students, under varying pose conditions, illumination variations, and occlusion conditions. For each student, at least 300 images are tested under those conditions. Moreover, an ID is provided for each student in the database such as TCE_ECE_IP_01, TCE_ECE _IP_02, TCE_ECE_IP_03... TCE_ECE_IP_30 (as shown in **Figure 6a**). Once a student enters the lab, her face is detected using Faster R-CNN. **Figure 6b** shows some of the sample detection results on the real-time TCE dataset, where the red color bounding boxes are ground-truth annotations and the yellow color bounding boxes are detection results, using Faster R-CNN.

The detected face is recognized, using the joint Bayesian model after finding facial landmarks, by means of the SDM algorithm. Afterward, the images in the

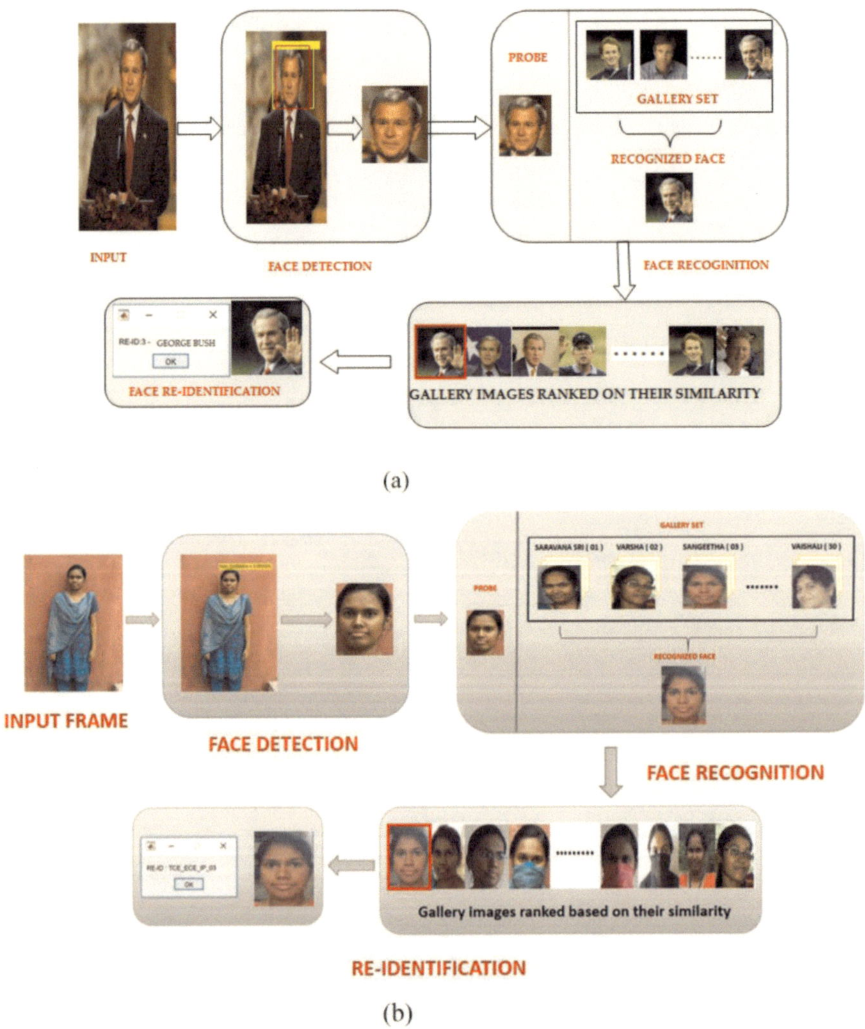

Figure 7.
The proposed facial feature-based Re-ID results for LFW and TCE dataset.

gallery set are arranged, based on their similarity. Finally, from the ranking list, the image with lower distance (rank 1) or with higher similarity score is displayed along with the Re-ID. The overall schematic representation of the proposed framework's result for a sampled query frame is shown in **Figure 7**.

5.3 Comparative analysis

The performance of face detection is measured in terms of recall and intersection over union (IoU). Each detection is considered as positive, if the IoU ratio is >0.5, matched with ground-truth annotation. The threshold of the detected scores is varied to generate a set of true positives and false positives. Finally, ROC curve is plotted. The larger the threshold is, the fewer the proposals that are considered to be true objects. **Figure 8a** and **b** illustrates the quantitative comparisons of using 300–2000 proposals. RPN is compared with other approaches including selective search (SS) and edge box (EB), and the N proposals are the top N-ranked ones, based on the confidence generated by these methods. The recall of SS and EB drops

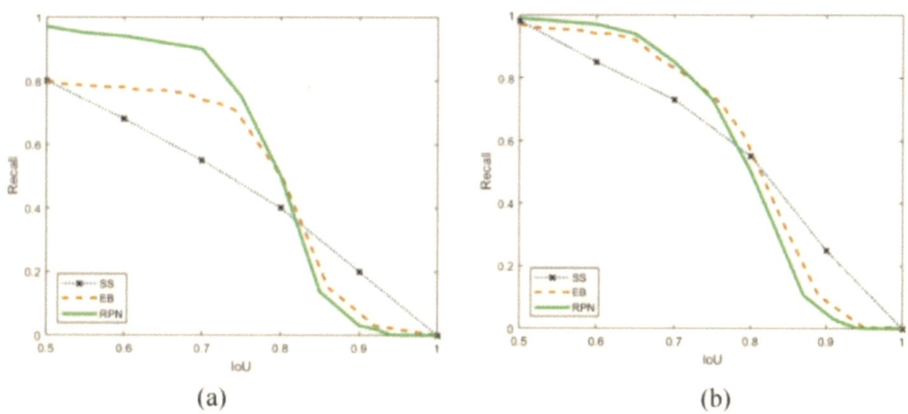

Figure 8.
(a) Recall vs. IoU overlap ratio with 300 proposals and (b) recall vs. IoU overlap ratio 2000 proposals.

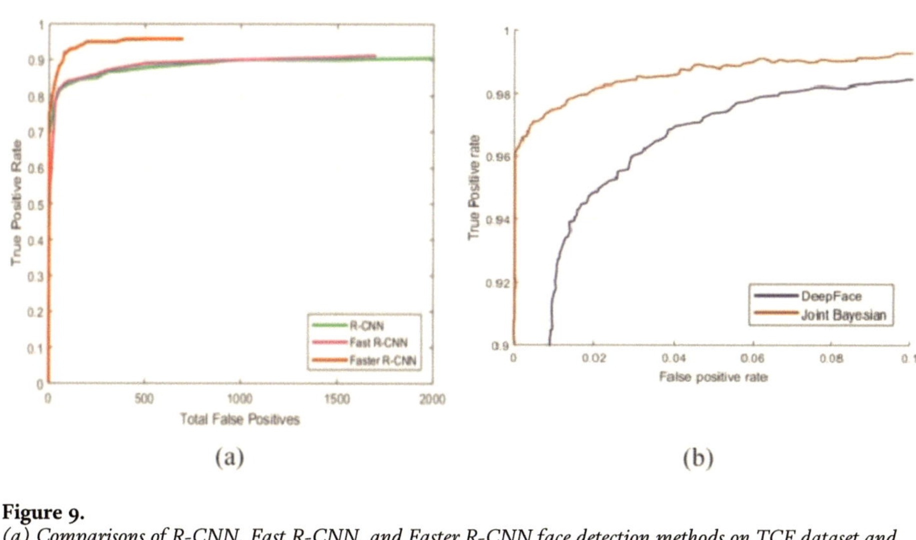

Figure 9.
(a) Comparisons of R-CNN, Fast R-CNN, and Faster R-CNN face detection methods on TCE dataset and (b) ROC comparison with the deep face method.

more quickly than RPN for fewer proposals. The plots show that using RPN yields a much faster detection system than using either SS or EB, when the number of proposals drops from 2000 to 300.

In addition the face detection performance of the R-CNN is compared with the Fast R-CNN and the Faster R-CNN on TCE dataset. As observed from **Figure 9a**, the Faster R-CNN significantly outperforms the other two. Deeply trained network

METHOD	ACCURACY (%)
Deep Face	91.4±1.9
Joint Bayesian	98.3±1.1

Table 3.
Accuracy comparison on TCE dataset.

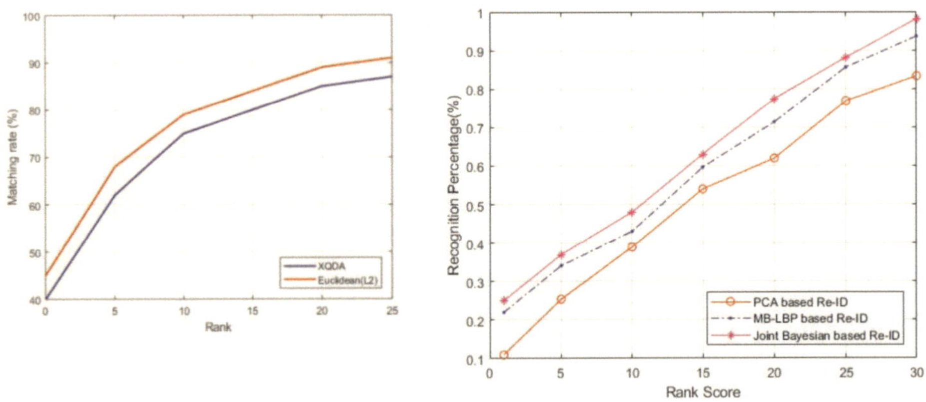

(a) (b)

Figure 10.
(a) CMC curve for different ranking methods and (b) CMC curve for various face recognition methods.

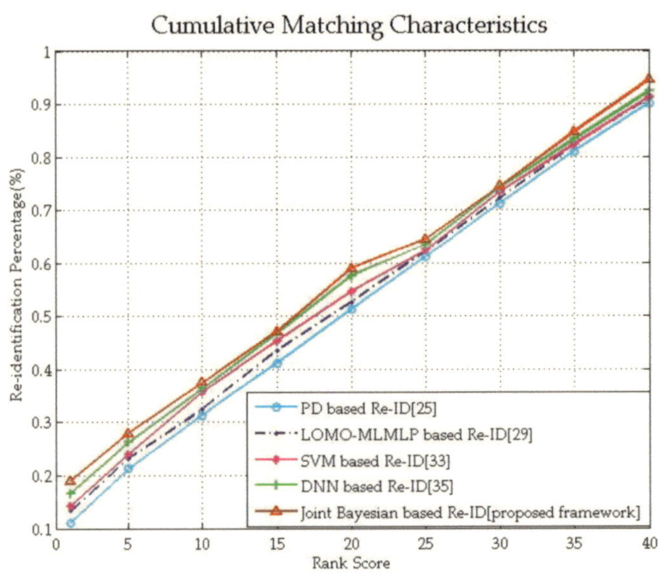

Figure 11.
CMC curve for various state-of-the-art facial feature-based Re-ID methods.

	Success cases			Failure cases	
Query	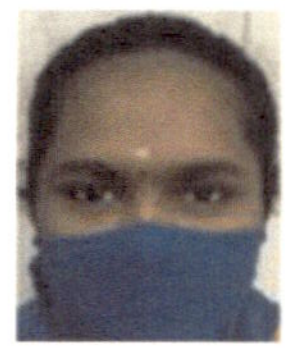				
Image with rank 1 (first image in the ranking list)				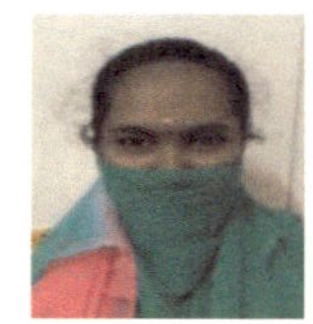	
Distance with the query image	0.5460	0.6989	0.60341	1.6792	1.710

Table 4.
Success and failure cases of the proposed frame work.

such as RPN boosts the performance of Faster R-CNN. Also, the Faster R-CNN has high computational speed than R-CNN and Fast R-CNN.

The comparison of the joint Bayesian method with the recent state-of-the-art deep face method in terms of the mean accuracy and ROC curves are presented in **Table 3** and **Figure 9b**, respectively. It can be observed that the joint Bayesian method advances the state-of-the-art deep face method, closely approaching human performance in face recognition. An accuracy of about $98.3 \pm 1.1\%$ in face recognition is achieved on TCE dataset.

The most widely used evaluation methodology for Re-ID is the cumulative matching characteristics curve, also known as CMC curve. This performance metric is adopted since Re-ID is intuitively posed as a ranking problem, where each element in the gallery is ranked, based on its comparison to the probe face. **Figure 10a** represents the comparison of rank vs. matching rate of Euclidean (L2) method with the XQDA method. It is evident from the plot that Euclidean (L2) method achieves better Re-ID matching rate than XQDA method on TCE dataset.

Recognition rate indicates probabilities of recognizing an individual, depending on how similar their measurements are to other individuals measurements in the gallery set and compared with performance of a biometric system, operating in the closed-set identification task. The probability of the equivalent match is ranked, and the value has been plotted against the size of the gallery set. **Figure 10b** represents the comparison of the recognition rate of joint Bayesian with the PCA-based eigenface approach algorithm. This shows PCA algorithm fails in some low-resolution images, wearing goggles, and different hairstyles. **Figure 11** represents the comparison of the reidentification rate of joint Bayesian method with other recent methods. **Table 4** shows the success and failure cases of the proposed frame work on TCE dataset and LFW dataset.

6. Conclusion

This chapter has presented an approach to robustly detect human facial regions from image sequences collected under various challenging conditions, such as partial occlusions, low resolutions, varying face poses, illumination variations, etc., and to reidentify a person even under those conditions. The well-established Faster R-CNN method is adopted to confirm whether the detected region proposals are human faces. Although the Faster R-CNN is designed for generic object detection, it manifests the impressive face detection performance, when attempted on a suitable face detection training set. The approach is tested on challenging benchmark datasets such as the WIDER FACE dataset, the FDDB, HALLWAY, and on own TCE dataset as well. The experimental results and various performance measures depict that the facial feature-based Re-ID results achieved are competitive and exclusive approach even in the presence of partial occlusions and other challenging conditions as mentioned above.

7. Future work

Till now, the scope of the algorithm (as shown in **Table 5**) is limited for frontal and profile face verifications, handling partial occlusions in a sparse crowd. Future work focuses on person Re-ID in a high-dense crowd under severe occlusions.

SCOPE	Algorithm works for multi-view faces, illumination changes and partial occlusions (wearing mask, specs and goggles)
CONSTRAINT	Completely occluded faces throughout the video cannot be re-identified. However, if partial face is available even in few frames, it is possible for the re-id process.

Table 5.
Scope and constraint of the proposed frame work.

Acknowledgements

This work has been supported under Video Analytics and Development System (VADS) project sponsored by IISC Bangalore under DST.

Author details

Yogameena Balasubramanian[1*], Nagavani Chandrasekaran[2], Sangeetha Asokan[1] and Saravana Sri Subramanian[1]

1 Department of Electronics and Communication Engineering, Thiagarajar College of Engineering, Madurai, India

2 Department of Electronics and Communication Engineering, Kamaraj College of Engineering and Technology, Madurai, India

*Address all correspondence to: ymece@tce.edu

References

[1] Bedagkar-Gala A, Shah SK. A survey of approaches and trends in person re-identification. Image and Vision Computing. 2014;**32**:270286. DOI: 10.1016/j.imavis.2014.02.001

[2] Bazzani L, Cristani M, Murino V. Symmetry-driven accumulation of local features for human characterization and re-identification. Computer Vision and Image Understanding. 2013;**117**:131-144. DOI: 10.1016/j.cviu.2012.10.008

[3] Liangliang R, Jiwen L, Jianjiang F, Jie Z. Multi-modal uniform deep learning for RGB-D person re-identification. Pattern Recognition. 2017;**72**:446-457. DOI: 10.1016/j.patcog.2017.06.037

[4] Sarattha K, Worapan KR. Human identification using mean shape analysis of face images. In: Proceedings of the 2017 IEEE Region 10 Conference. (TENCON); Penang: Malaysia; 5-8 November 2017. pp. 901-905

[5] Artur G, Marcin K, Norbert P. Face re-identification in thermal infrared spectrum based on thermal facenet neural network. In: Proceedings of 2018 22nd International Microwave and Radar Conference (MIKON); Warsaw Univ. of Technology: Polan; 2018. pp. 179-180

[6] Li P, Prieto ML, Patrick JF, Mery D. Learning face similarity for re-identification from real surveillance video: A deep metric solution. In: Proceedings of the Joint Conference on Biometrics (IJCB); Denver: CO, USA; 1-4 October 2017. pp. 243-252

[7] Li P, Joel B, Patrick JF. toward facial re-identification: Experiments with data from an operational surveillance camera plant. In: Proceedings of the 2016 IEEE 8th International Conference on Biometrics Theory, Applications and Systems (BTAS); Niagara Falls: NY, USA; September 2016

[8] De-la-Torre M, Granger E, Sabourin R, Gorodnichy DO. Individual specific management of reference data in adaptive ensembles for face reidentification. IET Computer Vision. 2015;**9**:732-740. DOI: 10.1049/iet-cvi.2014.0375

[9] Zheng L, Yang Y, Hauptmann AG. Person Re-identification: Past, present and future. Journal of Latex Class Files. 2016;**14**:1-20. DOI: arxiv.org/abs/1610.02984

[10] Mazzeo PL, Spagnolo P, D'Orazio T. Object tracking by non-overlapping distributed camera network. In: Blanc-Talon J, Philips W, Popescu D, Scheunders P, editors. Advanced Concepts for Intelligent Vision Systems. Vol. 5807. Berlin, Heidelberg: Springer; 2009. pp. 516-527. DOI: 10.1007/978-3-642-04697-1.ch48. ACIVS 2009. Lecture Notes in Computer Science

[11] Masi I, Lisanti G, Bartoli F, Del Bimo A. Person Re-Identification: Theory and Best Practice. 2015. Available from: http://www.micc.unifi.it/reid-tutorial [Accessed: September 02, 2015]

[12] Vezzani R, Baltieri D, Cucchiara R. People Re-identification in surveillance and forensics: A survey. ACM Computing Surveys. 2013;**46**:1-37. DOI: 10.1145/2543581.2543596

[13] Brendel W, Amer M, Todorovic S. Multi object tracking as maximum weight independent set. In: Proceedings of the IEEE International Conference on Computer Vision and Pattern Recognition; Colorado Springs: CO, USA; 20-25 June 2011. pp. 1273-1280

[14] Madrigal F, Hayet JB. Multiple view, multiple target tracking with principal axis-based data association. In: Proceedings of the IEEE International Conference on Advanced Video and Signal-Based Surveillance; Klagenfurt:

Austria; 30 August-2 September 2011. pp. 185-109

[15] Dantcheva A, Dugelay JL. Frontal-to-side face re-identification based on hair, skin and clothes patches. In: Proceedings of the IEEE International Conference on Advanced Video and Signal-Based Surveillance; Klagenfurt: Austria; 30 August-2 September 2011. pp. 309-313

[16] Albiol A, Albiol A, Oliver J, Mossi J. Who is who at different cameras: People re-identification using depth cameras. IET Computer Vision. 2012;**6**:378-387. DOI: 10.1049/iet-cvi.2011.0140

[17] Bak S, Corvee E, Bremond F, Thonnat M. Person re-identification using spatial covariance regions of human body parts. In: Proceedings of the IEEE Conference on Advanced Video and Signal Based Surveillance 29 August-1 September 2010; Boston, MA: USA: IEEE; 2010.pp. 435-440

[18] Bazzani L, Cristani M, Perina A, Murino V. Multiple-shot person re-identification by chromatic and epitomic analyses. Pattern Recognition Letters. 2012;**33**:898-903. DOI: 10.1016/j.patrec. 2011.11.016

[19] Chen L, Chen H, Li S, Wang Y. Person Re-identification by color distribution fields. Journal of Chinese Computer System. 2017;**38**:1404-1408. DOI: Xwxt.sict.ac.cn/EN/Y2017/V38/I6/1404

[20] Miyazawa K, Ito K, Aoki T, Kobayashi K, Nakajima H. An effective approach for iris recognition using phase-based image matching. IEEE Transactions on Pattern Analysis and Machine Intelligence. 2007;**30**: 1741-1756. DOI: 10.1109/TPAMI. 2007.70833

[21] Cheng DS, Cristani M, Stoppa M, Bazzani L, Murino V. Custom pictorial structures for re-identification. In: Proceedings of the British Machine Vision Conference (BMVC'11); 29 August-2 September 2011. pp. 1-11

[22] Fischer M, Ekenel H, Stiefelhagen R. Person re-identification in TV series using robust face recognition and user feedback. Multimedia Tools and Applications. 2011;**55**:83-104. DOI: 10.1007/s11042-010-0603-2

[23] Baltieri D, Vezzani R, Cucchiara R. SARC3D: A new 3D body model for people tracking and re-identification. In: Proceedings of the IEEE International Conference on Image Analysis and Process; September 14-16; Ravenna: Italy; 2011. pp. 197-206

[24] Caroline S, Thierry B, Carl F. AneXtended center-symmetric local binary pattern for background modelling and subtraction in videos. In: Proceedings of the International Joint Conference Computer Vision, Imaging and Computer Graphics Theory and Applications; VISAPP Berlin: Germany; March 2015. pp. 1-9

[25] Milborrow S, Nicolls F. Locating facial features with an extended active shape model. In: Proceedings of European conference on computer vision. Lecture Notes in Computer Science; Springer: Berlin, Heidelberg; 2008. pp. 504-513

[26] Miguel D, Eric G, Robert S, Dmitry OG. Individual-specific management of reference data in adaptive ensembles for face re-identification. IET Computer Vision. 2015;**9**:732-740

[27] Xu X, Li W, Xu D. Distance metric learning using privileged information for face verification and person Re-identification. IEEE Transactions on Neural Networks and Learning Systems December 2015;**26**: 3150–3162. DOI: 10.1109/TNNLS. 2015.2405574

[28] Cui Z, Li W, Xu D, Shan S, Chen X. Fusing robust face region descriptors via multiple metric learning for face recognition in the wild. In: Proceedings of IEEE Conference Computer Vision Pattern Recognition; Portland: USA; Jun 2013. pp. 3554-3561

[29] Xie P, Xing EP. Multi-modal distance metric learning. In: Proceedings of 23rd International Joint Conference Artificial Intelligence; Beijing: China; August 2013. pp. 1806-1812

[30] Schroff F, Kalenichenko D, Philbin JF. A unified embedding for face recognition and clustering. In: Proceedings of the IEEE Conference on Computer Vision and Pattern Recognition; 2015. pp. 815-823

[31] Hu J, Lu J, Tan Y, Zhou J. Deep transfer metric learning. IEEE Transactions on Image Processing. 2016; **25**:5576-5588. DOI: 10.1109/TIP.2016. 2612827

[32] Mai G, Cao K, Pong CY. On the reconstruction of face images from deep face templates. IEEE Transactions on Pattern Analysis and Machine Intelligence. 2018;**99**:1-15. DOI: 10.1109/TPAMI.2018.2827389

[33] Kobri H, Jones M. Improving face verification and person re-identification accuracy using hyper plane similarity. In: Proceedings of International Conference Computer Vision Workshops; Venice: Italy; October. 2017. pp. 1555-1563

[34] Sanping Z, Jinjun W, Deyu M. Deep self-paced learning for person Re-identification. Pattern Recognition. 2017;**76**:739-751. DOI: 10.1016/j. patcog.2017.10.005

[35] Varior RR, Haloi M, Wang G. Gated Siamese convolutional neural network architecture for human re-identification. In: Proceedings of European Conference on Computer Vision; Amsterdam: The Netherlands; 2016. pp. 791-808

[36] Borgia A, Hua Y, Kodirov E, Robertson N. GAN-Based pose-aware regulation for video-based person re-identification. In: Proceedings of IEEE Winter Conference on Applications of Computer Vision (WACV); Waikoloa Village, HI: USA; 2019. pp. 1175-1184

[37] Huang Z et al. Contribution-based multi-stream feature distance fusion method with k-distribution Re-ranking for person Re-identification. IEEE Access. 2019;**7**:35631-35644. DOI: 10.1109/ACCESS.2019.2904278

[38] Ross G, Jeff D, Trevor D, et al. Rich feature hierarchies for accurate object detection and semantic segmentation. In: Proceedings of International Conference Computer Vision and Pattern Recognition; Columbus, OH: USA; June 2014. pp. 580-587

[39] Ross G. Fast R-CNN. In: Proceedings of International Conference on Computer Vision; Santiago: Chile; December 2015. pp. 1440-1448

[40] Huaizu J, Miller EL. Face detection with the faster R-CNN. In: Proceedings of International Conference on Automatic Face and Gesture Recognition; Washington, DC: USA; June 2017. pp. 650-657

[41] Ranjan R, Sankaranarayanan S, Castillo CD, Chellappa R. An all-in-one convolutional neural network for face analysis. In: Proceedings of 12th IEEE International Conference on Automatic Face and Gesture Recognition (FG 2017); Washington: DC; 2017. pp. 17-24

[42] Xiong X, De la Torre F. Supervised descent method and its applications to face alignment. In: Proceedings of 2013 IEEE Conference on Computer Vision

and Pattern Recognition; Portland: OR; 2013. pp. 532-539

[43] Chen D, Cao X, Wipf D, Wen F, Sun J. An efficient joint formulation for Bayesian face verification. IEEE Transactions on Pattern Analysis and Machine Intelligence. 2017;**39**:32-46. DOI: 10.1109/TPAMI.2016.2533383

Chapter 5

Object Re-Identification Based on Deep Learning

Xiying Li and Zhihao Zhou

Abstract

With the explosive growth of video data and the rapid development of computer vision technology, more and more relevant technologies are applied in our real life, one of which is object re-identification (Re-ID) technology. Object Re-ID is currently concentrated in the field of person Re-ID and vehicle Re-ID, which is mainly used to realize the cross-vision tracking of person/vehicle and trajectory prediction. This chapter combines theory and practice to explain why the deep network can re-identify the object. To introduce the main technical route of object Re-ID, the examples of person/vehicle Re-ID are given, and the improvement points of existing object Re-ID research are described separately.

Keywords: object re-identification, deep learning, person re-identification, vehicle re-identification, feature extraction

1. Introduction

In a surveillance camera without overlapping vision, a recognized object is identified again after imaging conditions (including monitoring scene, lighting conditions, object pose, etc.) change, which is called object re-identification (Object Re-ID). Object Re-ID technology has important research significance in intelligent monitoring, multi-object tracking and other fields. In recent years, scholars have paid extensive attention to it. The main application areas of object Re-ID are person Re-ID and vehicle Re-ID.

Person re-identification (Re-ID) is a technology that uses computer vision technology to judge whether there is a specific person in the image or video sequence. It is widely regarded as a sub-problem of image retrieval. Given a monitor person image, retrieve the image of the row of people across the device. It aims to make up for the visual limitations of the current fixed cameras, and can be combined with person detection and pedestrian tracking technology, which can be widely used in intelligent video monitoring, intelligent security and other fields.

Vehicle re-identification (Re-ID) aims to quickly search, locate and track the target vehicles across surveillance camera networks, which plays key roles in maintaining social public security and serves as a core module in the large-scale vehicle recognition, intelligent transportation, surveillance video analytic platforms. Vehicle Re-ID refers to the problem of identifying the same vehicle in a large scale vehicle database given a probe vehicle image. In particular, vehicle Re-ID can be regarded as a fine-grained recognition task that aims at recognizing the subordinate category of a given class. The wide popularization and use of road video monitoring makes vehicle matching based on video image become the hot spot in current intelligent traffic research, and the typical applications are vehicle origin-destination analysis and vehicle trajectory reconstruction. In some cases which license plate number could be recognized clearly and accurately, vehicle Re-ID could be realized by match the license plate number. However, in more cases, such as license plate can't be recognized (for most surveillance video), license plate occlusion and so on in the criminal investigation, it is necessary to realize the vehicle Re-ID without license plates by using computer vision and other related technologies.

2. Related work of object Re-ID

As an emerging research topic, object Re-ID has attracted great efforts. Existing research directions of object Re-ID are mainly divided into person Re-ID and vehicle Re-ID. In this section, we will review the relevant works from person Re-ID and vehicle Re-ID.

2.1 Person Re-ID

We will review the relevant work [1] of person Re-ID from following aspects: person Re-ID based on representation learning, metric learning, local features and video sequence.

2.1.1 Person Re-ID based on representation learning

Methods based on representation learning are a kind of very common person Re-ID methods, which is mainly thanks to the deep learning, especially the Convolutional neural network (CNN) development. Sunderrajan et al. [2] propose a clothing context-aware color extraction method to learn color drift patterns in a non-parametric manner using the random forest distance (RFD) function. Geng et al. [3] proposed a person Re-ID algorithm which used Classification loss and verification loss to train the network (including Classification Subnet and Verification Subnet), and the network inputs several pairs of pedestrian images. The classification subnetwork makes ID prediction on the image, and calculates the classification error loss according to the predicted ID. The sub-network integrates the features of two images and judge whether these two images belong to the same pedestrian. The sub-network is essentially equivalent to a binary classification network. After enough data training, input a test image again, and the network will automatically extract a feature, which is used for person Re-ID. For the problem that pedestrian ID information alone is not enough to learn a model with strong generalization ability, the researchers added attributes such as gender, hair and clothing to the pedestrian images. By introducing the pedestrian attribute label, the model should not only accurately predict the pedestrian ID, but also predict the correct pedestrian attributes, which greatly increases the generalization ability of the model. Most papers also show that this method is effective. Lin et al. [4] proposed a person Re-ID algorithm based on multiple attributes. In this algorithm, the features of network output are not only used to predict the ID information of pedestrians, but also to predict the attributes of each pedestrian. The combination of ID loss and attribute loss can improve the generalization ability of the network. Currently, there is still a lot of work based on representational learning. Representational learning has also become a very important baseline of Re-ID field. Moreover, the method of representational learning is more robust, the training is more stable, and the results are easier to reproduce. However, representation learning is easy to be overfitted in the domain of the data set, and when the training ID is increased to a certain extent, it will be weak.

2.1.2 Person Re-ID based on metric learning

Metric learning is a method widely used in the field of image retrieval. Unlike representational learning, metric learning aims to learn the similarity between two images through the network. In the problem of person Re-ID, the similarity of different images of the same pedestrian is greater than that of different images of the different pedestrians. Finally, the loss function of the network makes the distance between the same pedestrian images (positive sample pairs) as small as possible, and the distance between different pedestrian images (negative sample pairs) as large as possible. Common measures of learning loss include Contrastive loss, Triplet loss, Quadruplet loss, Triplet hard loss with batch hard mining (TriHard loss) and Margin sample mining loss (MSML). Varior et al. [5] proposed Siamese Network, and trained the network model by contrast loss. By reducing the contrast loss, the distance between positive sample pairs is gradually reduced, and the distance between negative sample pairs is gradually increased, so as to meet the need of person Re-ID. Triplet loss is a widely used metric learning loss and a lot of metric learning methods have evolved based on triples. Ding et al. [6] considered the re-identification problem as a ranking issue and used triplet loss to obtain the relative distance between images. Chen et al. [7] designed a quadruplet loss process, which can lead to model outputs with larger inter-class variation and smaller intra-class variation compared with the triplet loss method. Hermans et al. [8] proposed a batch training based online difficult sample sampling method, which is named TriHard Loss. Traditional triplet sample mining strategy randomly select three images from training data, and most of the sampled images are simple and easily distinguishable sample pairs, which is not conducive to better representation of network learning. This paper proposes a sample mining strategy that can obtain more difficult samples which can improve the generalization ability of the network. Xiao et al. [9] proposed Margin sample mining loss which introduces the idea of hard sample sampling. MSML losses are calculated by picking only the hardest positive sample pair and the hardest negative sample pair. It is a measure learning method that takes into account both relative distance and absolute distance and introduces the idea of difficult sample sampling.

2.1.3 Person Re-ID based on local features

In the early stage of ReID's research, people still focused on global feature, but later the global feature encountered a bottleneck, so they began to study local feature gradually. The commonly used methods to extract local features include image segmentation, positioning of skeleton key points and posture correction, etc. Image segmentation is a very common way to extract local features. Wei et al. [10] develop a pedestrian image descriptor named Global-Local-Alignment Descriptor, this descriptor explicitly leverages the local and global cues in human body to generate a discriminative and robust representation. In order to solve the failure of manual image slice in the case of image misalignment, some papers first align pedestrians with some prior knowledge, which mainly includes pre-trained human Pose and Skeleton key points model. Su et al. [11] proposed a pose-driven deep convolutional model to alleviate the pose variations and learn robust feature representations from both the global images and different local parts. Liang et al. [12] first estimated the key points of pedestrians with the model of attitude estimation, and then made the same key points align with affine transformation. To extract local features at different scales, they set three different PoseBox combinations; afterwards, the three PoseBox corrected images were sent to the network together with the original corrected images to extract features, which contained both global and local information. In order to solve the problem of local feature alignment, most methods need an additional skeleton key point or pose estimation model. Zhang et al. [13] proposed an automatic alignment model based on SP distance (AlignedReID), which automatically aligned local features without requiring additional information.

2.1.4 Person Re-ID based on video sequence

The main difference between video sequence-based methods is that such methods not only consider the content information of the image, but also consider the motion information between frames. Liu et al. [14] propose an algorithm called Accumulative motion context network (AMOC), the input of AMOC includes the original image sequence and the extracted optical flow sequence. AMOC has Spatial network and Motion network. Each frame of an image sequence is input into Spat Nets to extract the global content features of the image, the two adjacent frames will be sent to the Moti Nets to extract the optical flow pattern features; then the spatial features and optical flow features are merged and input into an RNN to extract the temporal features. Through the AMOC network, each image sequence can be extracted with a feature that integrates content information and motion information. The network adopts classification loss and comparison loss to train the model. Sequential image features with motion information can improve the accuracy of person Re-ID. Mazzeo et al. [15] propose a multi camera architecture for wide area surveillance and a real time people tracking algorithm across non overlapping cameras, they proposed different methodologies [16] to extract the color histogram information from each object patches for the intra-camera and compared different methods to evaluate the colour Brightness Transfer Function (BTF) between non overlapping cameras for inter-camera tracking. This method outperforms the performance in terms of matching rate between different cameras.

2.2 Vehicle Re-ID

We will review the relevant works of vehicle Re-ID from three aspects: vehicle re-identification based on artificial design feature, vehicle re-identification based on deep learning feature and vehicle re-identification based on fusion feature.

2.2.1 Vehicle Re-ID based on artificial design feature

In the initial vehicle matching problem, sensor tag matching is adopted. Tian et al. [17] proposed an algorithm for vehicle Re-ID based on multiple sensor nodes. According to the matching results of the same vehicle label obtained by different nodes, the vehicle state was determined and the label segmentation was modified. Meanwhile, the time difference between vehicles was modified according to the relationship between different acquired labels. Coifman [18] proposed a matching algorithm for individual vehicles measured on the highway detector and made corresponding measurements on another detector upstream. Rios-Cabrera et al. [19] proposed a comprehensive scheme for solving the problems of vehicle detection, recognition and tracking in view of the practical application of tunnel monitoring, and proposed compact binary features to improve the recognition effect for the influence of poor imaging conditions and vehicle lights in tunnel monitoring.

Due to the late rise of vehicle Re-ID research, when traditional methods have not been applied to this problem too much, the deep learning technology has developed in a big bang. Almost all subsequent studies are based on deep learning technology, which greatly improves the effect of Re-ID.

2.2.2 Vehicle Re-ID based on deep learning feature

In recent years, convolutional neural network has been widely used in the field of computer vision and achieved remarkable effects. Because the depth features extracted by deep convolutional networks have stronger description ability, more and more scholars have applied them in vehicle Re-ID. Liu et al. [20] proposed a large-scale vehicle Re-ID data set "VeRi," and puts forward a method of feature Fusion FACT by combining the depth of the vehicle network features, color features and SIFT features to match the same vehicle, the follow-up of vehicle recognition of other study, a large number of experiment based on the data set, thereby evaluating effectiveness and superiority of the proposed algorithm. Liu et al. [21] solved the problem of difficulty in triplet loss convergence by adding a feature representation between the sample and each individual vehicle into the triplet network to model intra-class variance. Li et al. [22] proposed DJDL (Deep Joint Discriminative Learning) model, which projects the original vehicle image into Euclidean space through a two-branch Deep convolution network. Zhang et al. [23] proposed a guided Triplet network, which added classification loss to the original triplet loss function and strongly restricted the original training network, thus improving the Re-ID efficiency. Marin et al. [24] designed a metric learning model based on the supervision of the local constraints, its use in pairs and triple constraints to train a network, the network is able to share the same identity of the sample distribution of high similarity, and keep a distance of different identity in the feature space, the algorithm is one of the biggest advantage is to use the vehicle tracking to automatically generate a set of weak tag data, and will automatically generate data sets used in depth training network to complete the vehicles Re-ID task.

2.2.3 Vehicle Re-ID based on fusion feature

For monitoring video, in addition to appearance information of images, information other than appearance features (such as, space-time information) is also of great mining significance. Liu et al. [25] proposed a segmented vehicle Re-ID algorithm, which first used appearance features for preliminary screening, then used license plate information for matching, and finally used spatial and temporal information for reordering. After the method was integrated with spatial and temporal information, the effect was improved to a certain extent. Jiang et al. [26] proposed a vehicle Re-ID algorithm based on multiple attribute training and sort by spatial-temporal similarity, the vehicle image color, models, vehicle feature extraction with individual respectively. Through the fusion of multiple features for the initial Re-ID, the Re-ID results are reordered by the spatial-temporal similarity, and good results are obtained. Shen et al. [27] proposed a two-stage architecture containing complex spatiotemporal information, given a pair of vehicle images with spatio-temporal information, candidate visual spatio-temporal paths (where each visual spatio-temporal state corresponds to an actual vehicle image with spatio-temporal information) are generated by an MRF chain model with a deep learning function, and then candidate paths and paired queries are used to generate their similarity scores for the model. In addition to fusion of information other than the apparent features of images, many scholars have also studied fusion of manual features and deep convolution features, fusion of various attribute features or feature fusion between different image regions. Li et al. [28] proposed a vehicle Re-ID algorithm based on fusion features extract from different part of vehicle, firstly, a part detection algorithm [29] is used to obtain the attention area with big difference between different vehicles. Then, feature extraction was carried out on the detected area, and features of the two areas were fused to generate new fusion features. Liang et al. [30] put forward a new method of supervision and the depth of the hash to handle large-scale vehicle search problem, the use of multitasking learning to learn, vehicle model, vehicle image color depth features of individual ID hash code, the experimental results show the effectiveness of the proposed method, the method in classification loss and triple loss case depth hash method is superior to single task.

3. Some public database for object Re-ID

With the development of Re-ID research, many scholars have published the data sets of relevant fields. The following are some commonly used person Re-ID data sets and vehicle Re-ID data sets.

3.1 Person Re-ID data sets

Person Re-ID data sets commonly used in deep learning methods include VIPeR [31], PRID2011 [32], CUHK03 [33], Market1501 [34], CUHK-SYSU [35], MARS [36], DukeMTMC-reID [37]. In addition to the common data sets that are already open source, there are several newer data sets, such as SYSU-MM01 [38], LPW [39], MSMT17 [40], LVreID [41], the download link is not yet open. The following is a detailed description of CUHK03 and Market1501.

3.1.1 CUHK03

The dataset includes 13,164 images of 1360 pedestrians. The whole dataset is captured with six surveillance cameras. Each identity is observed by two disjoint camera views and has an average of 4–8 images in each view. Some examples are shown in **Figure 1**. Besides the scale, it has the following characteristics.

This dataset is partitioned into training set (1160 persons), validation set (100 persons), and test set (100 persons). Each person has roughly 4–8 photos per view, which means there are almost 26,000 positive training pairs before data augmentation.

3.1.2 Market1501

During dataset collection, a total of six cameras were placed in front of a campus supermarket, including five 1280 × 1080 HD cameras, and one 720 × 576 SD camera. Overlapping exists among these cameras. This dataset contains 32,668 boxes of 1501 identities. Due to the open environment, images of each identity are captured by at most six cameras. Each annotated identity is captured by at least two cameras, so that cross-camera search can be performed. Overall, the dataset has the following featured properties.

The dataset is randomly divided into training and testing sets, containing 750 and 751 identities, respectively. During testing, for each identity, it selects one query image in each camera. Note that, the selected queries are hand-drawn, instead of DPM-detected as in the gallery. The reason is that in reality, it is very convenient to interactively draw a box, which can yield higher recognition accuracy. The search process is performed in a cross-camera mode, i.e., relevant

Figure 1.
Person samples selected from the CUHK03 dataset.

Figure 2.
Person samples selected from the Market1501 dataset.

images captured in the same camera as the query are viewed as "junk." In this scenario, an identity has at most six queries, and there are 3368 query images in total. Dataset examples are shown in **Figure 2**.

3.2 Vehicle Re-ID data sets

Vehicle Re-ID data sets commonly used in deep learning methods include VRID-1 [42], VeRi-776 [25], VehicleID [21].

3.2.1 VRID-1

The open dataset VRID-1 for vehicle re-identification contains 10,000 images, which are captured by 326 surveillance cameras within 14 days. The resolutions of images are distributed from 400 × 424 to 990 × 1134. VRID collects 1000 vehicle IDs (vehicle identities) of top 10 common vehicle models (**Table 1**) to reconstruct the interference with the same vehicle model in the real world. The vehicle IDs belong to the same model have very similar appearance and their differences appears in the area of the logo and accessories. Besides, each vehicle IDs contains 10 images which are in various illuminations, poses and weather condition. Dataset examples are shown in **Figure 3**.

The attributes of VRID is illustrated in **Table 2**. The vehicle model column represents the vehicle model information. The license plate column is used for the correlation of the same vehicle. The window location column shows the location of vehicle window area. The vehicle color column contains the vehicle color information. Besides, with the rich attributes of vehicles, the dataset could also be used for vehicle fine-grained recognition as well as vehicle color recognition.

3.2.2 VeRi-776

To collect high-quality videos in real-world surveillance scene, we select 20 cameras deployed along a circular road of a 1.0 km^2 area as shown in **Figure 4**.

Vehicle model	Vehicle IDs	Total images
Audi_A4	100	1000
Honda_Accord	100	1000
Buick_Lacrosse	100	1000
Volkswagen_Magotan	100	1000
Toyota_Corolla_I	100	1000
Toyota_Corolla_II	100	1000
Toyota_Camry	100	1000
Ford_Focus	100	1000
Nissan_Tiida	100	1000
Nissan_Sylphy	100	1000

Table 1.
The 10 vehicle models in the dataset.

Figure 3.
Vehicle samples selected from the VRID-1 dataset.

Image_ID	Vehicle model	License plant number	Window location	Color
IDs_1	Toyota_Corolla	License_1	X1, Y1, X2, Y2	Yellow
IDs_12	Toyota_Corolla	License_2	X1, Y1, X2, Y2	Black
IDs_1000	Honda_Accord	License_10	X1, Y1, X2, Y2	White

Table 2.
The attributes of VRID.

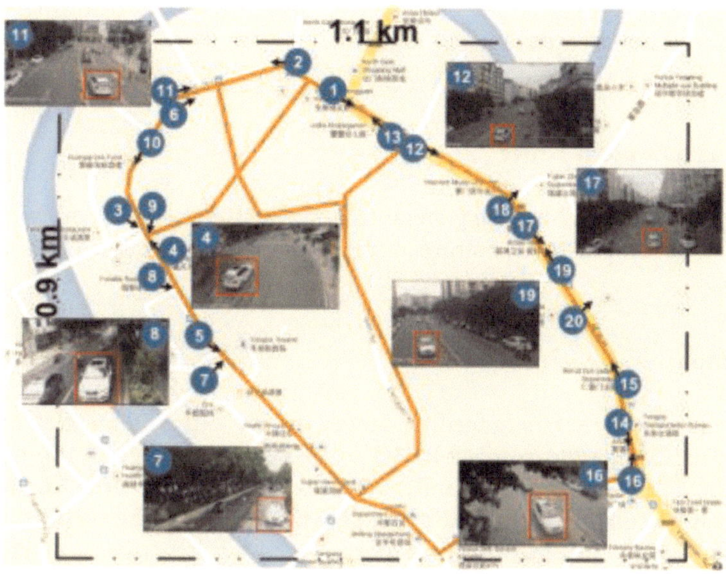

Figure 4.
The urban surveillance environments and cameras distribution for the VeRi dataset.

Figure 5.
Vehicle samples selected from the VeRi dataset.

The scenes of the cameras include two-lane roads, four-lane roads, and crossroads. All cameras are set to 1920 × 1080 resolution and 25 fps. The cameras are deployed with arbitrary orientations and tilt angles. Besides, there are overlaps for part of the cameras.

The VeRi dataset is collected with 20 cameras in real-world traffic surveillance environment. A total of 776 vehicles are annotated. Two hundred vehicles are used for testing. The remaining 576 vehicles are for testing. There are 11,579 images in the test set, 1678 images as queries and 37,778 images in the training set. Each vehicle is captured by at least two cameras. One advantage of this data set is that the camera ID and timestamp (frame ID) are reserved with tracks for further annotation. Dataset examples are shown in **Figure 5**.

4. General technical route

In deep learning method, the general technical route of object Re-ID includes three stages: data input stage, feature extraction model and distance measurement (**Figure 6**).

4.1 Data input

Data input mainly refers to feeding data to feature extraction model, and the commonly used data type in object Re-ID is three-channel image. In this part, we do not describe the input data, but mainly introduce data augmentation. In the training stage of deep learning model, insufficient data often leads to the situation that the model cannot converge or overfit. In order to avoid this situation, data augmentation is one of the solutions. Common operations for data augmentation are as follows:

- Color Jittering. Color data enhancement, such as Change image brightness, saturation, contrast and so on.

- Random Scale. Randomly change the original size of the image.

- Horizontal/vertical flip. Flip the original image horizontally or vertically.

In the data input stage, we need to pay attention to not only the data amplification, but also, in some special cases such as contrast loss or triplet loss model, we may need to construct the image pair or triplet sample in advance. Due to the limitation of GPU memory, it is impossible to input a batch of data includes all images, so it is possible that there is no negative sample which might result in the failure of image pair or triplet sample construction, at the same time, due to the large number of target individuals in the re-identification problem, the imbalance between positive and negative samples is very likely to exist, which easily leads to the unscientific network model trained. Therefore, we need to set some rules in the data input stage to correctly construct these image pairs or triplet samples.

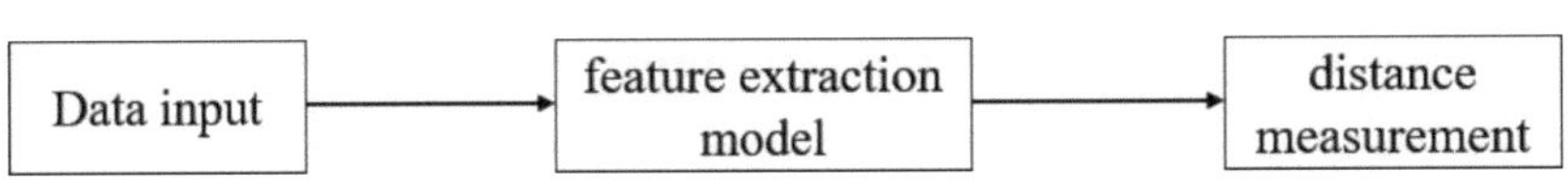

Figure 6.
General technical route of object re-identification.

4.2 Feature extraction model

The core of object Re-ID algorithm is feature extraction model, the effectiveness of the whole algorithm is also almost determined by this part. In other words, the essence of Re-ID is to compare the similarity or distance between the features extracted from two images. Image features mainly include color feature, texture feature, shape feature and spatial relationship feature. Feature extraction is a concept in computer vision and image processing. It refers to the use of computer to extract image information to determine whether each image pixel belongs to an image feature. Features are the best way to describe patterns, and we often think that each dimension of a feature can describe a pattern from a different perspective. Ideally, the dimensions are complementary and complete. In the field of image recognition or image Re-ID, traditional methods of feature extraction include Histogram of Oriented Gradient (HOG), scale-invariant feature transform (SIFT), Speeded Up Robust Features (SURF), Local Binary Pattern (LBP) and so on; the deep learning methods of feature extraction include Convolution Neural Network (CNN), Recurrent Neural Network (RNN) and so on. We present a feature extraction method in detail in both traditional and deep learning methods.

4.2.1 Histogram of oriented gradient (HOG)

The essence of HOG feature extraction is to constitute features by computing and statistics the histogram of gradient direction in the local area of the image. Hog feature combined with SVM classifier has been widely used in image recognition, especially in pedestrian detection, which has achieved great success. How to extract HOG feature? Firstly, the image is divided into small connected regions, which are called cell units. Then the direction histogram of the gradient or edge of each pixel in the cell is collected. Finally, these histograms can be combined to form a feature descriptor.

4.2.2 Convolution neural network (CNN)

It is a kind of feedforward neural network with deep structure including convolution calculation. A convolutional neural network contains three types of neural network layers: convolutional layer, pooling layer and fully connection layer. As is shown in **Figure 7**.

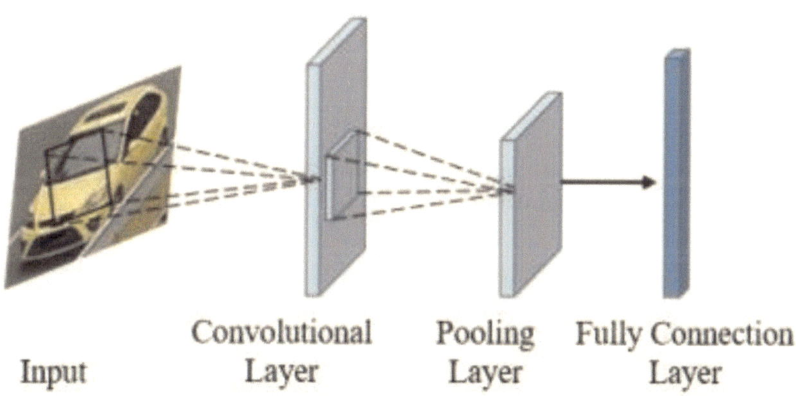

Figure 7.
Basic structure diagram of convolutional neural network.

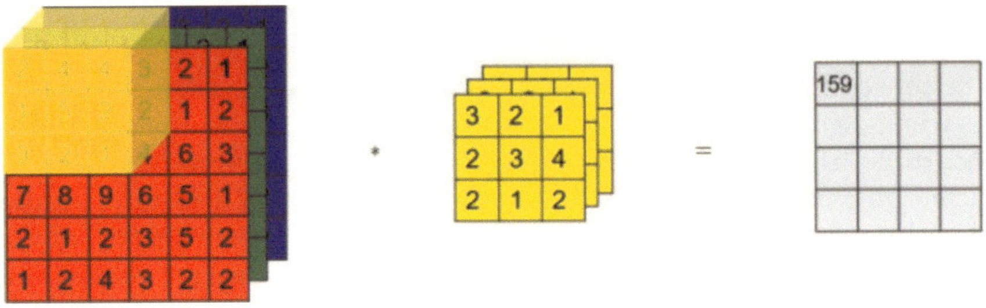

Figure 8.
Convolution diagram.

4.2.2.1 Convolutional layer

The convolution layer is mainly used for learning the feature representation of input data. The convolution layer is composed of multiple convolution kernels, and the convolution operation is carried out on the input image to calculate different feature maps.

In general, the input data is RGB image, as shown in **Figure 8**. If the color image is 6*6*3, the three refers to three color channels, and the convolution operation is carried out with a 3*3*3 convolution kernel, corresponding to the red, green and blue channels. Take the 27 numbers in turn, multiply them by the Numbers in the corresponding red, green and blue channel, and then add them all up to get the first number in the output of the feature graph.

The convolution layer principle is shown in equation:

$$x_j^l = f\left(\sum_i x_i^{l-1} * k_{ij}^l + b_j^l\right) \tag{1}$$

where $f(*)$ is activation functions; x_j^l denotes the $j-th$ feature map of output layer l, x_i^l is the $i-th$ feature map of the layer l; K_{ij}^l represents the convolution kernel of the $i-th$ feature graph of the current input layer and the $j-th$ feature graph of the output layer on the layer l; b_j^l is the bias term of the $j-th$ feature graph in the layer l.

4.2.2.2 Pooling layer

Pooling layer is often used in the convolutional network to reduce the size of the model, improve the computational speed, and improve the robustness of extracted features. Pooling operation can maintain the invariance of translation, rotation and scale. Common pooling layer operations are averaging and pooling. The maximum pooling operation is as shown in **Figure 9**. The input of 4*4 is divided into different regions. For the output of 2*2, each element output is the maximum element value in its corresponding color region.

4.2.2.3 Fully connection layer

Each node of the fully connection layer is connected to all nodes of the previous layer to integrate the features extracted from the previous layer. Due to its fully connected nature, the general fully connected layer also has the most parameters. The full join layer act as a mapping of the learned "distributed feature representation" into the sample tag space. It's essentially a linear transformation from one

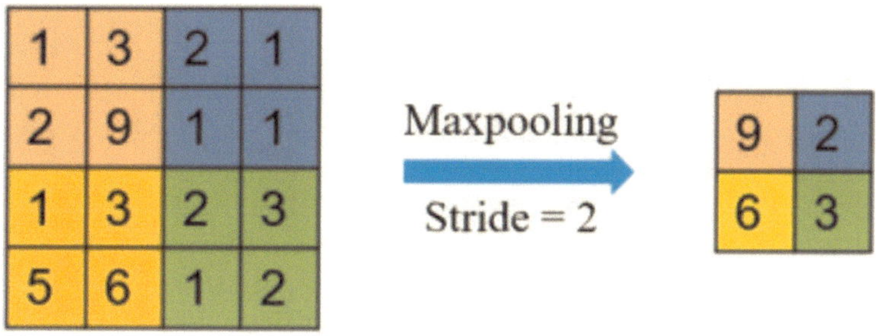

Figure 9.
Max pooling diagram.

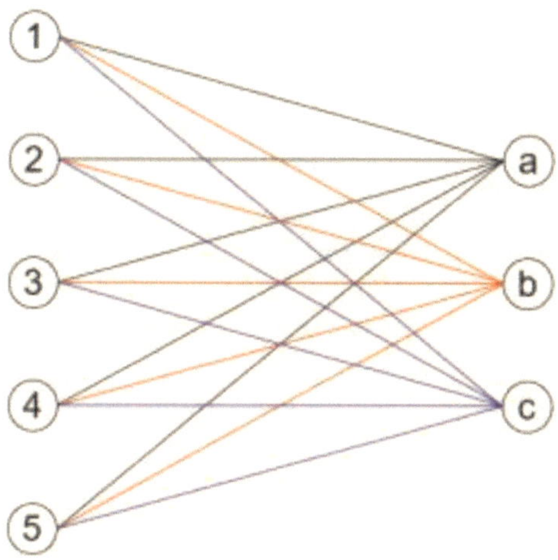

Figure 10.
Fully connection layer.

eigenspace to another eigenspace. Any dimension of the target space is affected by every dimension of the source space. In CNN, the full connection is often found in the last few layers, which is used to make a weighted sum of the features designed before. The schematic diagram of the entire connection layer is shown in **Figure 10**.

4.3 Distance measurement

After feature extraction, we need to compare the distance between the query image and all images in the retrieval set, and there are many ways you can measure the difference between two features, It is divided into distance measure (such as, Euclidean distance, Manhattan Distance etc.) and similarity measure (such as, Cosine Similarity, Jaccard Coefficient, etc.).

Distance measure is used to measure the distance of an individual in space, the greater the distance, the greater the difference between individuals. Similarity measurement is to calculate the degree of similarity between individuals. Contrary to distance measurement, the smaller the value of similarity measurement is, the smaller the similarity between individuals is, and the greater the difference is. Therefore, we can judge which images are more likely to be the same individual by the value of the difference between image features.

5. One case of person Re-ID

Person Re-ID is a technology that uses computer vision technology to judge whether there is a specific person in the image or video sequence. It is widely regarded as a sub-problem of image retrieval. Given a monitor person image, retrieve the image of the row of people across the device. It aims to make up for the visual limitations of the current fixed cameras, and can be combined with person detection and pedestrian tracking technology, which can be widely used in intelligent video monitoring, intelligent security and other fields. In this section, we show a classic person Re-ID algorithm Part-based Convolutional Baseline (PCB) [43].

5.1 Structure of PCB

PCB can take any network without hidden fully-connected layers designed for image classification as the backbone, e.g., Google Inception and ResNet. Original paper employs ResNet50 as the backbone network to reproduce the PCB algorithm.

The structure of PCB illustrated in **Figure 11**. The input image goes forward through the stacked convolutional layers from the backbone network to form a 3D tensor T. PCB replaces the original global pooling layer with a conventional pooling layer, to spatially down-sample T into p pieces of column vectors g. A following 1×1 kernel-sized convolutional layer reduces the dimension of g. Finally, each dimension-reduced column vector h is input into a classifier, respectively. Each classifier is implemented with a fully-connected (FC) layer and a sequential Softmax layer. During training, each classifier predicts the identity of the input image and is supervised by Cross-Entropy loss. During testing, either p pieces of g or h are concatenated to form the final descriptor of the input image.

5.2 Experimental results

5.2.1 Dataset

The original paper tested this algorithm on person Re-ID dataset Market-1501. The Market-1501 dataset contains 1501 identities observed under six camera viewpoints, 19,732 gallery images and 12,936 training images detected by DPM.

5.2.2 Performance comparison

It compares PCB and PCB + RPP with state of the art. Comparisons on Market-1501 are detailed in **Table 3**. PCB + RPP get mAP = 81.6% and Rank-1 = 93.8% for Market-1501, setting new state of the art on this dataset. All the results are achieved under the single-query mode without re-ranking. Reranking methods will further

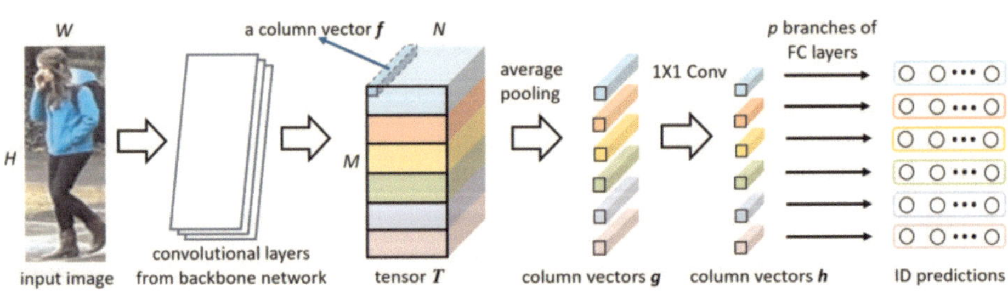

Figure 11.
Structure of PCB [43].

Methods	Rank-1	Rank-5	Rank-10	mAP
KLFDA	46.5	71.1	79.9	—
Triplet Loss	84.9	94.2	—	69.1
DML	87.7	—	—	68.8
MultiScale	88.9	—	—	73.1
GLAD	89.9	—	—	73.9
PCB	92.3	97.2	98.2	77.4
PCB + RPP	**93.8**	**97.5**	**98.5**	**81.6**

Table 3.
Comparison of the proposed method with the art on Market-1501.

boost the performance especially mAP. For example, when "PCB + RPP" is combined with the reranking method, mAP and Rank-1 accuracy on Market-1501 increases to 91.9 and 95.1%, respectively.

6. One case of vehicle Re-ID

Considering the spatiotemporal logic of vehicle driving process, we present a vehicle re-identification (Re-ID) algorithm based on multi-camera data's spatiotemporal information and joint learning mechanism without license plate. The algorithm is divided into feature extraction and spatiotemporal re-rank. In the feature extraction stage: on the basis of convolutional neural network (CNN), triplet loss and Softmax loss were used for joint training to model a feature extractor and calculate the feature distance measurement matrix between query image and retrieval set images. In the spatiotemporal re-rank stage: we calculate the spatiotemporal distance matrix and fuse the spatiotemporal distance with the normalized feature distance metric. The final distance measurement matrix is sorted to obtain the vehicle re-identification result. Extensive experiments were carried out on the benchmark datasets "VeRi" to verify the effectiveness of the proposed method and the result have shown that the proposed algorithm outperforms the state-of-the-art approaches for vehicle Re-ID.

6.1 Mathematical principles of joint learning

The architecture of proposed algorithm is illustrated in **Figure 12**. The algorithm is divided into two steps: feature extraction and spatiotemporal re-rank. In the feature extraction phase, triplet loss and Softmax loss are integrated for joint training, triplet loss is used to calculate the distance of the sample features, increasing the distance between the anchor and negative sample, reducing the distance between the anchor and the positive sample. Softmax loss performs label-level

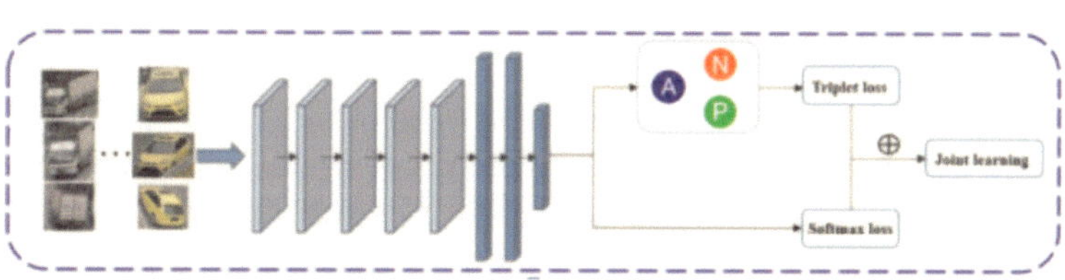

Figure 12.
The proposed algorithm for vehicle Re-ID.

supervision and constraint on the feature extraction network. In the spatiotemporal re-rank stage, calculating the spatiotemporal distance between images, and re-rank the retrieval results by merging the spatiotemporal distance and the feature distance.

6.1.1 Triplet loss

In order to learn high discriminative features from images to Euclidean space, where the distance can measure the discrepancy between two images. The idea of learning to rank has gradually been applied to many fields, such as face recognition [12], person Re-ID, and so on. One of the important steps in learning to rank is to find a good similarity function, and triplet loss is a very broad one. In the calculation of the triple loss, the feed data includes an anchor, a positive sample, and a negative sample, and the sample similarity calculation is realized by optimizing the distance between the anchor and the positive sample being smaller than the distance between the anchor and the negative sample. We suppose $T = \{x_i|i = 1, 2...m\}$ denotes the training set, where x_i is the i − th image in the training set and m denotes the total amount of training images. For an image triplet $\{x_i^a, x_i^p, x_i^n\}$, where x_i^a denotes an anchor, x_i^p denotes a positive of the same class as the anchor, x_i^n denotes a negative of a different class as the anchor, the triplet loss is calculated as Eq. (2).

$$L_{triplet} = \sum_{i}^{m} \max\left(0, \|f(x_i^a) - f(x_i^p)\|_2^2 - \|f(x_i^a) - f(x_i^n)\|_2^2 + \alpha\right) \tag{2}$$

where $f(x_i)$ denotes the embedded of the image, α denotes the parameter of expected gap between the distance of $\{x_i^a, x_i^p\}$ and $\{x_i^a, x_i^n\}$

6.1.2 Triplet sampling

This algorithm directly performs on-line triplet mining on image features, which is to compute useful triplets on the fly. For each batch of inputs, given a batch of N examples, we compute the N embeddings and we then can find a maximum of N^3 triplets. For three indices a, p, n ∈ [1, N], if examples a and p have the same label but are distinct, and example n has a different label, we say that (a, p, n) is a valid triplet. We suppose that have a batch of vehicle images as input of size N = PK, composed of P different vehicle ID with K images each. Choose the batch hard strategy: for each anchor, select the hardest positive and the hardest negative among the batch, finally we can obtain PK triplets.

$$d(a, b) = \|a - b\|^2 = \|a\|^2 - 2\langle a, p\rangle + \|b\|^2 \tag{3}$$

6.1.3 Softmax loss

We impose a strong constraint on distinguishing different vehicle label by adding Softmax loss to the loss function. The embedded obtained by CNN tend to clusters, and the embedded of same vehicle ID will be similar, so the convergence time of triplet loss will be cut down. In Softmax loss stream, each vehicle ID in the training set is considered as a category, the Softmax loss function is formulated as:

$$L_{softmax} = -\frac{1}{m}\left[\sum_{i=1}^{m}\sum_{j=1}^{k} 1\left\{y^{(i)} = j\right\} \log \frac{e^{\theta_j^T x^{(i)}}}{\sum_{l=1}^{k} e^{\theta_l^T x^{(i)}}}\right] \tag{4}$$

where m is the total amount of classes, k is the number of training image, $1(*)$ is the indicator function (if * is true, then the value set 1, or 0), and $\theta's$ are the parameters of the final full-connection layer of the CNN.

6.1.4 Joint multiple loss

The joint learning mechanism is mainly applied to the training phase of vehicle images. After the shared images pass through the shared CNN layer, they are divided into two branch streams, one is subjected to online triplet mining for the calculation of triplet loss, and the other stream enters the Softmax layer for Softmax loss calculation. The final joint learning loss function can be formulated as:

$$L_{JL} = L_{\text{softmax}} + L_{triplet} \tag{5}$$

6.2 Experimental results

6.2.1 Dataset

In order to verify the validity of the algorithm, we conduct experiments in the latest version of the vehicle re-identification dataset "VeRi." The dataset has a total of 49,357 images, which are taken for actual road monitoring and contains various angles and various vehicle models, as shown in **Figure 13**.

It is divided into two subsets for training and testing. The train set has 576 vehicle IDs with 37,778 images and the test set has 200 vehicle IDs with 11,579 images. For the vehicle re-identification task, we divided the test set to query set (1678 images) and retrieval set (9901 images).

Figure 13.
Vehicle samples selected from the VeRi dataset.

6.2.2 Experimental setting

All of the experiments are based on the deep learning framework Tensorflow. The base network is VGG_CNN_M, and the model was pre-trained on the ImageNet. In the calculation of triplet loss, we set $\alpha = 1$, the learning rate is set to 0.001, and the mini-batch is set to 32.

In order to evaluate the effect of this algorithm objectively, we set up two algorithms to compare with the method proposed to verify that the improvement of the algorithm. These algorithms are: (1) VGG + Softmax loss; (2) VGG + Triplet loss; (3) VGG + Softmax loss + Triplet loss (our method). All of network based on VGG16, "Softmax loss" denotes use Softmax loss to train the network, and "Triplet loss" denotes use triplet loss to train the network. At the same time, we also make comparison our experiment results with some state-of-the-art algorithms on the same dataset "VeRi."

6.2.3 Performance comparison on VeRi dataset

We conduct the experiment as described in experimental setting, and use cumulative matching curve (CMC), HIT@1, HIT@5 as metrics to evaluate the performance. In our method, S, T denote using Softmax loss and using triplet loss respectively. **Table 4** and **Figure 14** illustrate the performances of the proposed methods and some state-of-the-art algorithms in vehicle Re-ID field.

The results show that the proposed method "VGG + S + T" achieves the best results, the HIT@1 and HIT@5 hit 89.75 and 95.05% respectively. It is obvious that the CNN-based method has a significant improvement over the handcraft feature-based approach when compare BOW-CN and LOMO algorithm with other algorithms based on CNN feature. Compared with "VGG + S" which only utilizes Softmax loss, our method has much better results, improving 16.81% in HIT@1 and 11.38% in HIT@5. Compared with "VGG + T" which only utilizes triplet loss, our method makes improvement about 16.81% in HIT@1 and 8.67% in HIT@5. Compare to "FACT + Plate-SNN + STR" which additionally utilizes license plate information (Plate-SNN) and spatiotemporal relation (STR), our method improves 28.31% in HIT@1 and 16.27% in HIT@5. In summary, the proposed algorithm is feasible in vehicle re-identification task, and achieves outstanding results compared to other algorithms.

Method		**HIT@1**	**HIT@5**
BOW-CN		33.91	53.69
LOMO		25.33	46.48
ABLN		58.14	74.41
FACT + Plate-SNN+ STR		61.44	78.78
VAMI		77.03	90.92
JFSDL		82.90	91.60
This method	VGG+ S	72.94	83.67
	VGG + T	72.94	86.83
	VGG + S + T	**89.75**	**95.05**

Table 4.
Comparison of the proposed method with the art on VeRi.

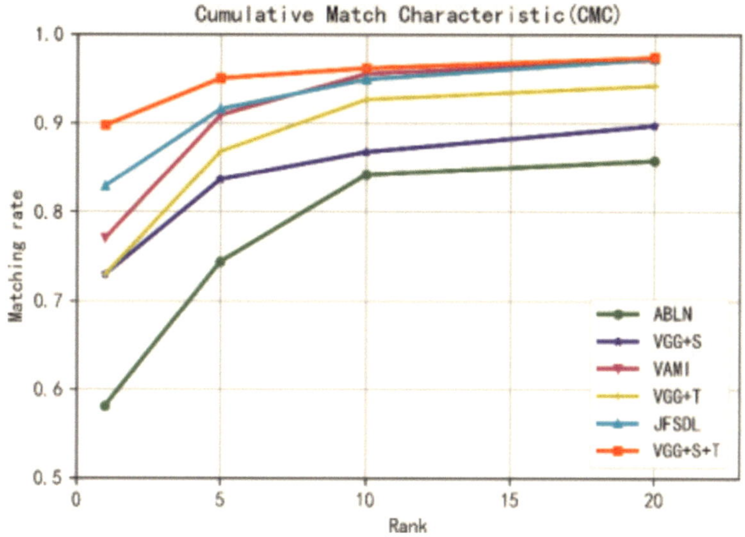

Figure 14.
The CMC curves on VeRi.

7. Summary

This chapter mainly introduces the concept of object Re-ID and two core applications: person Re-ID and vehicle Re-ID. In this chapter, the definitions of person Re-ID and vehicle Re-ID are given, some research methods of the two applications are reviewed, and the commonly used public data sets are described in detail.

In this chapter, the general process of object Re-ID by deep learning method is given, and the data input, feature extraction network structure, distance measurement and other parts are described in detail. At the same time, two examples are given to illustrate the algorithm in detail and experiment comparison. Person Re-ID refers to the network structure and experimental results of PCB algorithm [43]. Vehicle Re-ID is introduced in detail in terms of feature extraction and measurement calculation. The influence of parameters in the deep learning method is illustrated through the analysis of experimental results, and the evaluation comparison is given.

These can help relevant researchers to understand the context of technology, the general implementation process, as well as important parameters and evaluation indicators in this field, so that they can quickly start relevant research.

The object Re-ID is the basis of realizing cross-camera tracking. Person and vehicles are just two typical applications. In the future, with the gradual solution of the following problems, we will have a more extensive application:

- High-quality standard database is important to generalization performance of Re-ID algorithm. The database should be more suitable for the real environment and including different and varying scenes.

- Deep networks have poor interpretability. Although the deep learning method has achieved good performance in Re-ID tasks, few studies have shown which information has a greater impact on Re-ID behind the continuous improvement in accuracy.

- At present, most methods are carried out under the prior condition that object has been detected, but this requires a very robust detection model. We need to combine object Re-ID with object detection, which is more in line with practical application requirements.

- The research should focus on semi-supervised, unsupervised and transfer learning methods. The collected data are limited after all, and the cost of labeling data is also very high. Therefore, although the semi-supervised and unsupervised learning methods may not be as good as the supervised learning methods in terms of performance, they are valuable.

Acknowledgements

This work is supported by the National key Research and Development Program of China under Grant No. 2018YFB1601101 of 2018YFB1601100 and National Natural Science Foundation of China under Grant No. U1611461.

Author details

Xiying Li[1,2,3*] and Zhihao Zhou[1,2,3]

1 School of Intelligent Systems Engineering, Sun Yat-sen University, Guangzhou, Guangdong, People's Republic of China

2 Guangdong Provincial Key Laboratory of Intelligent Transportation System, Guangzhou, Guangdong, People's Republic of China

3 Laboratory of Video and Image Intelligent Analysis and Application Technology, Ministry of Public Security, Guangzhou, Guangdong, People's Republic of China

*Address all correspondence to: stslxy@mail.sysu.edu.cn

References

[1] Luo H, Wei J, Xing F, Si-Peng Z. A survey on deep learning based person re-identification. Acta Automatica Sinica. 2019. DOI: 10.16383/j.aas.c180154

[2] Sunderrajan S, Manjunath BS. Context-aware hypergraph Modeling for Re-identification and summarization. IEEE Transactions on Multimedia. 2016;**18**(1):51-63

[3] Geng M, Wang Y, Xiang T, Tian Y. Deep transfer learning for person reidentification. arXiv preprint arXiv: 1611.05244; 2016

[4] Lin Y, Zheng L, Zheng Z, Wu Y, Yang Y. Improving person re-identification by attribute and identity learning. arXiv preprint arXiv: 1703.07220; 2017

[5] Varior RR, Haloi M, Wang G. Gated siamese convolutional neural network architecture for human re-identification. In: European Conference on Computer Vision; Springer; 2016. pp. 791-808

[6] Shengyong D, Liang L, Guangrun W, et al. Deep feature learning with relative distance comparison for person reidentification. Pattern Recognition. 2015;**48**(10):2993-3003

[7] Chen W, Chen X, Zhang J, Huang K. Beyond triplet loss: A deep quadruplet network for person re-identification. 2017;**1**:1320-1329

[8] Hermans A, Beyer L, Leibe B. In defense of the triplet loss for person reidentification. arXiv preprint arXiv: 1703.07737; 2017

[9] Qiqi X, Hao L, Chi Z. Margin sample mining loss: A deep learning based method for person re-identification. arXiv preprint arXiv: 1710.00478; 2017

[10] Longhui W, Shiliang Z, Hantao Y, et al. GLAD: Global-local-alignment descriptor for scalable person re-identification. IEEE Transactions on Multimedia. 2019;**21**(4):986-999

[11] Chi S, Jianing L, Shiliang Z, et al. Pose-driven deep convolutional model for person reidentification. IEEE International Conference on Computer Vision (ICCV). 2017;**1**:3980-3989

[12] Zheng L, Huang Y, Lu H, Yang Y. Pose invariant embedding for deep person reidentification. arXiv preprint arXiv:1701.07732; 2017

[13] Xuan Z, Hao H, Xing F, et al. AlignedReID: Surpassing human-level performance in person re-identification. arXiv preprint arXiv:1711.08184

[14] Liu H, Jie Z, Jayashree K, et al. Video based person re-identification with accumulative motion context. IEEE Transactions on Circuits and Systems for Video Technology. 2018;**28**(10): 2788-2802

[15] Mazzeo PL, Spagnolo P, D'Orazio T. Object tracking by non-overlapping distributed camera network. In: International Conference on Advanced Concepts for Intelligent Vision Systems; 2009;**5807**:516-527

[16] Mazzeo P, Giove L, Moramarco GM, Spagnolo P, Leo M. HSV and RGB color histograms comparing for objects tracking among non-overlapping. In: 2011 8th IEEE International Conference on Advanced Video and Signal Based Surveillance (AVSS); IEEE; 2011. pp. 498-503

[17] Tian Y, Dong H-h, Jia L-m, et al. A vehicle re-identification algorithm based on multi-sensor correlation. Journal of Zhejiang University-Science C (Computers & Electronics). 2014; **15**(5):372-382

[18] Coifman B. Vehicle reidentification and travel time measurement, part II: Uncongested freeways and the onset of congestion. Journal of Transportation Engineering. 2003;**129**(5)

[19] Rios-Cabrera R, Tuytelaars T, Van Gool L. Efficient multi-camera vehicle detection, tracking, and identification in a tunnel surveillance application. Computer Vision and Image Understanding. 2012;**116**(6):742-753

[20] Liu X, Liu W, Ma H, et al. Large-scale vehicle re-identification in urban surveillance videos. In: 2016 IEEE International Conference on Multimedia and Expo (ICME); Barcelona, Spain: IEEE; 2016

[21] Liu H, Tian Y, Wang Y, et al. Deep relative distance learning: tell the difference between similar vehicles. In: Computer Vision and Pattern Recognition; Las Vegas, USA: IEEE; 2016. pp. 2167-2175

[22] Li Y, Li Y, Yan H, et al. Deep joint discriminative learning for vehicle re-identification and retrieval. In: 2017 IEEE International Conference on Image Processing (ICIP); Beijing, China: IEEE; 2017

[23] Zhang Y, Liu D, Zha ZJ. Improving triplet-wise training of convolutional neural network for vehicle re-identification. In: Proceedings of the IEEE International Conference on Multimedia and Expo (ICME); 2017. pp. 1386-1391

[24] Marin-Reyes PA, Bergamini L, Lorenzo-Navarro J, et al. Unsupervised vehicle re-identification using triplet networks. In: 2018 IEEE Conference on Computer Vision and Pattern Recognition Workshops (CVPRW); IEEE; 2018

[25] Liu X, Liu W, Mei T, et al. Provid: Progressive and multimodal vehicle reidentification for large-Scale Urban surveillance. In: IEEE Transactions on Multimedia; 2017. p. 99

[26] Na J, Yue X, Zhou Z, et al. Multi-attribute driven vehicle re-identification with spatial-temporal re-ranking. In: ICIP; 2018

[27] Yantao S, Tong X, Hongsheng L, et al. Learning deep neural networks for vehicle Re-ID with visual-spatio-temporal path proposals. In: 2017 IEEE International Conference on Computer Vision (ICCV); IEEE; 2017

[28] Li X, Zhou Z, Qiu M. A vehicle re-identification algorithm based on component fusion feature. Computer Engineering. DOI: 10.19678/j.issn.1000-3428.0052284

[29] Zhou Z, Li X, Qiu M. A car face parts detection algorithm based on faster R-CNN. In: 18th COTA International Conference of Transportation Professionals: Intelligence, Connectivity, and Mobility (CICTP 2018); 2018

[30] Liang D, Yan K, Wang Y, et al. Deep hashing with multi-task learning for large-scale instance-level vehicle search. In: 2017 IEEE International Conference on Multimedia & Expo Workshops (ICMEW); IEEE Computer Society; 2017

[31] Gray D, Brennan S, Tao H. Evaluating appearance models for recognition, reacquisition, and tracking. In: Proceedings of the 10th IEEE International Workshop on Performance Evaluation of Tracking and Surveillance (PETS). Rio de Janeiro: IEEE; 2007. pp. 1-7

[32] Hirzer M, Beleznai C, Roth PM, et al. Person re-identification by descriptive and discriminative classification. In: Proceedings of Scandinavian Conference on Image Analysis. Berlin, Heidelberg: Springer; 2011. pp. 91-102

[33] Li W, Zhao R, Xiao T, et al. DeepReID: Deep filter pairing neural network for person re-identification. In: Proceedings of the 2014 IEEE Conference on Computer Vision and Pattern Recognition; Columbus, OH, USA: IEEE; 2014. pp. 152-159

[34] Zheng L, Shen L, Tian L, et al. Scalable person re-identiflcation: A benchmark. In: Proceedings of the 2015 IEEE International Conference on Computer Vision; Santiago, Chile: IEEE; 2015. pp. 1116-1124

[35] Tong X, Shuang L, Bochao W, et al. End-to-end deep learning for person search. arXiv preprint arXiv: 1604.01850; 2016

[36] Zheng L, Bie Z, Sun Y, et al. Mars: A video benchmark for large-scale person reidentification. In: Proceedings of European Conference on Computer Vision; Cham: Springer; 2016. pp. 868-884

[37] Ristani E, Solera S, Zou R, Cucchiara R, et al. Performance measures and a data set for multi-target, multicamera tracking. In: Proceedings of European Conference on Computer Vision; Cham: Springer; 2016. pp. 17-35

[38] Wu A, Zheng WS, Yu HX, et al. RGB-infrared cross-modality person re-identification. In: Proceedings of the 2017 IEEE International Conference on Computer Vision; Venice, Italy: IEEE; 2017. pp. 5390-5399

[39] Song G, Leng B, Liu Y, et al. Region-based quality estimation network for large-scale person reidentification. In: Proceedings of Association for the Advancement of Artificial Intelligence; New Orleans: AAAI; 2018

[40] Wei L, Zhang S, Gao W, et al. Person transfer GAN to bridge domain gap for person re-identification. arXiv: 1711.08565; 2018

[41] Li J, Zhang S, Wang J, et al. LVreID: Person re-identification with long sequence videos. arXiv preprint arXiv: 1712.07286; 2017

[42] Li X, Yuan M, Jiang Q, et al. VRID-1: A basic vehicle re-identification dataset for similar vehicles. In: IEEE, International Conference on Intelligent Transportation Systems; IEEE; 2017. pp. 1-8

[43] Sun Y, Zheng L, Yang Y, et al. Beyond part models: Person retrieval with refined part pooling (and a strong convolutional baseline). 2018

Section 3

Face Recognition

Chapter 6

Spatial Domain Representation for Face Recognition

Toshanlal Meenpal, Aarti Goyal and Moumita Mukherjee

Abstract

Spatial domain representation for face recognition characterizes extracted spatial facial features for face recognition. This chapter provides a complete understanding of well-known and some recently explored spatial domain representations for face recognition. Over last two decades, scale-invariant feature transform (SIFT), histogram of oriented gradients (HOG) and local binary patterns (LBP) have emerged as promising spatial feature extraction techniques for face recognition. SIFT and HOG are effective techniques for face recognition dealing with different scales, rotation, and illumination. LBP is texture based analysis effective for extracting texture information of face. Other relevant spatial domain representations are spatial pyramid learning (SPLE), linear phase quantization (LPQ), variants of LBP such as improved local binary pattern (ILBP), compound local binary pattern (CLBP), local ternary pattern (LTP), three-patch local binary patterns (TPLBP), four-patch local binary patterns (FPLBP). These representations are improved versions of SIFT and LBP and have improved results for face recognition. A detailed analysis of these methods, basic results for face recognition and possible applications are presented in this chapter.

Keywords: spatial domain representation, face recognition, scale-invariant feature transform, histogram of oriented gradients, local binary patterns

1. Introduction

Face recognition is a powerful biometric system in today's highly technological world. It is widely accepted over other biometric systems like, finger print, iris or speech recognition for security, surveillance, and commercial applications. Face recognition system is generally a procedure of multiple major stages: face detection, preprocessing, feature extraction and verification. A complete structure of face recognition system is shown in **Figure 1**. Face detection detects a single face or number of faces present in a given image. Viola-Jones face detection algorithms using Haar features [1], faster R-CNN face detector [2], and face detection based on Histograms of Oriented Gradient [3] are popular methods for detecting faces in an image. Generally, images are captured under unconstrained environment and hence needed to be preprocessed before feeding to feature extraction stage. Preprocessing mainly aims to reduce noise effect, difference of illumination, color intensity, background, and orientation. The correct recognition of image depends upon quality of captured image, lighting condition etc. [4]. Recognition rate can be improved by performing pre-processing on the captured image. Various pre-processing

IntechOpen

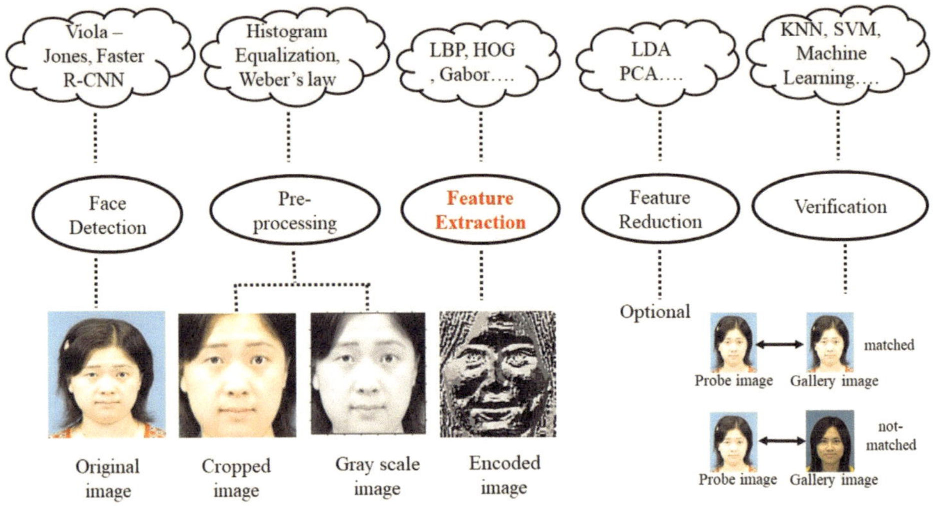

Figure 1.
A complete structure of face recognition system.

techniques are used in image processing to improve the recognition rate such as cropping, image resizing, histogram equalization and de-nosing filtering as described below.

1. Face Detection and Cropping: - Face detection involves detecting face image from whole image. Cropping can be done based on one or more features of the image such as eyes, lips, nose etc.

2. Image Resizing: - Variation in face image size, shape, pose etc. raises difficulty for designing face recognition algorithms. So it is very important to resize image before feature extraction. For this, face images are cropped again into a standard size. Affine transformation can be applied on face with Bilinear Interpolation algorithm.

3. Image Equalization: - Illumination variation problem in the original resized image is overcome by using histogram equalization.

4. Image De-noising and Filtering: - Raw images are captured with many noise during the time of capturing the image and later also. Wiener filter and median filter are used to remove noises [5].

Next is feature extraction which is considered as the most prominent stage in face recognition system to extract discriminative facial features. Extracted features are then represented as feature vector and are fed to verification stage. Feature selection is an optional stage before verification which reduces feature vector dimensions using dimensional reduction techniques [6]. Final stage is verification to identify an unknown by finding closest matching in gallery.

2. Existing face databases

There are a number of benchmark face databases for fair face recognition evaluation by researchers. These databases are designed with images or videos of a number of individuals with varying conditions and resolutions. A summary of benchmark face databases is tabulated in **Table 1**.

A detailed structure of some of these face databases are provided below.

2.1 A&T Database

A&T Database originally known as ORL database has face images captured in the interval April 1992 to April 1994. This database is collected by researchers of Cambridge University Engineering department for face recognition project. There are total 400 images in A&T database captured by taking 10 different images of 40 individuals. All images are captured in a dark homogeneous background with resolution 92 × 112 pixels. Different varying conditions under which images captured are- times, lighting, open eyes, closed eyes, smiling, not smiling, glasses, no glasses, some images also have rotation variation. This database has 40 different directories, each with 10 images of an individual stored as .pgm format. Samples of images of A&T database is shown in **Figure 2**.

2.2 CAS-PEAL-R1

CAS-PEAL-R1 Database is collected under sponsors of National Hi-Tech Program and ISVISION by the Face Recognition Group of JDL, ICT, CAS. This database contains 30,900 images of 1040 individuals captured under different conditions as such, variation in pose, facial expression, accessory, illumination, background, distance, and time. For pose variation, each of 1040 individuals has approximately 21 different poses. Facial expression is captured for 377 individuals with 6 different

Database	No. of individual	Conditions	Image Resolution	Images
A&T Database [7]	40 40 40 40 40	Lighting, Open eye, closed eyes, smiling, not smiling, glasses, no glasses	92 × 112	400
CAS-PEAL-R1 [8]	1040 377 438 233 297 296 66	Pose Facial expressions Accessory Illumination Background Distance Time	360 × 480	30,900
CMU Multi-PIE Database [9]	68	Pose Illumination Facial expressions	640 × 486	41,368
FERET [10]	1199	Pose Illumination Facial expressions Time	256 × 384	14,051
Korean Face Database (KFDB) [11]	1000	Pose Illumination Facial expressions	640 × 480	52,000
Yale Face Database B [12]	10	Pose Illumination	640 × 480	5850

Table 1.
Summary of benchmark face recognition databases.

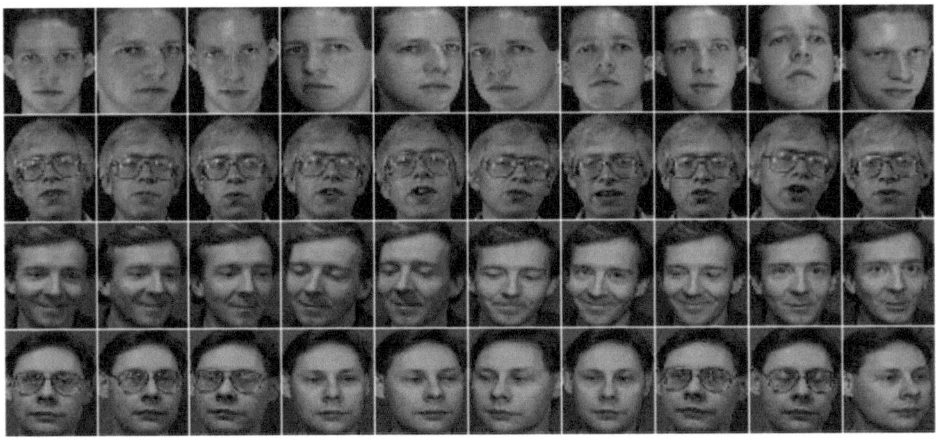

Figure 2.
Samples of images of A&T database with 10 varying conditions [7].

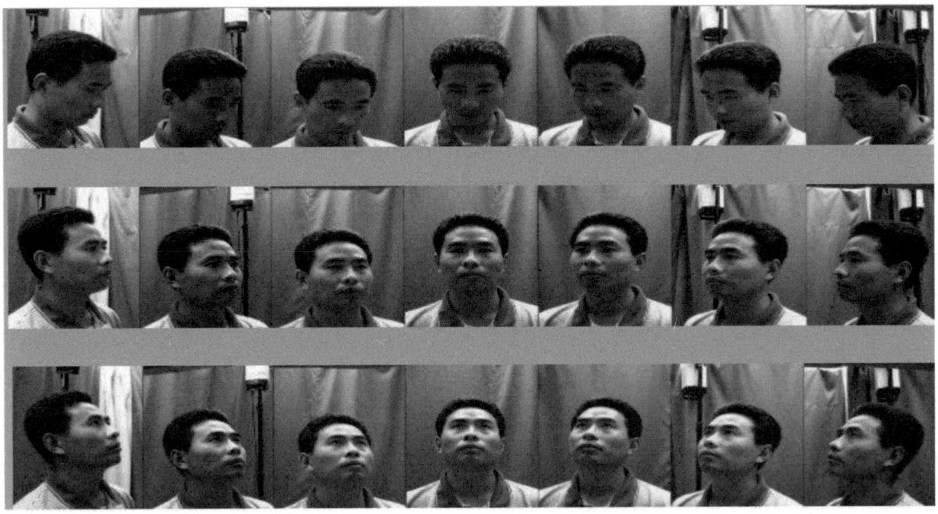

Figure 3.
Samples of images of CAS-PEAL-R1 database [8].

expressions, similarly for accessory, 6 different images of 438 individuals with different accessory are used. Illumination variation has images of 233 individuals captured for minimum 10 and maximum 31 lighting variations. Background variation has images of 297 individuals for 2 to 4 different backgrounds. Further distance and time parameters have 296 and 66 individuals at an interval of 6-month. Samples of images of CAS-PEAL-R1 database are shown in **Figure 3**.

2.3 CMU Multi-PIE Database

CMU Multi-PIE Database is collected from October 2000 to December 2000 by taking 41,368 images of 68 individuals designed for 14 different poses, 43 illumination variation, and 4 different expressions. This database is known as CMU Multi-PIE by its varying conditions- pose, illumination, and expression. Image resolution is set to resolution 640 × 486 pixels. Samples of images of CMU Multi-PIE database is shown in **Figure 4**.

This chapter mainly focuses on feature extraction stage in face recognition. It presents some well-known and recently explored spatial domain representations for

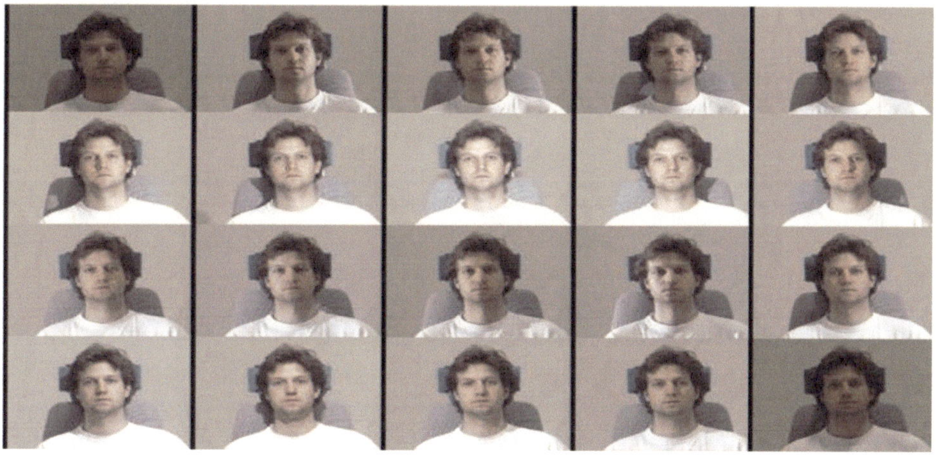

Figure 4.
Samples of images of CMU Multi-PIE Database [9].

face recognition. Scale-invariant feature transform (SIFT), histogram of oriented gradients (HOG), and local binary patterns (LBP) are most commonly used spatial feature representations over past decade. Recently, other relevant feature representations, such as, spatial pyramid learning (SPLE), linear phase quantization (LPQ), variants of LBP such as improved local binary pattern (ILBP), compound local binary pattern (CLBP), local ternary pattern (LTP), three-patch local binary patterns (TPLBP), four-patch local binary patterns (FPLBP) are effectively used for face recognition.

3. Histogram of oriented gradients (HOG)

Histogram of oriented gradients (HOG) is introduced by Dalal et al. [13] in 2005 for human detection. HOG is an effective descriptor for face recognition by computing normalized histograms of face gradient orientations in dense grid [14]. Basically, HOG generates local appearance and shape of face rather than local intensity gradients. HOG is based on computation, fine orientation binning, normalization and descriptor blocks.

A detailed implementation for extracting HOG features for face recognition is given as:

1. Facial image is first divided into small regions called cells. For an image of size 64×64, overlapping cells of 8×8 pixels are obtained. Gradient directions over pixels are computed for each cell. Simple 1-D derivatives are used in horizontal and vertical directions with the following masks:

$$D_x = [-1\ 0\ 1] \tag{1}$$

$$\text{and } D_y = \begin{bmatrix} -1 \\ 0 \\ 1 \end{bmatrix} \tag{2}$$

Results for a sample facial image using horizontal (D_x) and vertical(D_y) derivative masks are shown in **Figure 5**.

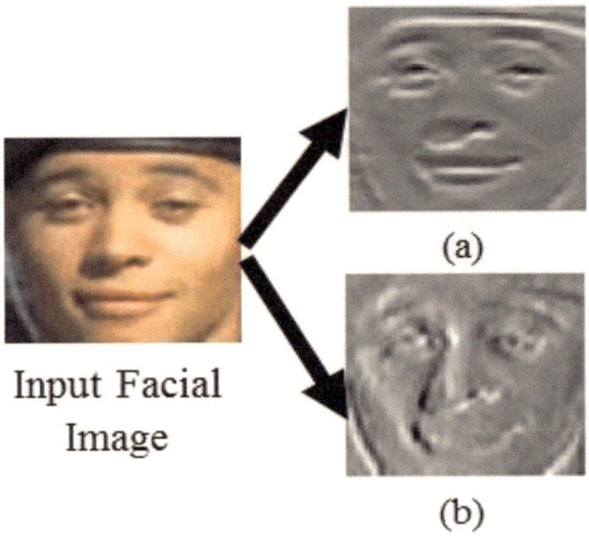

Figure 5.
Sample facial image and resultant derivatives. (a) Horizontal derivative. (b) Vertical derivative.

2. Next step is fine orientation binning for extracting HOG features. Histogram channels are evenly selected in the range 0–180° for unsigned and 0–360° for signed gradient. Each cell can contribute in the form of pixel magnitude, gradient magnitude, square root or square of magnitude. In general, gradient magnitude yields the best results while square root reduces the performance [13].

3. Gradients in each cell are normalized for local contrast normalization. Cell gradients are normalized from all blocks and are concatenated to form HOG feature vector. Dalal et al. [13] proposed 9 histogram channels (bins) to be computed for unsigned gradient. Hence, for 64 × 64 image, 1764 dimensional HOG feature vector is obtained representing full facial appearance. It can be explained as:

$$\frac{64 \times 64}{8 \times 8} \times 50\% \text{ overlapping} = 196 \text{ blocks} \tag{3}$$

$$196 \text{ blocks} \times 9 \text{ bin} = 1764 \text{ dimensional HOG vector} \tag{4}$$

4. Different normalization schemes are presented in [15] for block normalization. Let ν represents un-normalized block with $\| \nu\|_k$ as k^{th} norm for k = *1, 2* and

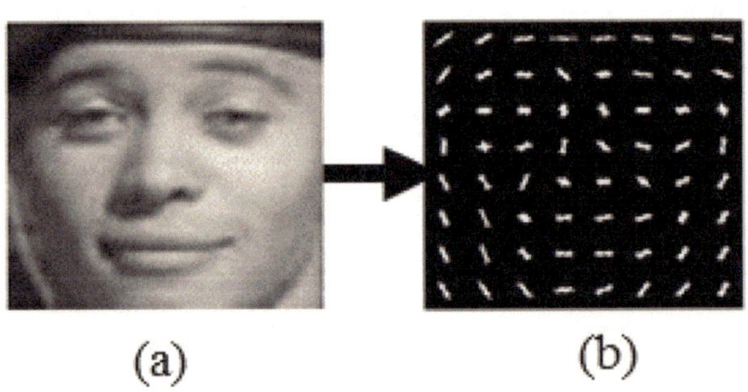

Figure 6.
Sample example of (a) Input facial image of size 64 × 64. (b) Resultant HOG features (1764 dimensions).

ϱ a small constant. Different normalization schemes used are L1-norm, L1-sqrt, L2-norm and L2-hys. Generally, L2-hys is used for block normalization. L2-hys is obtained by first computing L2-norm and then clipping such that maximum value of ν is limited to 0.2 and then renormalizing.

Sample input facial image and resultant HOG features are shown in **Figure 6**.

4. Scale invariant feature transform (SIFT)

Scale invariant feature transform (SIFT) is introduced by Lowe et al. [16] for extracting discriminative invariant features in an image. SIFT descriptor is widely used for facial feature representation by extracting blob-like local features [17]. These features are invariant to scale, translation and rotation resulting reliable matching. SIFT is described in four sections as: (1) Detection of scale-space extrema, (2) Detection of local extrema, (3) Orientation assignment, and (4) Keypoint descriptor representation.

4.1 Detection of scale-space extrema

First step is to identify keypoints in scale-space of grayscale input image $f(a,b)$which is defined as:

$$L(a,b,\sigma) = G(a,b,\sigma) * f(a,b) \tag{5}$$

$$\text{such that, } G(a,b,\sigma) = \frac{1}{2\Pi\sigma^2} e^{-\left(a^2+b^2\right)/2\sigma^2} \tag{6}$$

where σ is standard deviation of Gaussian $G(a,b,\sigma)$.

Two closest scales of image with difference of multiplication factor k are used to effectively detect extrema in scale-space. Difference of Gaussian (DOG) is computed by taking difference of these two scaled versions of image convolved with original image given as:

$$\begin{aligned} D(a,b,\sigma) &= (G(a,b,k\sigma) - G(a,b,\sigma)) * f(a,b) \\ &= L(a,b,k\sigma) - L(a,b,\sigma) \end{aligned} \tag{7}$$

4.2 Detection of local extrema

Local extrema (maxima/minima) of $D(a,b,\sigma)$ is calculated by comparing sample pixel with eight neighbors in 3×3 patch as well as nine neighbors above and below scaled images. To select sample point as local minima, it should be smaller than all 26 neighbors whereas for local maxima, selected point should be larger than all neighbors. After keypoint localization, low contrast and poorly localized points are removed by computing $|D(a,b,\sigma)|$ and discarding points with lower value to defined threshold.

4.3 Orientation assignment

Orientation assignment to each keypoint results in rotation invariance. For each Gaussian smoothened image $L(a,b)$, orientation is assigned by computing gradient magnitude $m(a,b)$, and gradient direction $\theta(a,b)$ by its neighbor using Eqs. (8) and (9) respectively.

$$m(a,b) = \sqrt{(L(a+1,b) - L(a-1,b))^2 + (L(a,b+1) - L(a,b-1))^2} \tag{8}$$

$$\theta(a,b) = \tanh(L(a,b+1) - L(a,b-1))/L(a+1,b) - L(a-1,b)) \tag{9}$$

4.4 Keypoint descriptor representation

Finally, each detected keypoint is represented as 128 dimensional feature vector. This is obtained by computing magnitude and orientation of gradient at each point in 16 × 16 sized patch of an image. Each 16 × 16 patch is subdivided into 4 × 4 non-overlapping regions such that each 4 × 4 region is represented by 8 bins. Hence, each keypoint descriptor is represented by 4 × 4 × 8 = 128 length vector.

Figure 7 shows an example of assignment of SIFT descriptor for 8 × 8 neighborhood. Length of each arrow corresponds sum of gradient magnitude in a specific direction for 4 × 4 region.

Processing flow to generate SIFT features for face recognition is shown in **Figure 8**. Input original image is first preprocessed and difference of Gaussian

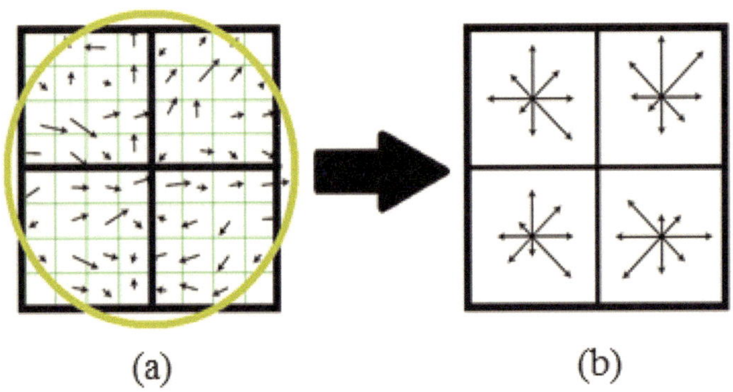

Figure 7.
Example of (a) Image gradients of 2 × 2 patch computed from 8 × 8 neighborhood. (b) Resultant SIFT keypoint descriptor.

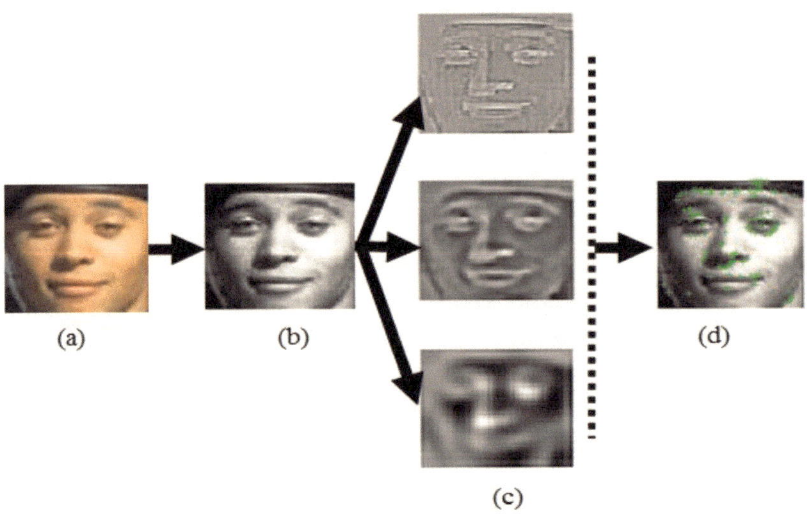

Figure 8.
Processing flow of SIFT for face recognition. (a) Original image. (b) Processed image. (c) Difference of Gaussian Pyramid. (d) SIFT keypoints.

pyramid is generated as in **Figure 8(c)**. Final resultant SIFT keypoints are then represented as feature vector to be fed to classifier for face recognition.

5. Linear phase quantization (LPQ)

Local phase quantization (LPQ) introduced by Ojansivu et al. [18, 19] is blur tolerant texture based descriptor. LPQ is based on blur invariance property of frequency domain phase spectrum of an image. LPQ for face recognition is investigated by Ahonen et al. [20] and reported improved results for blurred facial images.

LPQ on an image pixel is applied by using short-term Fourier transform (STFT) over $M \times M$ patch with image as center and four scalar frequencies. Imaginary and real components are then whitened and binary quantized to generate LPQ code for respective pixel. Complete process is detailed in **Figure 9** where LPQ code is obtained for an image pixel [21]. Similarly, final LPQ feature vector can be obtained by shifting $M \times M$ patch over the entire image.

Spatial blurring is performed by convolving grayscale input image $f(a, b)$ to point spread function (PSF). Frequency domain analysis can be represented as:

$$H(u,v) = F(u,v)\,.\,P(u,v) \tag{10}$$

here, $F(u,v)$ and $P(u,v)$ are DFT of original image and PSF respectively. $H(u,v)$ is DFT of resultant blurred image.

Phase spectrum is obtained as:

$$\angle H(u,v) = \angle F(u,v) + \angle P(u,v) \tag{11}$$

Now, if PSF is positive and even, then $\angle P(u,v)$ must be either 0 or Π, such that $\angle P(u,v) = 0$ for $P(u,v) \geq 0$ while, $\angle P(u,v) = \Pi$ for $P(u,v) < 0$.

Since, shape of $P(u,v)$ generally selected is similar to Gaussian function, low frequency value of $P(u,v)$ is positive. This results $\angle P(u,v) = 0$ and Eq. (11)

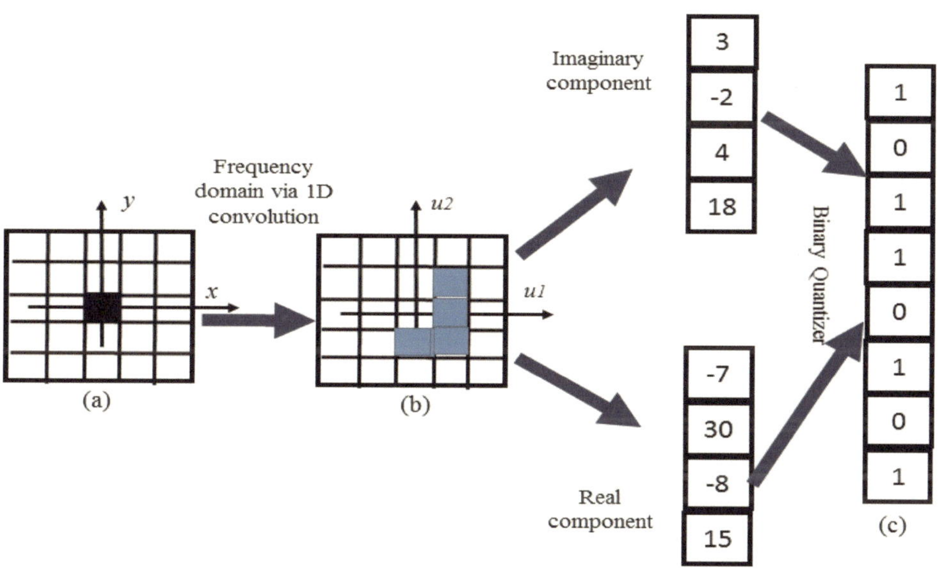

Figure 9.
LPQ encoding scheme. (a) Input 5 × 5 patch. (b) Frequency domain representation. (c) LPQ code.

becomes $\angle H(u,v) = \angle F(u,v)$. Hence, it can be stated that LPQ possesses blur invariant property. Detailed mathematical analysis of LPQ can be obtained from [21].

6. Local binary patterns (LBP)

Local Binary Patterns (LBP) is introduced by Ojala et al. [22] as rotation invariant texture based feature descriptor. LBP as feature representation for face recognition is proposed by Ahohen et al. [23]. It stated that texture analysis of a local facial region represents its local appearance and fusion of all regions can generate an encoded global geometry of face.

Consider an input image and let $f(a,b)$ be its preprocessed version. Basic LBP operator on 3×3 neighborhood of $f(a,b)$ and generated decimal code for center pixel is shown in **Figure 10**. LBP operator replaces each pixel of $f(a,b)$ with a calculated decimal code resulting in LBP encoded image $f_{LBP}(a,b)$. It is done by thresholding each pixel of 3×3 neighborhood with its center pixel. Resultant is a binary code which is then converted into corresponding decimal code. Center pixel is then replaced by decimal code of generated binary stream. LBP code assigned to center pixel is given by Eq. (12). Here, i_c represents center pixel, c_n is gray level of neighbor pixels, and c_p is gray level of center pixel.

$$LBP_{P,\ R}(i_c) = \sum_{m=0}^{P-1} s(c_n - c_p)2^m$$
$$s = \begin{cases} 1 & if\ c_n - c_p > 0 \\ 0 & otherwise \end{cases} \tag{12}$$

Ahohen et al. [23] proposed that LBP operator can be used with varying neighborhood size $M \times M$ and radius R to deal with different image scales. Notation (P, R) is used to represent P sampling points or neighbor pixels around center pixel for radius R. Thresholding is then performed by comparing center pixel with P neighbor pixels. Example of some selected values of (P, R) is shown in **Figure 11**.

LBP for face recognition processes by building local LBP descriptor to represent local region and then combined to obtain global representation for entire face. Encoded image $f_{LBP}(a,b)$ is evenly divided into non-overlapping blocks. Histogram for each block are calculated and final LBP feature vector is built by concatenating all regional histograms. LBP operator provides essential spatial information that plays a key role for face recognition. Complete processing flow to generate LBP feature vector is shown in **Figure 12**.

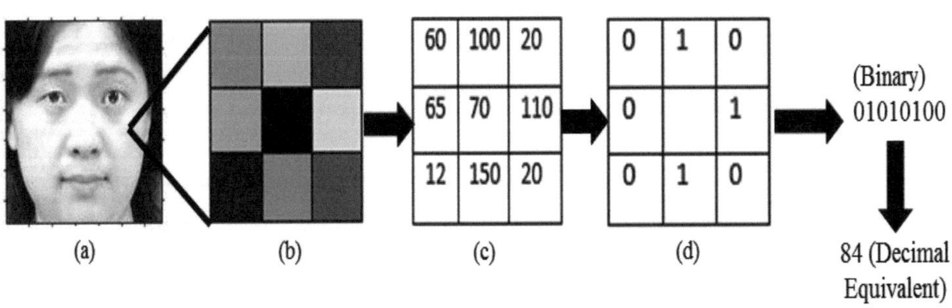

Figure 10.
Basic LBP operator on 3×3 neighborhood for $f(a,b)$. (a) Preprocessed image. (b) 3×3 Neighborhood. (c) Corresponding gray levels of each pixel. (d) Result after thresholding. Finally, center pixel is replaced by code 42.

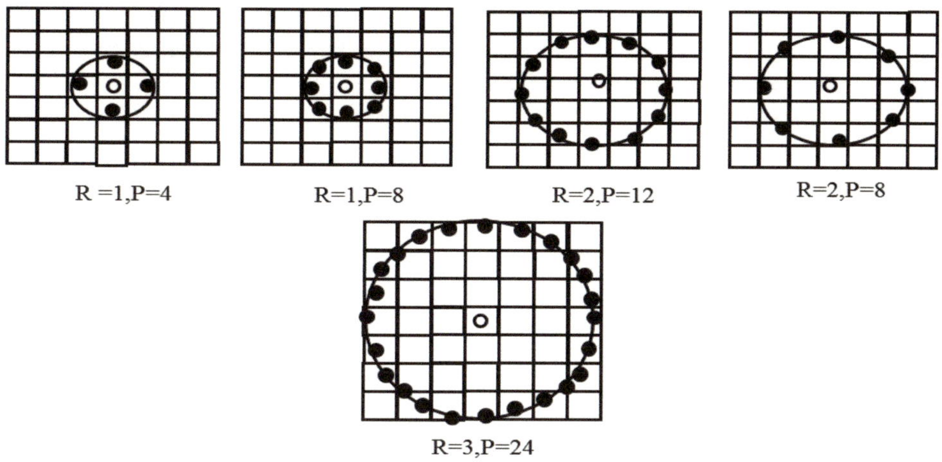

Figure 11.
Different P and R combinations for LBP operator.

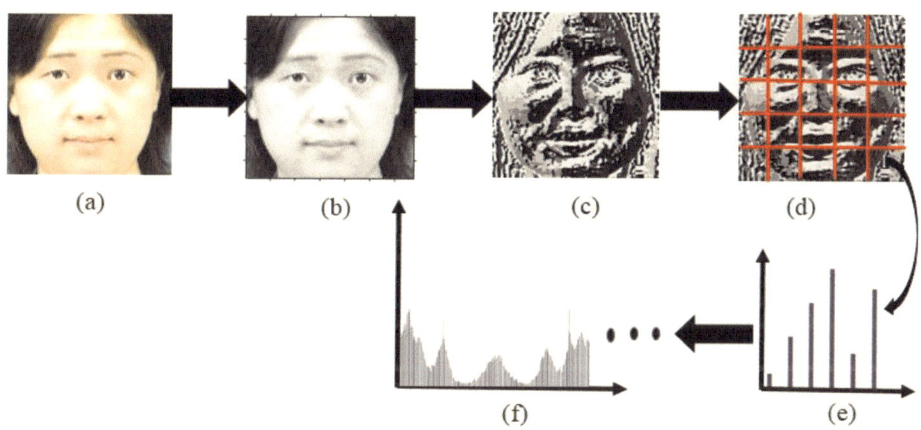

Figure 12.
Processing flow of LBP for face recognition. (a) Original input image. (b) Preprocessed image. (c) LBP Encoded image. (d) Divided non-overlapping patches for encoded image. (e) Histogram of selected non-overlapping patch. (f) Final LBP feature vector by concatenating histograms of all patches in image.

Major advantages of LBP over other spatial feature representations are simple calculations, comparatively smaller feature vector size, more powerful towards noises and illumination balance. In recent years, various variants of LBP are widely implemented in texture analysis. Local ternary patterns (LTP) proposed by Tan et al. [24] is based on a ternary threshold operator. LTP is an improved LBP variant by using two LBP vectors for building one LTP representation. Other variants of LBP are compound local binary pattern (CLBP) [25], three-patch LBP (TPLBP) [26], four-patch LBP (FPLBP) [26] and improved local binary pattern (ILBP) [27]. These representations are verified to be more efficient than LBP against illumination and noise conditions.

7. Local ternary patterns (LTP)

Local ternary patterns (LTP) [24] is a generalization of LBP with reduced sensitivity to noise and illumination variations. LTP generates a 3-valued code by including a threshold around zero and improves resistance to noise. LTP works well for noisy images and different lighting conditions.

In LBP, neighbor pixels are compared with center pixel directly. Hence, a small variation in pixel values due to noise can drastically change LBP code. To overcome this limitation, LTP introduces a threshold $\pm t$ around center pixel i_c and neighbor pixels are compared to generate 3-valued ternary code as:

$$LTP_{P,\,R}(i_c) = \sum_{m=0}^{P-1} s(c_{n-}c_p)2^m \tag{13}$$

$$s = \begin{cases} 1 & c_p \geq c_n + t \\ 0 & |c_p - t| < t \\ -1 & c_p \leq c_p - t \end{cases} \tag{14}$$

Here, c_p and c_n represent gray levels of center pixel and neighbor pixels respectively. Understanding of LTP encoding scheme to generate ternary LTP code is shown in **Figure 13**. Here, threshold t is set to 5, hence with center pixel value 40, the tolerance range is [35, 45]. Neighbor pixels with gray level values in this range is replaced by zero, those above are replaced by 1 and below are replaced by -1 as described in Eq. (14).

Resultant ternary LTP code is split into two sub-LTP codes which are treated as two separate channels as shown in **Figure 14**. Lower and upper sub-LTP codes are

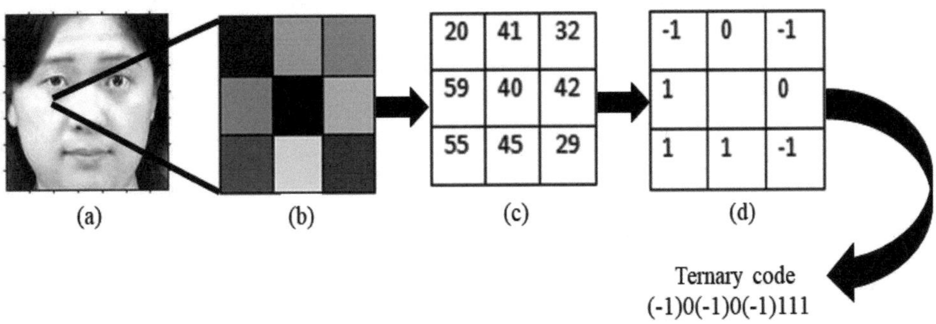

Figure 13.
LTP encoding scheme to generate ternary LTP code. (a) Preprocessed image. (b) 3 × 3 Neighborhood. (c) Corresponding gray levels of each pixel. (d) Ternary LTP code after thresholding.

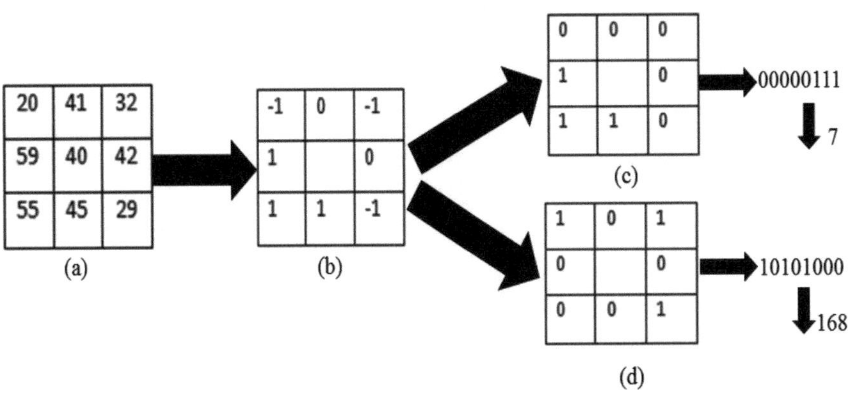

Figure 14.
Splitting of ternary LTP code to generate lower and upper sub-LTP codes. (a) 3 × 3 neighborhood of an image. (b) Ternary LTP code. (c) Lower sub-LTP code. (d) Upper sub-LTP code. Finally, lower and upper sub-LTP codes obtained are 7 and 168 respectively.

generated by replacing '-1' in original ternary code to '0' and '1' respectively. Hence, LTP represents each original image by two encoded images.

8. Compound local binary pattern (CLBP)

Compound local binary pattern (CLBP) proposed by Ahmed et al. [25] is an improved variant of LBP using $2P$ bits code. CLBP overcomes limitation of LBP by improving performance in case of flat image. LBP results poor for images with bright spots or dark patches i.e. in case of flat image LBP fails as shown in **Figure 15**.

Original LBP generates P bits code by taking gray level difference between center pixel and P neighbor pixels (sampling points). CLPB is an extension to LBP by generating $2P$ bits code for P neighbor pixels. Here, extra P bits encode magnitude information of difference between center pixel and P pixels. This way, CLBP increases robustness of texture representation mainly in case of flat images.

To generate $2P$ bits code, CLBP represents each neighbor pixel with two bits for sign and magnitude information. The first bit is same as LBP bit and represents sign of difference between center pixel and respective neighbor pixel. Second bit encodes magnitude of difference with respect to a calculated threshold M_{ab}. This threshold is obtained by taking mean of magnitudes of difference between center pixel and all P pixels.

First bit is set to '1' if gray level of neighbor pixel is greater than or equals to center pixel and '0' otherwise. Second bit is '1' if absolute magnitude of difference between neighbor pixel and center pixel is greater than threshold and '0' otherwise. CLBP

$$CLBP_{P,R}(i_c) = \sum_{m=0}^{P-1} s\left(c_n - c_p\right)2^m \tag{15}$$

$$s = \begin{cases} 00\ c_n - c_p < 0, & \left|c_n - c_p\right| \le M_{ab} \\ 01\ c_n - c_p < 0 & \left|c_n - c_p\right| > M_{ab} \\ 10\ c_n - c_p \ge 0 & \left|c_n - c_p\right| \le M_{ab} \\ 11 & otherwise \end{cases} \tag{16}$$

CLBP encoding scheme to generate $2P$ bits code for 3×3 neighborhood of an image is shown in **Figure 16**. A 16-bits CLBP code is generated after thresholding using Eq. (16). Resultant CLBP code is then split into two 8 bits sub-CLBP codes to reduce possible binary patterns from 2^{16} to (2×2^8). First 8-bits code is

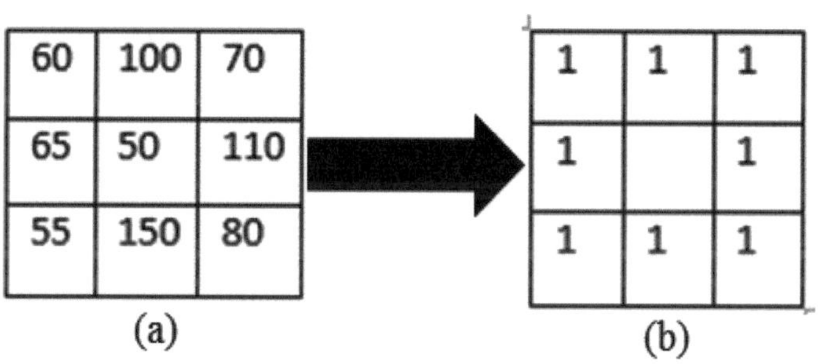

Figure 15.
LBP code for flat image. (a) 3×3 Neighbouhood of an image. (b) LBP encoded image.

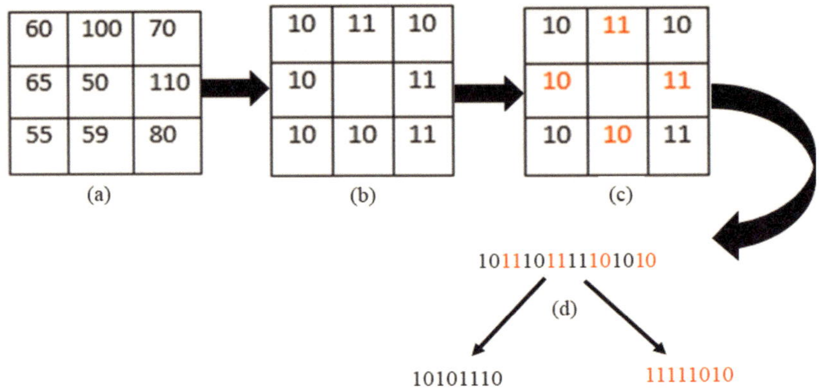

Figure 16.
CLBP encoding scheme to generate 2P bits code. (a) 3 × 3 neighborhood of an image. (b) 2P bits CLBP code after thresholding. (c) Separated sub-CLBP codes. (d) Resultant two 8-bit sub-CLBP codes.

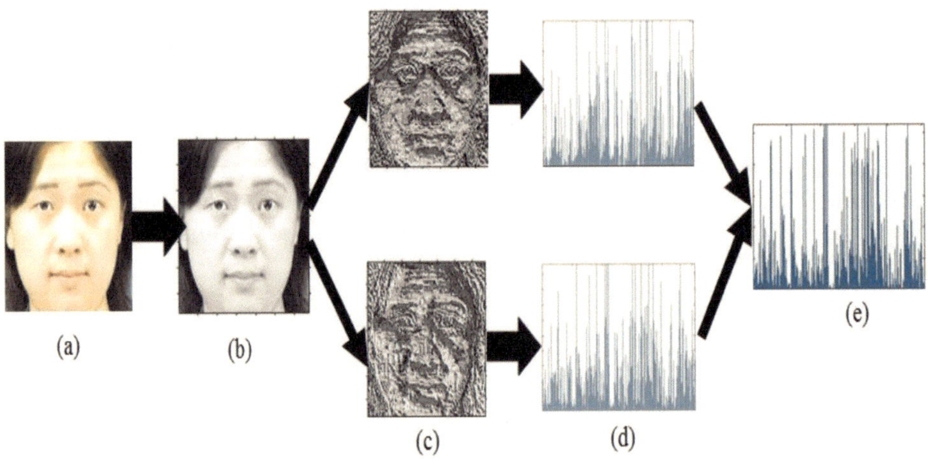

Figure 17.
Processing flow of CLBP for face recognition. (a) Original image. (b) Preprocessed image. (c) Separated sub-CLBP encoded images. (d) Respective histograms of each encoded image. (e) Concatenated histogram.

concatenation of bits from pixels marked red in **Figure 16(c)**. Again, second 8-bits code is obtained by concatenating bit values from left over pixels. Finally, these sub-CLBP codes are treated as channels for final feature vector representation.

Processing flow to generate histograms of CLBP encoded image for face recognition is shown in **Figure 17**. It explains how each pixel of original image is converted into CLBP encoded image. **Figure 17(c)** shows two sub-CLBP encoded images. Histogram of each encoded image are obtained as in **Figure 17(d)**. These histograms can be individually used as separate feature vectors for face recognition or can be concatenated as a single final vector.

9. Three-patch LBP (TPLBP)

Original LBP and different variants of LBP generate 1-bit value or 2-bit value (for CLBP) by comparing two pixels, one as center pixel and other as one of the *P* neighbor pixels. Wolf et al. [26] proposed two different variants of LBP, namely, Three-patch LBP (TPLBP and Four-patch LBP (FPLBP) by comparing center pixel with more than one neighbor pixels.

TPLBP assigns each neighbor pixel in encoded image with 1-bit value by comparing gray level of three patches. For each center pixel i_c, $M \times M$ patch is considered and P additional same sized patches with center at distance of radius R is selected. Center pixel i_c is compared with center pixels of two patches at δ distance apart along the ring of radius R. This way, TPLBP generates P bits code for i_c as:

$$TPLBP_{P,R,M,\delta}(i_c) = \sum_{m=0}^{P-1} f\left(d\left(c_m, c_p\right) - d\left(c_{m+\delta \text{ mod M}}, c_p\right)\right)2^m \tag{17}$$

here, c_p, c_m and $c_{m+\delta \text{ mod M}}$ are gray level of i_c, gray levels of center pixel of mth and $(m+\delta)^{th}$ patches respectively. $d(.)$ is L_2 norm and f is given as:

$$f(a) = \begin{cases} 1, & a \geq \tau \\ 0, & a < \tau \end{cases} \tag{18}$$

τ is a user-specific threshold selected slightly greater than zero (say τ=.01) to obtain stability in flat regions. **Figure 18** shows a sample example to generate TPBLP code for selected $P = 8$, $\delta = 2$, $M = 3$. TPLBP code generation for given sample using Eq. (17) is as:

$$\begin{aligned} &f\left(d\left(c_0, c_p\right) - d\left(c_2, c_p\right)\right)2^0 + f\left(d\left(c_1, c_p\right) - d\left(c_3, c_p\right)\right)2^1 + \\ &f\left(d\left(c_2, c_p\right) - d\left(c_4, c_p\right)\right)2^2 + f\left(d\left(c_3, c_p\right) - d\left(c_5, c_p\right)\right)2^3 + \\ &f\left(d\left(c_4, c_p\right) - d\left(c_6, c_p\right)\right)2^4 + f\left(d\left(c_5, c_p\right) - d\left(c_7, c_p\right)\right)2^5 + \\ &f\left(d\left(c_6, c_p\right) - d\left(c_0, c_p\right)\right)2^6 + f\left(d\left(c_7, c_p\right) - d\left(c_1, c_p\right)\right)2^7 \end{aligned} \tag{19}$$

Processing flow to obtain TPLBP feature vector for face recognition is shown in **Figure 19**. Input facial image of size 64 × 64 is first represented as TPLBP encoded image as in **Figure 19(c)**. TPLBP encoded image is then divided into non-overlapping patches of same size and histogram for each patch is obtained. These

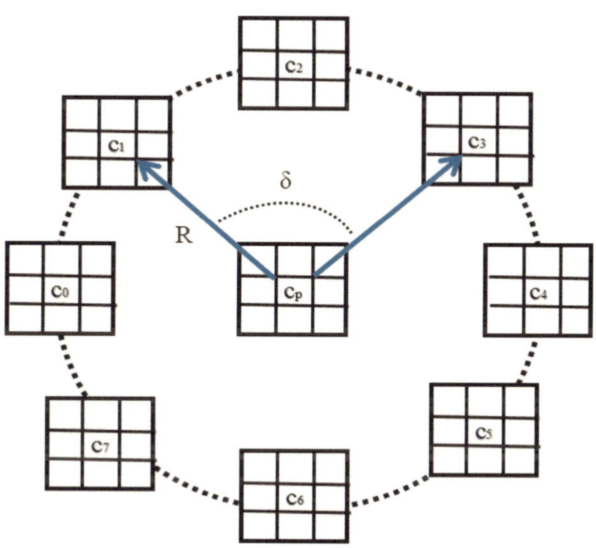

Figure 18.
TPLBP code generation for selected $P = 8, \delta = 2, M = 3$.

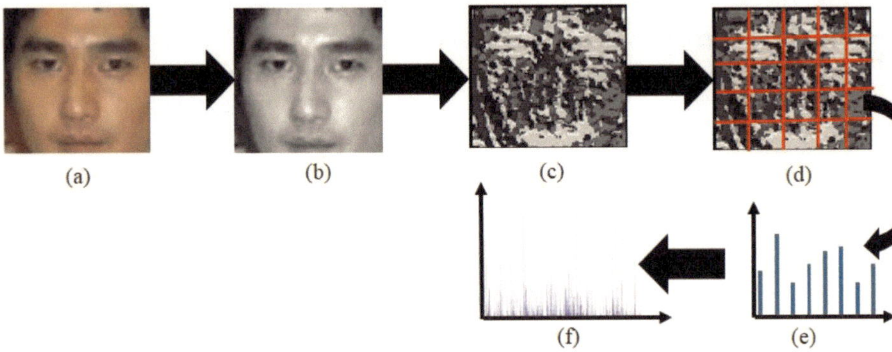

Figure 19.
Processing flow of TPLBP for face recognition. (a) Original input image. (b) Preprocessed image. (c) TPLBP Encoded image. (d) Divided non-overlapping patches for encoded image. (e) Histogram of selected non-overlapping patch. (f) Final TPLBP feature vector by concatenating histograms of all patches in image.

histograms are then normalized and truncated to value 0.2. Finally, TPLBP feature vector is obtained by concatenating all histograms.

10. Four-patch LBP (FPLBP)

Four-patch LBP (FPLBP) [26] is an extension to TPLBP by comparing center pixels of four patches to generate 1-bit value. Two different rings with radius $R1$ and $R2$ ($R1 < R2$) and P patches of size $M \times M$ for each ring are selected around center pixel i_c. Two patches with center symmetric are selected in inner ring and compared with corresponding patches in outer ring at distance δ along a circle. This way, FPLBP generates $P/2$ bit code for i_c by obtaining $P/2$ pairs as:

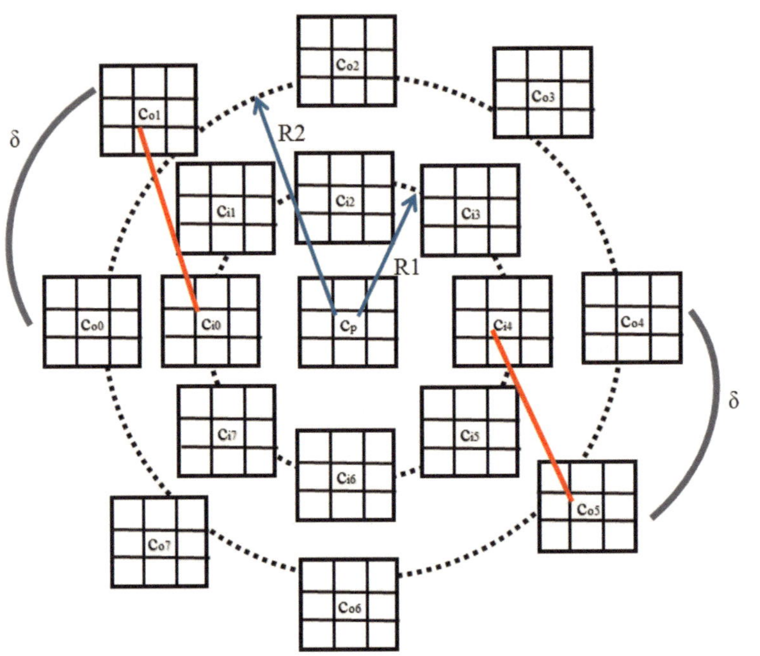

Figure 20.
FPLBP code generation for selected $P = 8, \delta = 2, M = 3$.

$$FPLBP_{P,R1,R2,M,\delta}(i_c) = \sum_{m=0}^{P/2-1} f\left(d\left(c_{i,m}, c_{o,m+\delta \bmod M}\right) - d\left(c_{i,m+P/2}, c_{o,m+P/2+\delta \bmod M}\right)\right)2^m \quad (20)$$

here, $c_{i,m}$ and $c_{o,m+\delta \bmod M}$ are gray levels of center pixel of mth patch in inner ring and $(m+\delta)^{th}$ patch in outer ring respectively. Again, $c_{i,m+P/2}$ and $c_{o,m+P/2+\delta \bmod M}$ are gray levels of center pixel of center symmetric $(m+P/2)^{th}$ patch in inner ring and $(m+P/2+\delta)^{th}$ patch in outer ring respectively. **Figure 20** shows a sample example to generate FPBLP code for selected $P = 8$, $\delta = 2$, $M = 3$. Also FPLBP code generation for given sample using Eq. (20) is as:

$$\begin{aligned} &f(d(c_{i0}, c_{o1}) - d(c_{i4}, c_{o5}))2^0 + f(d(c_{i1}, c_{o2}) - d(c_{i5}, c_{o6}))2^1 \\ &f(d(c_{i2}, c_{o3}) - d(c_{i6}, c_{o7}))2^2 + f(d(c_{i3}, c_{o4}) - d(c_{i7}, c_{o8}))2^3 \end{aligned} \quad (21)$$

Processing flow to obtain FPLBP feature vector for a sample facial image similar to TPLBP is shown in **Figure 21**.

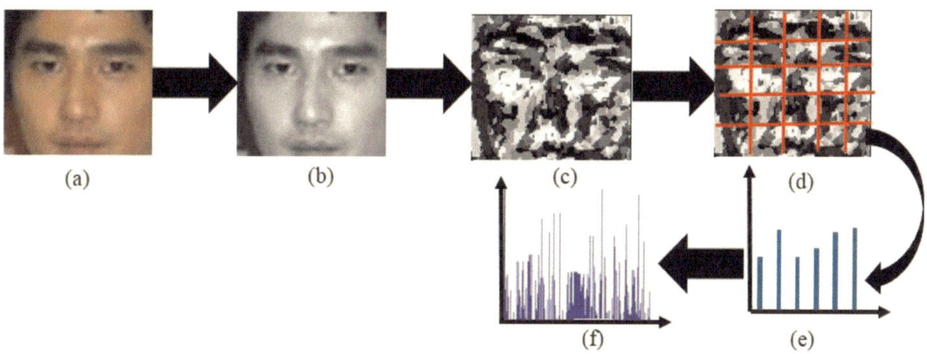

Figure 21.
Processing flow of FPLBP for face recognition. (a) Original input image. (b) Preprocessed image. (c) FPLBP Encoded image. (d) Divided non-overlapping patches for encoded image. (e) Histogram of selected non-overlapping patch. (f) Final FPLBP feature vector by concatenating histograms of all patches in image.

11. Improved LBP (ILBP)

Improved LBP (ILBP) originally named as CLBP (complete LBP) is proposed by Guo et al. [27]. It is termed as ILBP to distinguish its abbreviation from compound LBP (CLBP). In ILBP, neighbor pixels are represented by its center pixel and a local difference sign-magnitude transform (LDSMT). A complete processing flow to

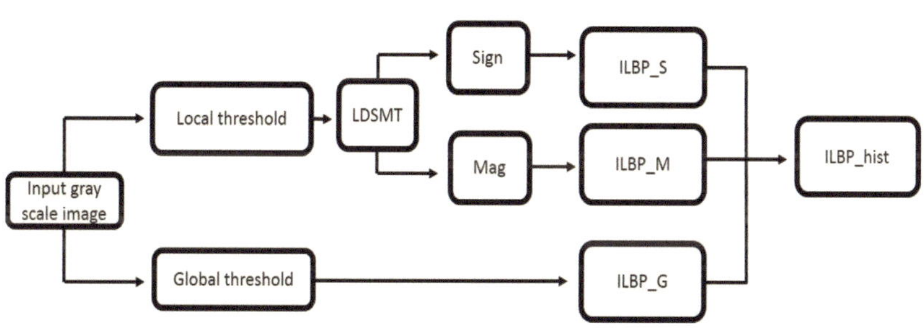

Figure 22.
Complete processing flow to generate ILBP code.

generate ILBP code is shown in **Figure 22**. ILPB generates 3*P* bits code for *P* neighbor pixels. An original image is first represented in terms of local threshold and global threshold. Local threshold is then further decomposed into sign and magnitude components. Consequently, three representations of *P* bits are obtained namely, ILBP_Sign (ILBP_S), ILBP_Magnitude (ILBP_M) and ILBP_Gobal (ILBP_G) and combined to form 3*P* bits ILBP code.

Let c_p and c_n represent gray levels of center pixel i_c and *P* neighbor pixels respectively. Local threshold is generated by taking difference $s_p = c_n - c_p$. Subtracted vector s_p is further divided into components, namely, magnitude of subtraction (m_p) and sign of subtraction (q_p) as:

$$s_p = q_p * m_p, \textit{where} \begin{cases} q_p = \text{sign}(s_p) \\ m_p = |sp| \end{cases} \tag{22}$$

$$q_p = \begin{cases} 1, & s_p \geq 0 \\ -1, & s_p < 0 \end{cases} \tag{23}$$

Understanding of ILPB encoding scheme to generate 3*P* bits ILBP code is shown in **Figure 23. Figure 23(a)** shows 3 × 3 neighborhood with center pixel value 50. ILBP encoded image after local thresholding is shown in **Figure 23(b)** as [−38, −15, 20, 15, 22, −6, −41, 35]. After LDSMT, sign and magnitude vectors are obtained. It is clearly seen that original LBP uses only sign as LBP encodes −1 as 0 in sign vector representation. LBP code for above sample block is [0, 0, 1, 1, 1, 0, 0, 1]. Hence, LBP considers only sign components of subtraction while ILBP combines three representations, ILBP_S, ILBP_M and ILBP_G. Local region around center pixel is represented by LDSMT, assigning threshold value w.r.t sign leads ILBP_S and assigning threshold value w.r.t. magnitude leads ILBP_M. Similarly, image is also encoded using global threshold is termed as ILBP_G.

A comparative analysis of various spatial domain feature representations is given in **Table 2**.

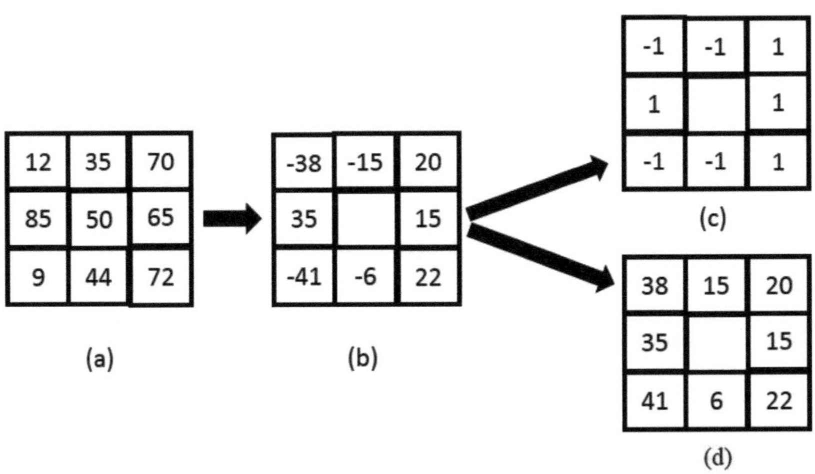

Figure 23.
ILBP encoding scheme. (a) 3 × 3 neighborhood of an image. (b) ILBP encoded image after thresholding. (c) Sign component. (d) Magnitude component.

Feature	Advantages	Disadvantages
HOG	• Rotation and scale invariant.	• Very sensitive to image rotation. Not good choice for classification of textures or objects.
SIFT	• Rotation and scale invariant.	• Mathematically complicated and computationally heavy. • It is not effective for low powered devices.
LBP	• High discriminative power. • Computational simplicity.	• Not invariant to rotations. • Size of feature vector increases exponentially with number of neighbors leading to an increase of computational complexity in terms of time and space. • The structural information captured by it is limited. Only pixel difference is used, magnitude information ignored. • Performance decreases for flat images.
LPQ	• Performance is better as compare to LBP in case of blurred illumination and facial expression variations images.	• LPQ vector is about four times longer than an LBP vector with 8 neighbor pixels.
CLBP	• It gives better performance as compared to LBP as it uses both difference sign and magnitude.	• Feature vector is too long so it increases computational time.
LTP	• Resistant to noise.	• Not invariant under gray-scale transform of intensity values as its encoding is based on a fixed predefined thresholding.
TPLBP	• Rotation invariant for texture descriptor. • Capture information for not only microstructure but also macrostructure.	• Complexity increases.
FPLBP	• Rotation invariant for texture descriptor. • Capture information for not only microstructure but also macrostructure.	• More complex.

Table 2.
Comparative analysis of spatial domain feature representations.

12. Result analysis for face recognition

Face recognition has been explored over last many years, hence there exists a large number of researches in this domain. In this section, we present existing face recognition results and analysis based on different spatial domain representations. Deniz et al. [28] proposed face recognition using HOG features by extracting features from varying image patches which resulted in an improved accuracy. Recognition accuracy is evaluated on FERET database with best result of 95.4%. Other related researches are [29] which used EBGM-HOG and showed robustness to change in illumination, rotation and small displacements. Some existing works on face recognition using SIFT features are [30, 31]. These works have also used variants of SIFT such as volume-SIFT (VSIFT), partial-descriptor-SIFT (PDSIFT), learning SIFT at specific locations to improve verification accuracy.

Face recognition using LPQ feature representation is inspired by [18, 19] which used LPQ as blur invariant descriptor. Damane et al. [32] presented face recognition using LPQ under varying conditions of light, blur, and illumination. Experiments are performed on extended YALE-B, CMU-PIE, and CAS-PEAL-R1 face databases and results showed that LPQ has more robustness to light and illumination variation. Chan et al. [33] presented multiscale LPQ for face recognition and evaluated results on FERET and BANCA face databases. Multiscale LPQ is obtained by applying varying filter size and combining LPQ images, which are then projected into LDA space. Best results of 99.2% for FB, 92% for DP1 and 88% for DP2 are achieved on FERET probe sets.

Face recognition using LBP feature representation is one of the most researched area [34–38]. Again, Tan et al. [24] evaluated face recognition under varying lighting condition using LTP feature representation on Extended Yale-B, and CMU PIE face databases. They showed that LTP is more discriminant and less sensitive to noise in uniform regions and improved results in case of flat images. Wolf et al. [26] proposed TPLBP and FPLBP features for face recognition. Accuracy results are validated on two well-known databases, labeled faces in the wild (LFW) and multi PIE. They showed that combining several descriptors from the same LBP boosts family recognition rate. This paper claimed that best accuracy of 80.75% for TPLBP and 75.57% for FPLBP are obtained with the combination of ITML with MultiOSS ID and pose variation. Ahmed et al. [25] proposed CLBP features for facial expression recognition. It is an extension of LBP features. Results are verified in Cohn-Kanade (CK) facial expression database. CLBP features are classified with the help of SVM classifier. They showed that classification rate can be effected by adjusting the number of regions into which expression images are partitioned. For this, they considered three cases by dividing images into 3×3, 5×5, and 7×6 patches. Best accuracy result for CLBP is 94.4% in case of image with 5×5 patch size.

13. Conclusion

This chapter presents well-known and some recently explored spatial feature representations for face recognition. These feature representations are scale, translation and rotation invariants for 2-D face images. This chapter covers HOG, SIFT and LBP feature representations and complete processing flow to generate feature vectors using these representations for face recognition. SIFT and HOG based on computing image gradients and local extrema are commonly used feature representations for face recognition. LBP performs texture based analysis to represent local facial appearance and an encoded facial image. Other relevant spatial domain representations, such as, LPQ and variants of LBP are explained and analyzed for face recognition. LPQ possesses blur invariant property and provides improved results for blurred facial image. Different variants of LBP, such as, LTP, CLBP, TPLBP and FPLBP are more robust to noise and lighting conditions. These representations characterize facial features more effectively and obtain discriminative feature vectors for face recognition.

Acknowledgements

The research work is supported by Science and Engineering Research Board (SERB), Department of Science and Technology (DST), Government of India for the research grant. The sanctioned project title is "Design and development of an Automatic Kinship Verification system for Indian faces with possible integration of AADHAR Database." with reference no. ECR/2016/001659.

Conflict of interest

The authors have no conflict of interest.

Author details

Toshanlal Meenpal*, Aarti Goyal and Moumita Mukherjee
Electronics and Telecommunication Department, National Institute of Technology, Raipur, Chhattisgarh, India

*Address all correspondence to: tmeenpal.etc@nitrr.ac.in

References

[1] Viola P, Jones MJ. Robust real-time face detection. International Journal of Computer Vision. 2004;**57**(2):137-154

[2] Ren S, He K, Girshick R, Sun J. Faster r-cnn: Towards real-time object detection with region proposal networks. In: Advances in Neural Information Processing Systems. 2015. pp. 91-99

[3] King DE. Dlib-ml: A machine learning toolkit. Journal of Machine Learning Research. 2009;**10**(Jul): 1755-1758

[4] Dharavath K, Talukdar FA, Laskar RH. Improving face recognition rate with image preprocessing. Indian Journal of Science and Technology. 2014;**7**(8):1170-1175

[5] Gross R, Brajovic V. An image preprocessing algorithm for illumination invariant face recognition. In: International Conference on Audio- and Video-Based Biometric Person Authentication. Berlin, Heidelberg: Springer; 2003. pp. 10-18

[6] Chandrashekar G, Sahin F. A survey on feature selection methods. Computers and Electrical Engineering. 2014;**40**(1, 1):16-28

[7] Available from: http://www.cl.cam.ac.uk/research/dtg/attarchive/facedatabase.html

[8] Gao W, Cao B, Shan S, Chen X, Zhou D, Zhang X, et al. The CAS-PEAL large-scale Chinese face database and baseline evaluations. IEEE Transactions on Systems, Man, and Cybernetics-Part A: Systems and Humans. 2008;**38**(1): 149-161

[9] Sim T, Baker S, Bsat M. The CMU pose, illumination, and expression (PIE) database. In: Proceedings of Fifth IEEE International Conference on Automatic Face Gesture Recognition. IEEE; 2002. pp. 53-58

[10] Phillips PJ, Moon H, Rauss P, Rizvi SA. The FERET evaluation methodology for face-recognition algorithms. In: Proceedings of IEEE Computer Society Conference on Computer Vision and Pattern Recognition. IEEE; 1997. pp. 137-143

[11] Hwang BW, Roh MC, Lee SW. Performance evaluation of face recognition algorithms on Asian face database. In: Sixth IEEE International Conference on Automatic Face and Gesture Recognition, 2004. Proceedings. IEEE; 2004. pp. 278-283

[12] Available from: http://vision.ucsd.edu/datasets/yale_face_dataset_original/yalefaces.zip

[13] Dalal N, Triggs B. Histograms of oriented gradients for human detection. In: International Conference on computer vision & Pattern Recognition (CVPR'05). Vol. 1. IEEE Computer Society; 2005. pp. 886-893

[14] Shu C, Ding X, Fang C. Histogram of the oriented gradient for face recognition. Tsinghua Science and Technology. 2011;**16**(2):216-224

[15] Dadi HS, Pillutla GK. Improved face recognition rate using HOG features and SVM classifier. IOSR Journal of Electronics and Communication Engineering. 2016;**11**(04):34-44

[16] Lowe DG. Distinctive image features from scale-invariant keypoints. International Journal of Computer Vision. 2004;**60**(2):91-110

[17] Bicego M, Lagorio A, Grosso E, Tistarelli M. On the use of SIFT features for face authentication. In: 2006 Conference on Computer Vision and

Pattern Recognition Workshop (CVPRW'06). IEEE; 2006. pp. 35-35

[18] Ojansivu V, Heikkilä J. Blur insensitive texture classification using local phase quantization. In: International Conference on Image and Signal Processing. Berlin, Heidelberg: Springer; 2008. pp. 236-243

[19] Rahtu E, Heikkilä J, Ojansivu V, Ahonen T. Local phase quantization for blur-insensitive image analysis. Image and Vision Computing. 2012;**30**(8): 501-512

[20] Ahonen T, Rahtu E, Ojansivu V, Heikkila J. Recognition of blurred faces using local phase quantization. In: 2008 19th International Conference on Pattern Recognition. IEEE; 2008. pp. 1-4

[21] Nguyen HT. Contributions to facial feature extraction for face recognition [Doctoral dissertation]. Université de Grenoble, Sep 2014

[22] Ojala T, Pietikäinen M, Harwood D. A comparative study of texture measures with classification based on featured distributions. Pattern Recognition. 1996;**29**(1, 1):51-59

[23] Ahonen T, Hadid A, Pietikainen M. Face description with local binary patterns: Application to face recognition. IEEE Transactions on Pattern Analysis and Machine Intelligence. 2006;**1**(12):2037-2041

[24] Tan X, Triggs W. Enhanced local texture feature sets for face recognition under difficult lighting conditions. IEEE Transactions on Image Processing. 2010;**19**(6):1635-1650

[25] Ahmed F, Hossain E, Bari AS, Hossen MS. Compound local binary pattern (clbp) for rotation invariant texture classification. International Journal of Computers and Applications. 2011;**33**(6):5-10

[26] Wolf L, Hassner T, Taigman Y. Effective unconstrained face recognition by combining multiple descriptors and learned background statistics. IEEE Transactions on Pattern Analysis and Machine Intelligence. 2011;**33**(10):1978-1990

[27] Guo Z, Zhang L, Zhang D. A completed modeling of local binary pattern operator for texture classification. IEEE Transactions on Image Processing. 2010;**19**(6): 1657-1663

[28] Déniz O, Bueno G, Salido J, De la Torre F. Face recognition using histograms of oriented gradients. Pattern Recognition Letters. 2011; **32**(12):1598-1603

[29] Albiol A, Monzo D, Martin A, Sastre J, Albiol A. Face recognition using HOG–EBGM. Pattern Recognition Letters. 2008;**29**(10):1537-1543

[30] Križaj J, Štruc V, Pavešić N. Adaptation of SIFT features for robust face recognition. In: International Conference Image Analysis and Recognition. Berlin, Heidelberg: Springer; 2010. pp. 394-404

[31] Sadeghipour E, Sahragard N. Face recognition based on improved SIFT algorithm. International Journal of Advanced Computer Science and Applications. 2016;7(1):547-551

[32] Damane Local Phase-Context for Face Recognition under Varying Conditions. Procedia Computer Science. 2014;**39**:12-19

[33] Chan CH, Kittler J, Poh N, Ahonen T, Pietikäinen M. (Multiscale) local phase quantisation histogram discriminant analysis with score normalisation for robust face recognition. In: 2009 IEEE 12th International Conference on Computer Vision Workshops, ICCV Workshops. IEEE; 2009. pp. 633-640

[34] Huang D, Shan C, Ardebilian M, Chen L. Facial image analysis based on local binary patterns: A survey. IEEE Transactions on Image Processing. 2011; **41**:1-14

[35] Shan C, Gong S, McOwan PW. Facial expression recognition based on local binary patterns: A comprehensive study. Image and Vision Computing. 2009;**27**(6):803-816

[36] Zhang G, Huang X, Li SZ, Wang Y, Wu X. Boosting local binary pattern (LBP)-based face recognition. In: Advances in Biometric Person Authentication. Berlin, Heidelberg: Springer; 2004. pp. 179-186

[37] Dadiz BG, Ruiz CR. Detecting depression in videos using uniformed local binary pattern on facial features. In: Computational Science and Technology. Singapore: Springer; 2019. pp. 413-422

[38] Liu L, Fieguth P, Zhao G, Pietikäinen M, Hu D. Extended local binary patterns for face recognition. Information Sciences. 2016;**358**:56-72

Chapter 7

Extended Binary Gradient Pattern (eBGP): A Micro- and Macrostructure-Based Binary Gradient Pattern for Face Recognition in Video Surveillance Area

Nuzrul Fahmi Nordin, Samsul Setumin, Abduljalil Radman and Shahrel Azmin Suandi

Abstract

An excellent face recognition for a surveillance camera system requires remarkable and robust face descriptor. Binary gradient pattern (BGP) descriptor is one of the ideal descriptors for facial feature extraction. However, exploiting local features merely from smaller region or microstructure does not capture a complete facial feature. In this paper, an extended binary gradient pattern (eBGP) is proposed to capture both micro- and macrostructure information of a local region to boost up the descriptor performance and discriminative power. Two topologies, the patch-based and circular-based topologies, are incorporated with the eBGP to test its robustness against illumination, image quality, and uncontrolled capture conditions using the SCface database. Experimental results show that the fusion between micro- and macrostructure information significantly boosts up the descriptor performance. It also illustrates that the proposed eBGP descriptor outperforms the conventional BGP on both the patch-based topology and the circular-based topology. Furthermore, a fusion of information from two different image types, orientational image gradient magnitude (OIGM) and grayscale image, attained better performance than using OIGM image only. The overall results indicate that the proposed eBGP descriptor improves the recognition performance with respect to the baseline BGP descriptor.

Keywords: surveillance system, face recognition, binary gradient pattern (BGP), facial feature extraction, patch-based topology, circular-based topology

1. Introduction

Face recognition is one of the biometric verification methods that offers a wide range of applications such as law enforcement, forensics, biometric authentication, surveillance, and health monitoring [1]. Face recognition has also been used to authenticate payment using mobile wallet, and the social media company like Facebook uses face recognition algorithm for the purpose of image tagging [2]. One of the advantages of face recognition is being contactless between the subject and camera. Given the advantages offered by face recognition and with the advancement in computing power, significant research and methods have been proposed over the years in face recognition domain. In fact, a robust facial recognition system must be able to work with various real-life situations or unconstrained conditions, such as but not limited to pose, lighting, image or camera quality, occlusion, rotation, and translation. The system must also be able to perform extremely well in a domain where limited sample is available. In surveillance monitoring applications, a typical approach is to sample face appearing in videos and then match them with facial models generated from high-quality target face image [3, 4].

Feature extraction is the process of capturing feature of interest from the face and represents it in the form of feature vector. The extraction process is usually done by a face descriptor. This descriptor must be able to work with multiple variations such as illumination, occlusion, face expression, and image quality [4]. Indeed, there is a collection of face descriptors proposed over the years such as scale-invariant feature transform (SIFT) [5], speeded up robust feature (SURF) [6], local binary pattern (LBP) [7], and histogram of oriented gradient (HOG) [8]. In terms of facial feature representation, there are two types of representations that many descriptors have evolved around over the years. They are global and local feature representations. Global-based feature extraction like principal component analysis [9], linear discriminant analysis [10], and independent component analysis [11] preserves the statistical information of the face by turning each face image into a high-dimensional feature vector. Meanwhile, local-based feature splits input image into smaller patches and extracts the micro textural details from each patch before fusing these features back to form the global shape information. Local-based feature extraction has shown to be resilient to multiple variations by enforcing spatial locality in both pixel and patch levels. For instance, local feature descriptor is robust to local deformation in expression and occlusion. LBP [7] is an example of feature extraction method that works on this principle which achieved reasonably good performance but heuristic in nature. Recently, LBP has drawn great intention as a face descriptor due its reputation as a powerful texture descriptor [9]. LBP extracts local-based spatial structure of an image by thresholding intensity of center pixel with its neighborhood. The product of this operation is characterized as local binary pattern, which then the distribution of binary pattern over the whole image is used to form the LBP histogram vector or feature vector. Neighborhood pixels are sampled on a circle, and any neighbor which does not fall exactly on the center of the pixel has an intensity computed from interpolation [7]. Due to some shortcomings of LBP, for instance, LBP produces long histogram, and therefore it is memory-consuming [12], LBP is very sensitive for image rotation and noise [13], and it only captures microstructure and ignores macrostructure of the texture resulting in missing extra discriminative power [14]. Several variants of LBP have been proposed in the literature, for example, rotation-invariant LBP [13], median robust extended local binary pattern (MRELBP) [15], and binary gradient pattern (BGP) [14]. This paper touches on a number of relevant existing LBP-based descriptors. The rest of this paper is organized as follows. In Section 2, two state-of-the-art descriptors (the LBP [7] and its variant, the BGP [14]) would be briefly reviewed since we would embed the proposed extended BGP (eBGP) into these two descriptors. Section 3 describes the proposed eBGP descriptor. The evaluating results are analyzed and discussed in Section 4. Finally, conclusions are drawn in Section 5.

2. From local binary pattern (LBP) to binary gradient pattern (BGP)

LBP [7] is one of various texture descriptors and is known for being computationally efficient [16]. It extracts local-based spatial structure of an image by thresholding intensity of center pixel with its neighborhood pixel P within a radius R. The product of this operation is characterized as local binary pattern, which then the distribution of binary pattern over the whole image is used to form the LBP histogram vector or feature vector. The original LBP works on 3 × 3 square neighborhood and only considers the sign information to form the LBP pattern. Neighborhood pixels are sampled on a circle, and any neighbor which does not fall exactly on the center of the pixel has an intensity computed from interpolation [7]. **Figure 1(a)** illustrates LBP neighborhoods around the center pixel with $R = 1$. Assuming all the pixels hold values as in **Figure 1(b)**, thresholding all eight neighborhood pixels with the center pixel using Eq. (1) will produce the result as in **Figure 1(c)**. This binary string is then multiplied with weights, and the sum of these values corresponds to the LBP label for that particular pixel. The distribution of LBP labels across the entire image is represented in a histogram as a feature vector:

$$LBP_{R,P}(c) = \sum_{i=0}^{P-1} s(g_i - g_c)\, 2^i, s(x) = \begin{cases} 1, x \geq 0 \\ 0, x < 0 \end{cases} \qquad (1)$$

where g_i and g_c are the gray values of the center pixel and its neighbors, respectively, P is the number of neighbors, and R is the radius of the neighborhood. LBP offers few advantages in terms of low computational complexity, illumination invariant, and ease of implementation, but it has significant disadvantages. In LBP implementation, the individual operator of particular (P,R) produces different histogram length. For instance, in (8,1) neighborhood, LBP generates $2^P = 256$ $(P = 8)$ histogram bins, while for (16,2) neighborhood, 2^{16} histogram bins are produced. This is a significant drawback as LBP produces long histogram and therefore memory-consuming. The LBP is also intolerant to image rotation and highly sensitive to noise where noise on the center pixel will dominate local characteristic [12]. Furthermore, the LBP only captures microstructure and ignores macrostructure of the texture resulting in missing extra discriminative power.

The success of LBP has continued since then. A variety of LBP-based descriptors have been proposed recently to overcome all shortcomings toward noise, illumination, color, and temporal information. Huang and Yin [14] proposed an improved version of LBP, called binary gradient pattern (BGP), by introducing structural pattern and image gradient orientation (IGO) implementation in multiple directions rather than on X and Y directions only, as in the conventional manner. The implementation of IGO in multiple directions helps to improve discriminative power of the proposed descriptor. **Figure 2** shows how BGP encodes binary string

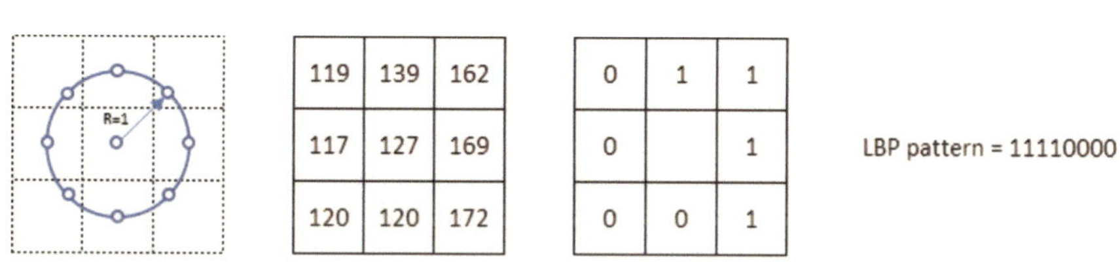

Figure 1.
LBP neighborhood and thresholding.

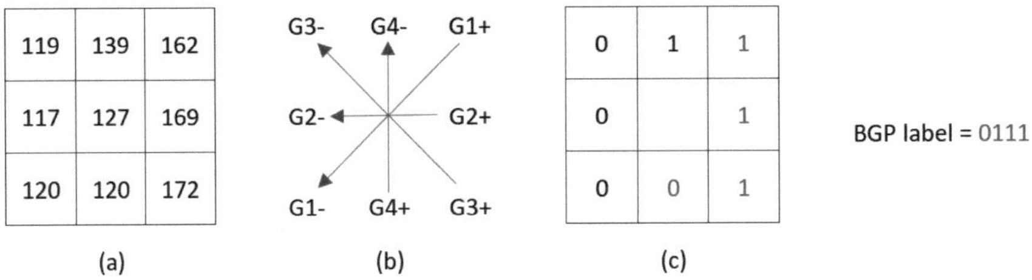

Figure 2.
Basic BGP operator with eight neighbors.

from a region of interest (ROI). Given a set of grayscale intensity value of 9 pixels as in **Figure 2(a)**, BGP computes binary correlations between symmetric neighbors of central pixel from multiple *k* directions. With the number of neighbors always twice than the number of directions *k*, in (8,1) spatial resolution, there are four different thresholding directions denoted as G1, G2, G3, and G4 as shown in **Figure 2(b)**. Principal binary, B_i^+, is computed from all directions using Eq. (2), and its associated binary B_i^- from Eq. (3), where G_i^+ and G_i^- are intensity values of the pixels. The resulting principal binary numbers and its associated are shown in **Figure 2(c)**:

$$B_i^+ = \begin{cases} 1, if\, G_i^+ - G_i^- \geq 0 \\ 0, if\, G_i^+ - G_i^- < 0 \end{cases} \tag{2}$$

$$B_i^- = 1 - B_i^+, i = 1, 2, \ldots, k \tag{3}$$

$$L = \sum_{i=1}^{k} 2^{i-1} B_i^+ \tag{4}$$

Binary string for the ROI is constructed from four principal binary numbers which is equivalent to 0111, and the label L is computed from Eq. (4). Because the principal and associated binary numbers are always complementary, only a single bit is required to describe the direction, this allowing for more compact representation of BGP label by only considering principal binary numbers. The total number of BGP label N_L is determined by the numbers of principal binary only, which is also equivalent to the number of directions *k*. At any spatial resolution, N_L equals to $2k$. Using **Figure 2(b)** as an example, features extracted from four directions in (8,1), spatial resolution will produce 24 or 16 different labels (i.e., from 0000 to 111/from 0 to 15). Structural pattern is a binary string which has continuous "1"s indicating a stable local change in texture and essentially describes the orientation of local edge texture. On the other hand, a nonstructural pattern is a binary string with a discontinuous "1"s, which contains arbitrary changes of local texture which is likely to indicate noise or outliers. From statistical experiment conducted by Huang and Yin [14] on 2600 face images, 95% of the patterns in typical BGP face having continuous "1"s.

The number of structural labels N_{sp} at any spatial resolution equals to the number of neighbors *P*. With eight neighbors, there will be 16 different labels where eight of it made up a structural label and the remaining belong to nonstructural label. For example, 0000, 0001, 0011, 0111, 1000, 1100, 1110, and 1111 are structural patterns in $BGP_{8,1}$, and each structural pattern location map is illustrated in **Figure 3**. In BGP implementation, nonstructural patterns are discarded and not given a label in contrast to nonuniform pattern in LBP implementation. Location map of nonstructural patterns in **Figure 3** shows that nonstructural patterns contain less meaningful information and are often caused by noise and outliers.

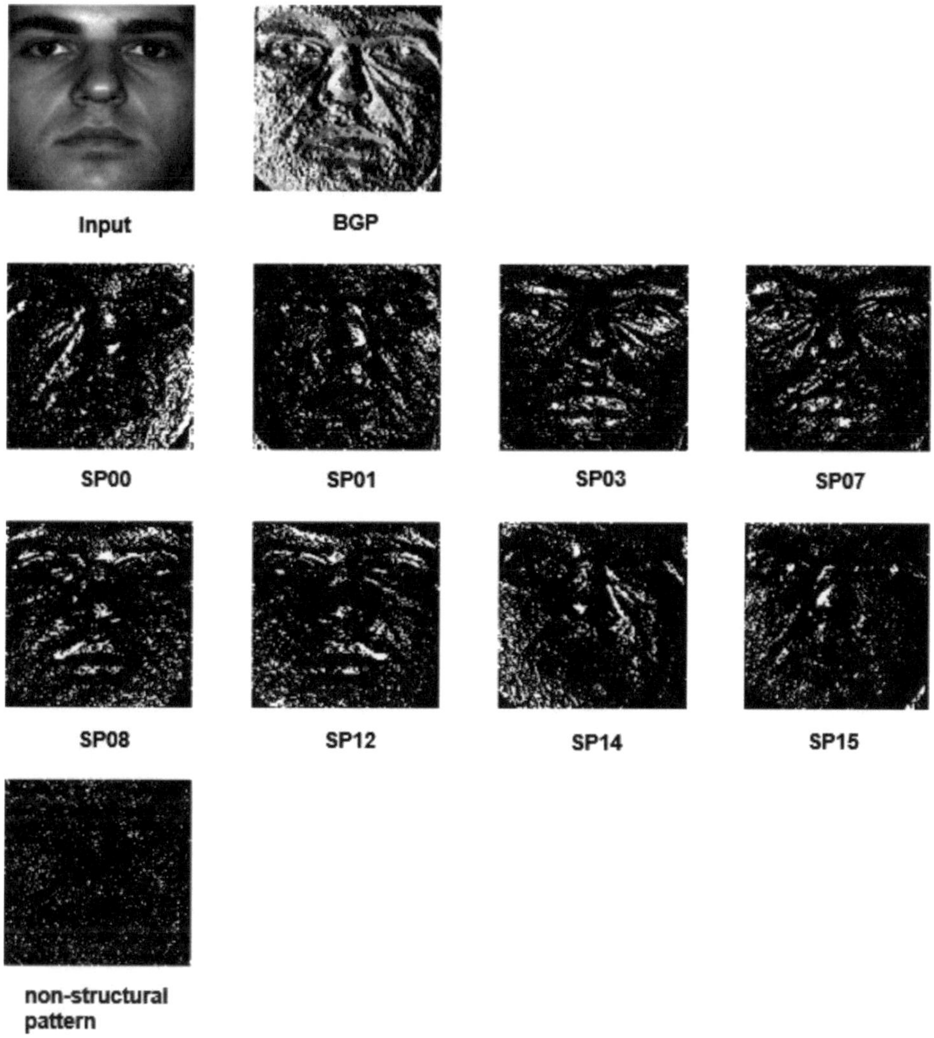

Figure 3.
Face and location maps of eight structural patterns (SP00-SP15) and nonstructural pattern.

To further enhance discriminative power and robustness of BGP, Huang and Yin [14] introduced another descriptor by applying BGP on orientational image gradient magnitude (OIGM) which is abbreviated as BGPM. The use of image gradient magnitude (IGM) enhances the strength of edge information which effectively allows BGPM to gain greater discriminant ability with only small increment in complexity. The overall process of BGPM descriptor is depicted in **Figure 4**.

Based on a series of results obtained from multiple databases such as Extended Yale B [17], AR [18], CMU Multi-PIE [19], FERET [20], and LFW [21] against a wide range of descriptors, BGPM is proven to be the best descriptor for each database. The BGPM descriptor has achieved invariance against illumination changes and local distortions while reducing the vector dimensionality. BGP compact representation makes BGP extremely fast and uses much fewer pattern labels than LBP at any spatial resolution. For instance, in a system with spatial resolution of (8,1), BGP histogram only needs 9 bins, with 8 bins for structural patterns, and 1 bin for nonstructural patterns, in contrast to the LBP which requires 59 bins. BGP and BGPM have been demonstrated to possess strong spatial locality and orientation properties which lead to effective discrimination.

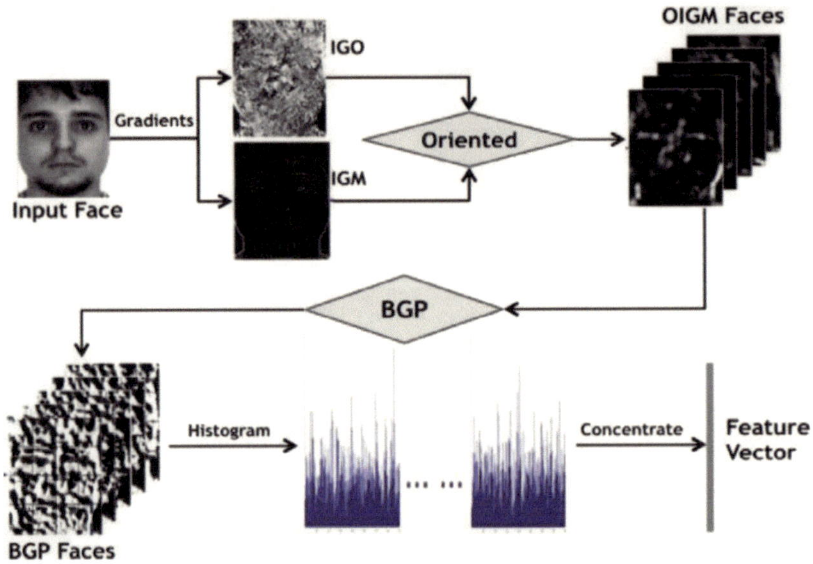

Figure 4.
Framework of BGPM descriptor [14].

Although BGP has shown to be efficient in processing time and achieving outstanding results in several databases, BGP was never being tested with a proper surveillance database like [22], which consists of low-resolution non-frontal face images taken by different camera quality. Like most of other local-based descriptors, BGP exploits information from microstructure only, however exploiting facial feature from macrostructure to complement the microstructure feature resulting in a more complete image representation [23–24], especially for surveillance applications where noise, occlusion, and head position might impact the descriptor performance. In this paper, information from both micro- and macrostructures are captured and integrated into the BGP descriptor to boost up its performance for video surveillance applications. The new proposed descriptor is termed as an extended BGP (eBGP).

3. Extended binary gradient pattern (eBGP)

An eBGP extends the BGP descriptor by exploiting macrostructure information from topology with larger spatial resolution. There are many different types of macrostructure topologies that have been proposed for other LBP variants [25]. In this paper, the patch-based topology with eight neighborhood patches and the circular topology are evolved with the proposed eBGP descriptor. Both topologies have been implemented by [24, 26], where each topology has its pros and cons with the implementation. Regardless of the topology, the microstructure information is always extracted using the same approach as in BGP. Herein, the eBGP is explained with the focus on extracting features from macrostructure based on the patch-based topology with eight neighborhood patches and the circular-based topology.

3.1 Patch-based topology

Patch-based topology is inspired by multi-scale block local binary pattern (MBLBP) [24]. In this topology, macrostructure is made up of nine patches of pixels as in **Figure 5**. All these patches have the same size and width, while the center patch represents the ROI microstructure. Thereby, a default BGP operator is applied

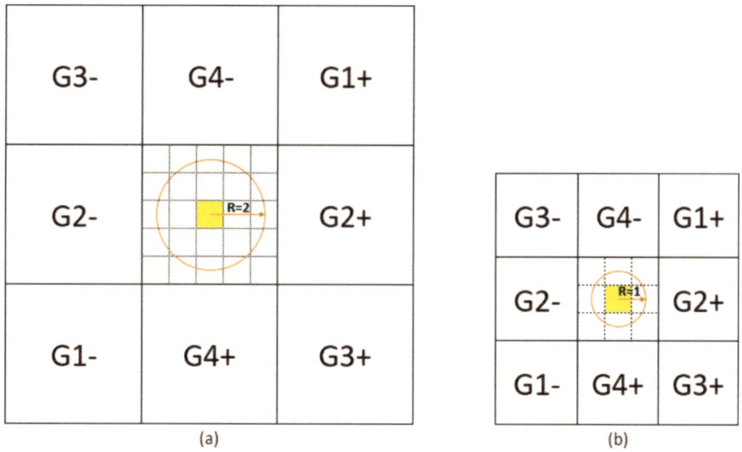

Figure 5.
Topology for macrostructure information extraction. (a) Patch of 5 × 5 pixels for R = 2. *(b) Patch of 3 × 3 pixels for* R = 1.

to the center patch in order to extract the microstructure information, whereas the macrostructure information is extracted from the eight neighborhood patches. Accordingly, multiple sizes of patches could be selected from this topology, and the size of the structure is determined by the spatial resolution of the center patch.

For instance, when exploiting microstructure information from (8,1) spatial resolution, the size of the center patch will be 3 × 3 pixels as illustrated in **Figure 5(b)**. In this implementation, all patches have the same size and do not overlap each other; therefore the macrostructure is formed from nine patches of 3 × 3 pixels. **Figure 5(a)** depicts the macrostructure topology formed from 9 patches of 5 × 5 pixels when microstructure information is exploited from (16,2) spatial resolution. For comparison purposes, this research will evaluate two structures as illustrated in **Figure 5(a)** and **(b)**, to match BGP results exploited from (8,1) and (16,2) spatial resolution. Using **Figure 5(a)** as an example, each neighborhood patch contains 25 pixels with each pixel having its own grayscale value. Unlike the center patch, no feature is extracted from the individual neighborhood patch. Instead, each neighborhood patch is represented by a single intensity value which will be used for thresholding. In this topology, the patch's mean and median will be applied to represent the patch intensity. The patch's mean (G) of a neighborhood patch (P), accounted from 25 pixels in a single 5 × 5 patch, is computed as follows:

$$G_P = \frac{1}{n}\sum_{i=1}^{n} x_i \tag{5}$$

where x is the intensity value of each pixel and n is the number of pixels in the patch P.

On the other hand, the patch median is computed by finding the middle value of ordered pixel values. Additional experiments are conducted in this research to find the best representation for the patch-based topology. As an example, feature extraction from macrostructure is illustrated in **Figure 6**. **Figure 6(a)** shows the patch-based topology with the size of 3 × 3 pixels and its intensity value. In each patch, a median is calculated from all pixels within the patch, and the median now represents the image intensity of the patch as shown in **Figure 6(b)**. The following steps are similar to what has been explained in BGP. By thresholding each patch with symmetric neighbors in four directions using Eqs. (2) and (3), four pairs of binary numbers are generated as shown in **Figure 6(c)**. Once all the principal bits are computed, the

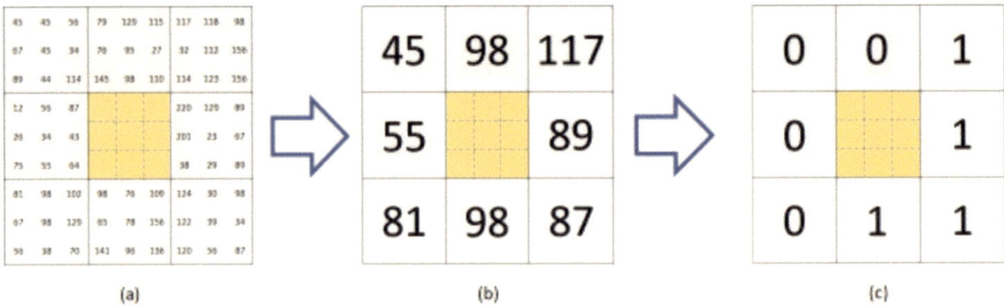

Figure 6.
Feature extraction from the macrostructure using median as the patch intensity.

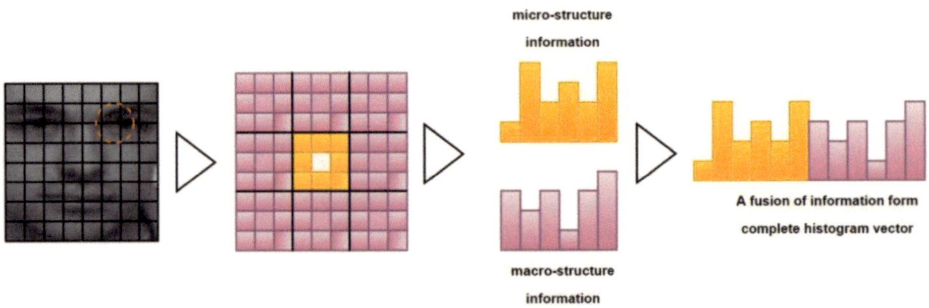

Figure 7.
Patch-based feature extraction flow. The center patch represented by the orange box and the neighborhood patches by the purple boxes.

label can be calculated using Eq. (4). In general, the flow for macrostructure extraction is like microstructure except for its representative value used during thresholding. Indeed, the microstructure information is extracted from neighborhood pixels, while the macrostructure information is extracted from neighborhood patches.

Since there are only eight neighbor patches, regardless of the structures' size, the generated histogram vector which represents the macrostructure information is bound to the maximum of 16 bins. Observing only a structural pattern will greatly reduce the dimensionality of macrostructure information to eight bins. The total length of the histogram vector (H_t) is computed as follows:

$$H_t = \sum_{k=1}^{N} (P_R + 8)_k \tag{6}$$

where N is the number of blocks and P_R is the number of neighborhood pixels used for extracting the microstructure information at the center patch and 8 is the length of the histogram vector extracted from the macrostructure. Using **Figure 6(b)** as an example, at each k_{th} block, the length of histogram vector is 16, where 8 comes from the microstructure and the other 8 from the macrostructure.

Subsequently, information fusion between micro- and macrostructures is conducted through concatenating the feature vectors of both the microstructure and the macrostructure, as illustrated in **Figure 7**. At this point, both feature vectors are contributed by the same weight. **Figure 8** demonstrates an example of face image represented using the patch-based topology. **Figure 8** illustrates that eBGP on the patch-based topology capable to capture the micro textural details and the macrostructure provides complementary information to the small details. Moreover, the macrostructure information contains less detailed information and may reduce the noise or outlier embedded in the image.

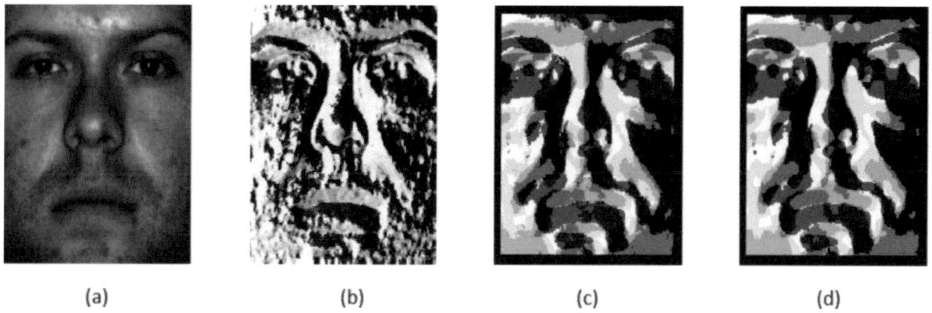

Figure 8.
Sample image with 5 × 5 pixel patch-based structure: (a) the original image, (b) the image extracted using the microstructure, (c) the image extracted using the macrostructure based on the local median, and (d) the image extracted from the macrostructure using the local mean.

3.2 Circular-based topology

Circular-based topology borrows the basic implementation of LBP which identifies a neighborhood as a set of pixels on a circular ring. In this topology, two levels of information are extracted from neighborhood at two different spatial resolutions. The first level of information is the microstructure information, which is extracted from a set of pixels on a circular ring with radius R_1. Meanwhile, the macrostructure information is extracted from neighborhood pixels that lie on a circular ring of radius R_2. The same BGP operator is used to extract information from the two different spatial resolutions with smaller spatial resolution that represents the microstructure and larger spatial resolution that represents the macrostructure. The visual illustration of circular-based topology implementation is presented in **Figure 9**. Circular rings with R_1 and R_2 represent the two different spatial resolutions $(P;R)$. Assuming R_1 is 1, running BGP descriptor on (8,1) neighborhood extracts the microstructure information of ROI. In this implementation, R_2 is always larger than R_1, and thus R_2 must be set to any number >1.

Figure 10(a) shows a sample of image intensity that falls on circular rings R_1 and R_2 with spatial resolution (8,1) and (24,3), respectively. In this example, the microstructure information is extracted from 8 pixels, while the macrostructure information is extracted from 24 pixels as shown in **Figure 10(b)**. Using the same method in BGP, principal and associated bits are calculated using Eqs. (2) and (3) by thresholding symmetric neighbors in multiple directions. The computed binary pairs are shown in **Figure 10(c)** with 4 and 12 principal bits generated from 8 and 24 neighbors, respectively. Finally, label for both micro- and macrostructures is computed using Eq. (4).

In BGP scheme, the length of histogram vector is equal to the number of neighbors at any spatial resolution. Similar to the patch-based topology, the generated histogram vector which embeds micro- and macrostructure information is concatenated to form a final representation of features for each ROI. The total length of histogram vector in this scheme can be computed using:

$$H_t = \sum_{k=1}^{N} (P_1 + P_2)_k \tag{7}$$

where N is the number of blocks and P_1 and P_2 are the number of neighborhood pixels on the circular rings of radius R_1 and R_2, respectively. For instance, if $R_1 = 2$ and $R_2 = 4$, features are exploited from 16 and 32 neighborhood pixels, respectively. Thus, the combination of the two spatial resolutions will produce a histogram vector with a length of 48 at each k_{th} block. Resulting from this observation, R_2 is set to

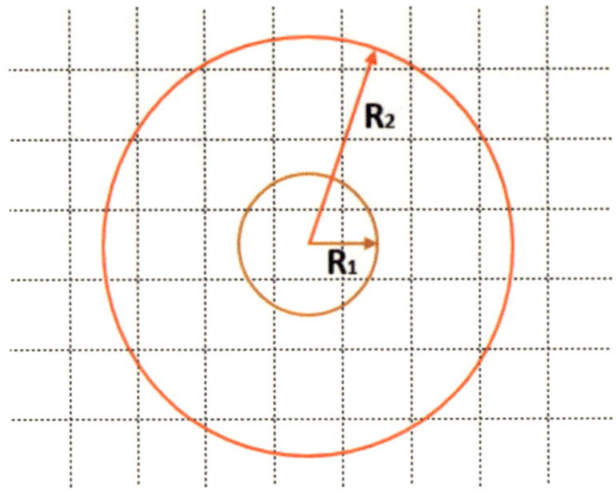

Figure 9.
Circular-based topology.

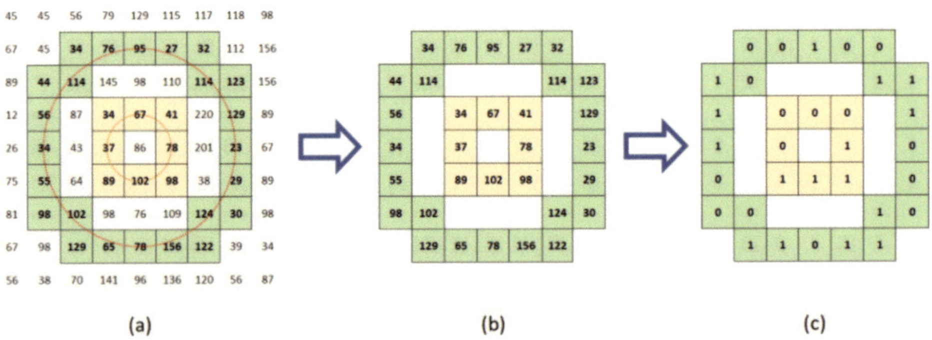

Figure 10.
The microstructure information is devised from 8 pixels on the smaller ring, while the macrostructure information is devised from 24 pixels on the larger ring without any interpolation.

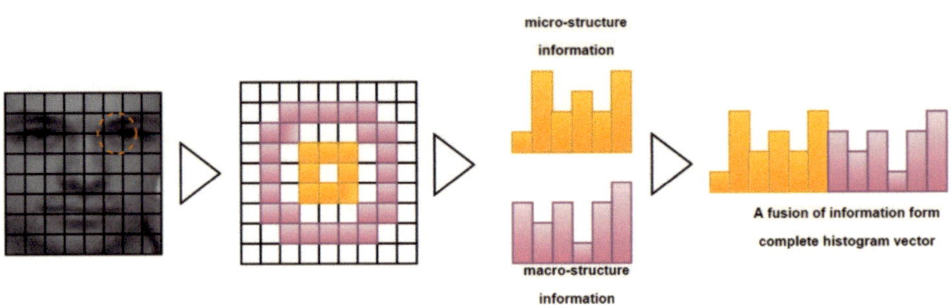

Figure 11.
Circular-based feature extraction flow with $R_1 = 1$ *and* $R_2 = 3$.

5 to limit the feature dimensionality of macrostructure to 40 because having larger spatial resolution will only increase the feature vector dimensionality. In contrast, R_1 is limited to 4 because larger spatial resolution will prevent BGP operator from capturing micro edge and micro texture features which are mostly exploited from a smaller region.

Figure 11 illustrates the general flow of feature extraction in the circular-based topology. Overall, this topology employs BGP operator on two different spatial resolutions, where the smaller resolution is for the microstructure information and the larger resolution is for the macrostructure information. In this research, no interpolation has been done to neighboring pixels where the circle does not fall

Figure 12.
Sample image with $R_1 = 2$ *and* $R_2 = 5$ *circular-based topology: (a) the original image, (b) the image extracted from the microstructure* ($R_1 = 2$)*, and (c) the image extracted from the macrostructure* ($R_2 = 5$)*.*

exactly on the center of pixels. **Figure 12** presents a sample image that is extracted from the two spatial resolutions $R_1 = 2$ and $R_2 = 5$.

Similar to the patch-based topology, BGP captures the micro-oriented edges from the small structure while capturing less details of information at a much larger spatial resolution. But the combination of these two information will complement each other in providing a complete face representation.

4. Results, discussion, and analysis

To illustrate a real-world video surveillance system, the effectiveness of the proposed eBGP descriptor was evaluated using the Surveillance Camera Face (SCface) database [22]. The SCface database consists of low-resolution non-frontal face images taken by different camera quality. A series of experiments were planned to test all proposed topologies and structures on the SCface database. The performance of the proposed eBGP descriptor was evaluated against illumination, image quality, single sample per person, and real-world capture condition.

In fact, the SCface database is the most challenging database for face recognition, where its images were taken in uncontrolled indoor environment. The SCface database consists of 4160 images from 130 subjects. All images were taken at three distinct distances from the camera, where the cameras are installed at 2.25 m above the floor. Images were captured at distance 1 while the subject position is 4.20 m away from the camera, whereas for distances 2 and 3, the subject positions were at 2.60 and 1.00 m, respectively. The outdoor light was only the source of illumination, which came through a window on one side. The images were captured from five different quality commercial surveillance video cameras and two infrared night-vision cameras, in uncontrolled lighting so as to mimic the real-world conditions. Furthermore, full frontal mug shot image for each subject was captured using a high-quality photo camera with the capture conditions exactly the same as would be expected for any law enforcement. The high-quality photo camera for capturing visible light mug shots was installed the same way as the infrared camera but in a separate room with the standard indoor lighting, and it was equipped with adequate flash. In our experiments, the high-quality mug shot image of each person was used as a training gallery, while the remaining images from the five surveillance cameras and distances were used as test images, as depicted in **Figure 13**. With the focus of this research toward images in visible spectrum and single sample per person, especially for real-world surveillance system, the images taken from IR night-vision cameras and mug shot rotation were not used in this research. As preprocessing

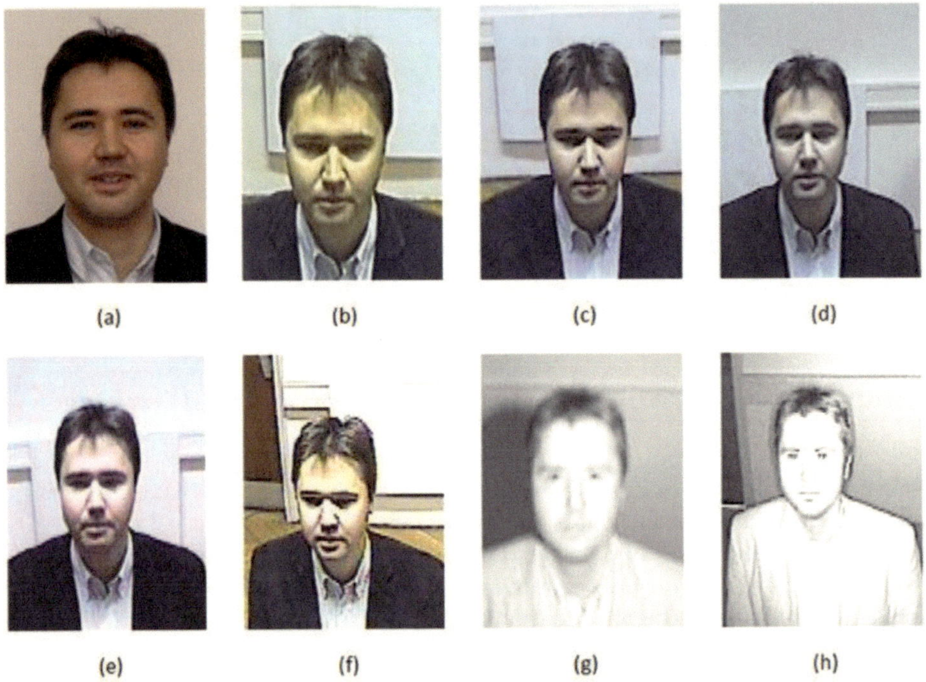

Figure 13.
Sample images from the SCface database of distance 3: (a) the high-quality mug shot. (b–f) The images taken from five different surveillance cameras. (g and h) The images were taken from IR night-vision cameras.

steps, all images in the SCface database were aligned based on the provided eye coordinates, so that the eyes' line lies on a straight line. The images were then scaled and cropped to 64x64 pixel as has been implemented in [22].

The performance of the proposed eBGP descriptor was evaluated using the histogram intersection, where the histogram intersection computes the similarity between two discretized probability distributions or histogram vectors. Given H^T is the histogram vector of a training image reference and H^P is the histogram vector of a probe image, each one containing n bins, the intersection between them is defined as follows:

$$H^T \cap H^P = \sum_{j=1}^{n} \min\left(H_j^T, H_j^P\right) \tag{8}$$

where H^T and H^P are generated from distribution of labels computed from eBGP operator and the *min* function takes as arguments two values and return the smallest one. Any histogram pair that returns the highest intersection value based on Eq. (8) than any other pairs is considered to be matched and assigned to the label. By comparing this label against ground truth label, the recognition rate is determined by counting the occurrence of the correct label over the number of test images. Recognition rate is computed as follows:

$$Recognition\ rate\ (\%) = \frac{N_L}{N} \times 100\% \tag{9}$$

where N_L is the total number of test images which are correctly matched and N is the total number of test images.

It is vital to stress that the classifier plays a decisive role in achieving better recognition rate. In this research, the experiments were dictated in such a way to focus on recognition rate improvement due to macrostructure information fusion. Hence, the recognition rate of the proposed eBGP descriptor and its baseline BGP descriptor were computed and compared to verify the recognition rate improvement. For comparative analysis, results of BGP descriptor on the SCface database are produced by running the BGP code requested from [14]. This is to ensure analysis of the result can be done without any concern on the validity of the results. In fact, Huang and Yin [14] do not use the SCface database in their work; thus BGP code was altered to work with the SCface database.

4.1 Experiment settings and preprocessing

As a preprocessing step, each image is first transformed into OIGM images using the same method used by the BGP descriptor. OIGM images are then divided into N numbers of non-overlapped blocks before applying eBGP descriptor, where N is set to 16 in this research.

4.2 Results of patch-based topology

For better presentation, several notations are used to describe the experiment setup and implementation. BGPM$_{(P;R)}$ is the implementation used in the BGP descriptor of spatial resolution (P,R), while eBGPM$_{(P;R)}$ is the implementation of the proposed eBGP descriptor with macrostructure information based on the patch-based topology. In this experiment, the patch-based topology uses the patch's median as a default scheme for the thresholding between patches.

Table 1 shows the performance of the proposed descriptor on the SCface database, where eBGPM$_{(16;2)}$ and eBGPM$_{(8;1)}$ represent the extended BGPM (eBGPM) with structures of **Figure 5(a)** and **Figure 5(b)**, respectively. Results of BGPM$_{(16;2)}$ and BGPM$_{(8;1)}$ represent the baseline descriptor. As mentioned before in this section, the images of SCface database were captured by five cameras with three different distances. **Table 1** shows the recognition rate results for each set and the average recognition rate over all cameras. The recognition rate for each set was calculated based on Eqs. (8) and (9).

Distance	Descriptor	Camera					
		1	2	3	4	5	Average
1	BGPM$_{(8;1)}$	3.08	0.77	3.08	3.08	5.38	3.08
	BGPM$_{(16;1)}$	6.15	4.62	4.62	3.85	5.38	4.92
	eBGPM$_{(8;1)}$	4.62	1.54	4.62	3.85	6.15	4.16
	eBGPM$_{(16;1)}$	3.85	7.69	5.38	5.38	8.46	6.15
2	BGPM$_{(8;1)}$	16.15	12.31	6.92	11.54	13.85	12.15
	BGPM$_{(16;1)}$	23.85	13.85	7.69	12.31	13.08	14.16
	eBGPM$_{(8;1)}$	20.77	13.85	10.77	16.92	16.15	15.69
	eBGPM$_{(16;1)}$	23.08	17.69	13.85	16.92	16.15	17.54
3	BGPM$_{(8;1)}$	15.38	19.23	10.00	16.92	11.54	14.61
	BGPM$_{(16;1)}$	18.46	20.00	16.15	14.62	11.54	16.15
	eBGPM$_{(8;1)}$	19.23	17.69	11.54	17.69	13.08	15.85
	eBGPM$_{(16;1)}$	16.15	16.15	15.38	16.15	17.69	16.30

Table 1.
Recognition rate (%) of the proposed eBGP descriptor on the SCface dataset using the patch-based topology.

From **Table 1**, it can be seen that none of the descriptors achieved recognition rate higher than 35% over all cameras and distances. Particularly, the images of distance 1 recorded the lowest recognition rate with an average of 4.58%, while the images of distances 2 and 3 achieved better recognition rates with an average of 14.89 and 15.73%, respectively. **Table 1** also shows that $eBGPM_{(8;1)}$ slightly boosted up the performance comparable with $BGPM_{(8;1)}$ for all distances, where it attained the highest recognition rate over $BGPM_{(8;1)}$ on the distance 2 with an average recognition rate which equals to 3.54%. On the contrary, $eBGPM_{(16;2)}$ has a mix result with respect to its baseline $BGPM_{(16;2)}$; the performance drop can be observed from camera 1 gallery results, where distance 1, distance 2, and distance 3 show lower recognition rate comparable with the baseline descriptor. Similar to $eBGPM_{(8;1)}$, $eBGPM_{(16;2)}$ presented the highest recognition rate on distance 2 gallery images compared to those from distance 1 and distance 3. This is because the gallery images of distance 1, which have been acquired at 4.20 m distance, are low in resolution and small in size. Moreover, the process of scaling and cropping the images into 64 × 64 size leads to loss of the quality and some dominant features. On the other hand, the images of distance 3 are higher in quality and details. However, as the subjects are closer to the camera, which is installed at 2.25 m from the floor, in most natural head position, the upper half of the subject face is more dominant in the captured images as depicted by **Figure 14**. Figure 14 demonstrates that the images of distance 2 are slightly better in quality than the other two distances, but they still suffer from head position. This interprets the superiority of descriptors on this distance.

Due to these discouraging results by both the proposed eBGP descriptor and its baseline BGP, extra experiments were conducted on the SCface database. Since **Table 1** illustrated that the recognition rate is improved with increase of the spatial resolution, consequently the BGPM descriptor is first extended to larger spatial resolution of (24,3). Even though recognition rate increased by including the macrostructure in eBGP, the overall recognition rate is still too low for realistic applications. It might be because the structural pattern and OIGM image were

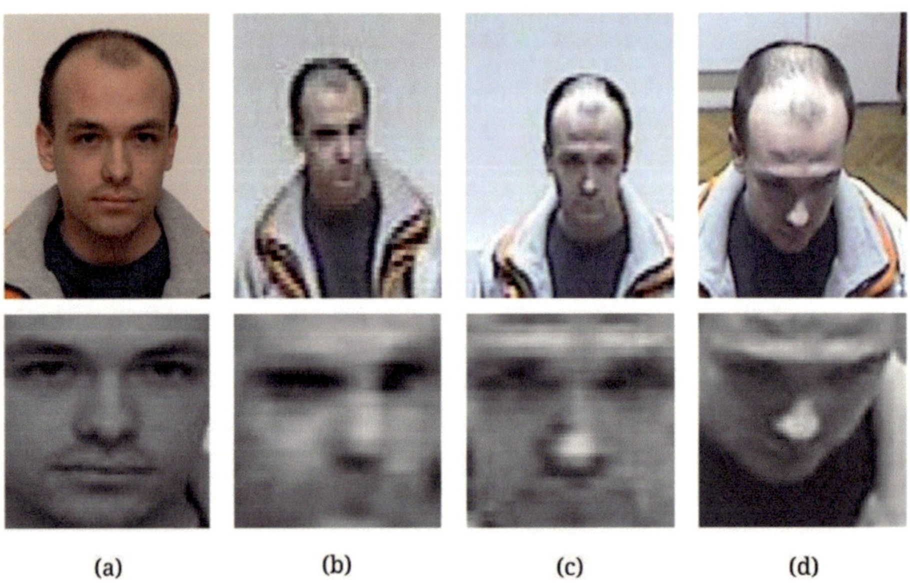

Figure 14.
Samples of the SCface database: (a) training image mug shot and (b–d) test images captured by camera 2 at distances 1, 2, and 3, respectively. The upper row shows the original images, while the lower row shows the images after alignment, scaling, and cropping to 64 × 64.

Distance	Descriptor	Camera					
		1	2	3	4	5	Average
1	$BGPM_{(24;3)}$	5.38	2.31	4.62	4.62	5.38	4.62
	Type I_P	3.85	6.92	4.62	6.92	3.85	6.00
	Type II_P	10.77	6.92	6.92	5.38	10.77	8.31
2	$BGPM_{(24;3)}$	21.54	16.15	13.08	16.15	15.38	16.46
	Type I_P	23.85	20.00	13.85	19.23	15.38	18.46
	Type II_P	34.62	25.38	20.00	25.38	21.54	25.38
3	$BGPM_{(24;3)}$	20.00	18.46	14.62	16.15	11.54	16.15
	Type I_P	16.92	16.92	14.62	16.92	16.15	16.31
	Type II_P	22.31	23.08	15.38	23.85	16.92	20.31

Table 2.
Recognition rate (%) of $BGPM_{(24;3)}$. Type I_P and Type II_P descriptors on the SCface database.

extracted from low-resolution and deformed images (after scaling and cropping have been done). Hence, two additional descriptors were then designed to investigate the effectiveness of structural patterns and OIGM image when exploiting the macrostructure information from low-resolution images. These descriptors still use BGPM in exploiting information from the microstructure, but they extract the macrostructure information in a different way.

The first additional descriptor, denoted as Type I_P in **Table 2**, is equivalent to the $eBGPM_{(16;2)}$ descriptor with one exception. The structural pattern concepts are ignored, and all labels which are produced by (16,2) spatial resolution are assumed to hold some unique features. In this setup, all information from 16 labels are used to populate the histogram vector. This descriptor is designed to investigate if there is any other feature that may be discarded by the structural patterns when dealing with low-quality images. The second descriptor, denoted as Type II_P in **Table 2**, is designed to extract information from both OIGM and grayscale intensity images. This descriptor extracts the microstructure information from the OIGM image and the macrostructure information from the grayscale image. Type II_P descriptor is similar to the other proposed descriptor, where the local microstructure information is extracted from the central patch of ROI using $BGPM_{(16;2)}$. However, instead of using BGP operator to assemble histogram vector from the macrostructure, a standard $LBP^{u2}_{8,1}$ operator is employed to extract the macrostructure information. The patch median of eight neighborhood patches is thresholded with the patch's median of the center patch, so as to produce a string of eight binaries or label. $LBP^{u2}_{8,1}$ descriptor generates over 256 labels, but only 58 uniform patterns are kept for histogram fusion and the remaining are discarded. Histograms from both domains are concatenated and given equal weights.

Results in **Table 2** expose that the Type II_P descriptor achieved better recognition rate than the rest of descriptors. The results also illustrate that Type II_P achieved better performance on images of distance 2 than those from distances 1 and 3. Furthermore, it is notable to mention that employing $BGPM_{(24;3)}$ at larger spatial resolution did not help much in improving the recognition rate as much as Type II_P has achieved.

4.3 Results of circular-based topology

As described in Section 3.2, the macrostructure information are exploited from the outer circle which always has larger spatial resolution ($P;R_2$) than

Circular eBGP		Camera						
$S^i_{(P,R)}$	$S^o_{(P,R)}$	Type	1	2	3	4	5	Average
(8,1)	(16,2)	I_c	5.38	3.85	3.85	3.08	4.62	4.12
		II_c	6.92	6.92	6.92	6.15	7.69	6.92
	(24,3)	I_c	5.38	4.62	4.62	3.08	5.38	4.62
		II_c	7.69	5.38	6.92	7.69	6.92	6.92
	(32,4)	I_c	5.38	6.15	5.38	6.15	6.15	5.84
		II_c	6.92	6.15	6.92	8.46	6.15	6.92
	(40,5)	I_c	5.38	7.69	4.62	6.15	6.15	6.00
		II_c	9.23	7.69	6.92	7.69	6.15	7.54
(16,2)	(24,3)	I_c	5.38	4.62	6.15	3.85	6.15	5.23
		II_c	6.92	6.92	5.38	6.15	7.69	6.61
	(32,4)	I_c	6.15	6.92	7.69	4.62	6.15	6.31
		II_c	10.00	6.92	3.85	7.69	7.69	7.23
	(40,5)	I_c	5.38	6.92	3.85	6.15	6.15	5.69
		II_c	8.46	7.69	6.15	8.46	6.92	7.54
(24,3)	(32,4)	I_c	5.38	3.85	6.92	3.85	6.15	5.23
		II_c	12.31	7.69	7.69	9.23	6.92	8.77
	(40,5)	I_c	6.15	6.15	5.38	2.31	6.92	5.38
		II_c	10.77	8.46	9.23	9.23	4.62	8.46
(32,4)	(40,5)	I_c	4.62	5.38	6.15	2.31	7.69	5.23
		II_c	9.23	7.69	10.00	10.77	5.38	8.61
Baseline	$BGPM_{(8;1)}$		3.08	0.77	3.08	3.08	5.38	3.08
	$BGPM_{(16;2)}$		6.15	4.62	4.62	3.85	5.38	4.92

Table 3.
Circular-based topology on the SCface dataset at distance 1.

$(P;R_1)$. In other words, more points are used for thresholding when extracting the macrostructure information. For the presentation purpose, $S^i_{(P,R)}$ and $S^o_{(P,R)}$ notations are used to represent the spatial resolution of inner circle and outer circle, respectively. In the circular-based topology, two types of descriptors are designed to evaluate the performance of this topology. Type I_c descriptor is similar to what has been discussed in Section 3.2. Learning from the results obtained based on the patch-based topology, Type II_c descriptor is designed to explore a fusion of texture extracted from grayscale image and OIGM image. This descriptor extracts the local microstructure information from the OIGM image and the macrostructure information from the grayscale image. The histograms generated from these two types of images are concatenated and given equal weights. In this topology, multiple combinations of spatial resolution of inner and outer circles are tested. By limiting R_2 to 5, there are 10 combinations of descriptors at different spatial resolutions. Overall, there are 20 different combinations of descriptors that were put to the test.

Performance of Type I_c and Type II_c descriptors on the SCface dataset at distance 1, distance 2, and distance 3 is presented in **Tables 3, 4**, and **5**, respectively. Similar to the results obtained by the patch-based topology, the average recognition rate of the images that belong to distance 1 from all cameras is the lowest compared to

Circular eBGP			**Camera**					
$S^{i}_{(P,R)}$	$S^{o}_{(P,R)}$	Type	1	2	3	4	5	Average
(8,1)	(16,2)	I_c	20.77	12.31	10.00	11.54	14.62	13.85
		II_c	25.38	19.23	15.38	17.69	14.62	18.46
	(24,3)	I_c	24.62	15.38	11.54	15.38	16.92	16.77
		II_c	25.38	21.54	16.15	19.23	14.62	19.38
	(32,4)	I_c	26.92	17.69	15.38	17.69	13.85	18.31
		II_c	23.85	19.23	16.92	18.46	15.38	18.77
	(40,5)	I_c	29.23	19.23	13.08	19.23	13.85	18.92
		II_c	23.08	19.23	15.38	17.69	16.92	18.46
(16,2)	(24,3)	I_c	26.15	16.15	11.54	13.08	15.38	16.46
		II_c	25.38	22.31	16.15	21.54	19.23	20.92
	(32,4)	I_c	25.38	18.46	13.85	13.85	13.85	17.08
		II_c	24.62	21.54	17.69	21.54	20.00	21.08
	(40,5)	I_c	25.38	20.00	13.08	20.77	15.38	18.92
		II_c	24.62	20.77	16.92	20.00	17.69	20.00
(24,3)	(32,4)	I_c	20.77	18.46	12.31	13.85	14.62	16.00
		II_c	28.46	24.62	16.92	20.77	20.77	22.31
	(40,5)	I_c	22.31	17.69	14.62	16.15	14.62	17.08
		II_c	28.46	23.85	15.38	16.15	16.92	20.15
(32,4)	(40,5)	I_c	22.31	16.92	13.85	17.69	13.85	16.92
		II_c	25.38	25.38	16.92	20.00	16.15	20.77
Baseline	$BGPM_{(8;1)}$		16.15	12.31	6.92	11.54	13.85	12.15
	$BGPM_{(16;2)}$		23.85	13.85	7.69	12.31	13.08	14.16

Table 4.
Circular-based topology on the SCface dataset at distance 2.

those from distance 2 and distance 3 as shown in **Table 3**. One noteworthy observation is that most of Type II_c descriptors at any spatial resolution achieved better recognition rate than Type I_c descriptors. Taking a closer look at the descriptor's performance in **Table 5**, Type II_c descriptor with spatial resolution of $s^{i}_{(16,2)}$ and $s^{o}_{(24,3)}$ recorded the best results for all cameras on the test gallery of distance 3. On the other hand, for distance 2 test gallery, Type II_c descriptor with spatial resolution of $s^{i}_{(24,3)}$ and $s^{o}_{(32,4)}$ achieved the best result against other combinations.

For further evaluation, **Table 6** demonstrates results of the proposed eBGP descriptor compared with state-of-the-art descriptors such as PCA [27], SIFT and sparse representation-based classification (SRC) [28], and edge-preserving super-resolution (SR) [29], on the SCface database at distance 2. All descriptors applied the same test conditions, where only one mug shot image per subject is used for training, while the remaining low-resolution images from all cameras are used as probe images. The results show that the proposed descriptors based on eBGP achieved the highest recognition rates compared to all other descriptors, especially $eBGPM_{(16;2)}$ (Type II_P) which has the best recognition rate over all camera images. Exploiting information from the macrostructure raised the BGPM results from the fifth highest to first. This indicates the importance of the macrostructure information in shaping a complete face representation in single-reference face recognition problem.

Circular eBGP			**Camera**					
$S^{i}_{(P,R)}$	$S^{o}_{(P,R)}$	Type	1	2	3	4	5	Average
(8,1)	(16,2)	I_c	20.77	21.54	13.85	15.38	13.85	17.08
		II_c	25.38	26.15	20.00	23.85	13.85	21.85
	(24,3)	I_c	23.08	20.77	13.08	20.00	11.54	17.69
		II_c	23.08	24.62	20.00	23.85	16.92	21.69
	(32,4)	I_c	20.00	21.54	14.62	17.69	11.54	17.08
		II_c	20.77	24.62	17.69	21.54	14.62	19.85
	(40,5)	I_c	19.23	17.69	15.38	18.46	10.77	16.31
		II_c	23.85	23.85	15.38	20.77	13.85	19.54
(16,2)	(24,3)	I_c	20.77	20.77	13.08	17.69	13.08	17.08
		II_c	26.15	25.38	20.77	24.62	19.23	23.23
	(32,4)	I_c	20.77	18.46	16.15	19.23	10.00	16.92
		II_c	24.62	22.31	16.15	22.31	16.92	20.46
	(40,5)	I_c	19.23	19.23	15.38	18.46	12.31	16.92
		II_c	26.15	21.54	16.15	22.31	11.54	19.54
(24,3)	(32,4)	I_c	17.69	16.15	13.85	17.69	9.23	14.92
		II_c	23.08	20.77	19.23	21.54	15.38	20.00
	(40,5)	I_c	20.00	16.15	13.85	19.23	10.77	16.00
		II_c	23.85	21.54	16.92	18.46	16.15	19.38
(32,4)	(40,5)	I_c	16.15	15.38	13.08	18.46	10.00	14.61
		II_c	20.77	20.77	16.92	21.54	10.77	18.15
Baseline	$BGPM_{(8;1)}$		15.38	19.23	10.00	16.92	11.54	14.61
	$BGPM_{(16;2)}$		18.46	20.00	16.15	14.62	11.54	16.15

Table 5.
Circular-based topology on the SCface dataset at distance 3.

Descriptor	**Camera**					
	1	**2**	**3**	**4**	**5**	**Average**
PCA [27]	7.70	7.70	3.90	3.90	7.70	6.18
SIFT [28]	13.08	12.31	8.46	15.38	9.23	11.69
$BGPM_{(16;2)}$	23.85	13.85	7.69	12.31	13.08	14.16
SRC [28]	29.23	16.15	12.31	25.38	13.08	19.23
Edge-preserving SR [29]	26.92	21.54	15.38	24.61	15.38	20.77
$eBGPM_{(24;3)(32;4)}$ (circular)	28.46	24.62	16.92	20.77	20.77	22.31
$eBGPM_{(16;2)}$ (Type II_P)	34.62	25.38	20.00	25.38	21.54	25.38

Table 6.
Comparison of recognition rate (%) of the proposed eBGP descriptor with state-of-the-art descriptors on the SCface database at distance 2.

5. Conclusion

In this paper, an extended BGP (eBGP) descriptor, which incorporates macrostructure information into BGP descriptor, has been proposed to improve the overall descriptor performance in single-reference face recognition problem.

Results obtained from a series of experiments on the SCface database showed that a fusion of information extracted from micro- and macrostructures is capable of boosting up the performance of BGP descriptor. The proposed eBGP descriptor was tested with the patch-based and circular-based topologies; in overall, the circular-based topology outperformed the patch-based topology in terms of recognition rate. In patch-based topology, 5 × 5 structure recorded better hike in recognition rate than 3 × 3 structure, while in circular-based topology, larger spatial resolution showed better hike in the recognition performance. Moreover, a fusion of micro- and macrostructure information extracted from OIGM and grayscale image, respectively, raised the recognition rate higher. In fact, Type II_c setup always illustrated a better performance boost than Type I_c. With regard to thresholding implementation, it is worth to mention that local mean is on par with the local median for the descriptor and does not offer additional boost in the patch-based topology.

Acknowledgements

The authors highly acknowledge Universiti Sains Malaysia for its fund Universiti Sains Malaysia Research University Grant (RUI) no. 1001/PELECT/8014056.

Author details

Nuzrul Fahmi Nordin[1], Samsul Setumin[1,2], Abduljalil Radman[1,3] and Shahrel Azmin Suandi[1]*

1 Intelligent Biometric Group, School of Electrical and Electronics Engineering, Universiti Sains Malaysia, Nibong Tebal, Malaysia

2 Faculty of Electrical Engineering, Universiti Teknologi MARA Pulau Pinang, Permatang Pauh, Malaysia

3 Faculty of Engineering and Information Technology, Taiz University, Taiz, Yemen

*Address all correspondence to: shahrel@usm.my

References

[1] Radman A, Suandi SA. Robust face pseudo-sketch synthesis and recognition using morphological-arithmetic operations and HOG-PCA. Multimedia Tools and Applications. 2018;**77**(19):25311-25332

[2] Matta F, Dugelay J-L. Person recognition using facial video information: A state of the art. Journal of Visual Languages and Computing. 2009;**20**(3):180-187

[3] De-la-Torre M, Granger E, Radtke PVW, Sabourin R, Gorodnichy DO. Partially-supervised learning from facial trajectories for face recognition in video surveillance. Information Fusion. 2015;**24**:31-53

[4] Zakaria Z, Suandi SA, Mohamad-Saleh J. Hierarchical skin-AdaBoost-neural network (H-SKANN) for multi-face detection. Applied Soft Computing. 2018;**68**:172-190

[5] Lowe DG. Object recognition from local scale-invariant features. In: Proceedings of the Seventh IEEE International Conference on Computer Vision. 20-27 September; Kerkyra, Greece; 1999. pp. 1150-1157

[6] Bay H, Tuytelaars T, Van Gool L. Surf: Speeded up robust features. In: European Conference on Computer Vision. 7-13 May; Graz, Austria; 2006. pp. 404-417

[7] Ahonen T, Hadid A, Pietikainen M. Face description with local binary patterns: Application to face recognition. IEEE Transactions on Pattern Analysis and Machine Intelligence. 2006;**28**(12):2037-2041

[8] Dalal N, Triggs B. Histograms of oriented gradients for human detection. In: International Conference on Computer Vision and Pattern Recognition. 20-25 June; San Diego, CA; 2005. pp. 886-893

[9] Wold S, Esbensen K, Geladi P. Principal component analysis. Chemometrics and Intelligent Laboratory Systems. 1987;**2**(1-3):37-52

[10] Belhumeur PN, Hespanha JP, Kriegman DJ. Eigenfaces vs. fisherfaces: Recognition using class specific linear projection. IEEE Transactions on Pattern Analysis and Machine Intelligence. 1997;**19**(7):711-720

[11] Bartlett MS, Movellan JR, Sejnowski TJ. Face recognition by independent component analysis. IEEE Transactions on Neural Networks. 2002;**13**(6):1450-1464

[12] Ren J, Jiang X, Yuan J. Noise-resistant local binary pattern with an embedded error-correction mechanism. IEEE Transactions on Image Processing. 2013;**22**(10):4049-4060

[13] Ojala T, Pietikäinen M, Mäenpää T. Gray scale and rotation invariant texture classification with local binary patterns. In: European Conference on Computer Vision. June 26-July 1; Dublin, Ireland; 2000. pp. 404-420

[14] Huang W, Yin H. Robust face recognition with structural binary gradient patterns. Pattern Recognition. 2017;**68**:126-140

[15] Liu L, Lao S, Fieguth PW, Guo Y, Wang X, Pietikäinen M. Median robust extended local binary pattern for texture classification. IEEE Transactions on Image Processing. 2016;**25**(3):1368-1381

[16] Ojala T, Pietikäinen M, Harwood D. A comparative study of texture measures with classification based on featured distributions. Pattern Recognition. 1996;**29**(1):51-59

[17] Lee K-C, Ho J, Kriegman DJ. Acquiring linear subspaces for face

recognition under variable lighting. IEEE Transactions on Pattern Analysis and Machine Intelligence. 2005;**27**(5):684-698

[18] Martinez AM. The AR face database. CVC Tech. Report. 1998. 24

[19] Gross R, Matthews I, Cohn J, Kanade T, Baker S. Multi-PIE. Image and Vision Computing. 2010;**28**(5):807-813

[20] Phillips PJ, Rizvi SA, Rauss PJ. The FERET evaluation methodology for face-recognition algorithms. IEEE Transactions on Pattern Analysis and Machine Intelligence. 2000;**22**(10):1090-1104

[21] Huang GB, Ramesh M, Berg T, Learned-Miller E. Labeled Faces in the Wild: A Database for Studying Face Recognition in Unconstrained Environments. In: European Conference on Computer Vision Workshop on Faces in Real-life Images. October 200. pp.1-11

[22] Grgic M, Delac K, Grgic S. SCface—surveillance cameras face database. Multimedia Tools Applications. 2011;**51**(3):863-879

[23] Liu L, Fieguth P, Zhao G, Pietikäinen M, Hu D. Extended local binary patterns for face recognition. Information Sciences. 2016;**358**:56-72

[24] Liao S, Zhu X, Lei Z, Zhang L, Li SZ. Learning multi-scale block local binary patterns for face recognition. In: International Conference on Biometrics. 27-29 August 2007; Seoul, Korea;. pp. 828-837

[25] Liu L, Fieguth P, Guo Y, Wang X, Pietikäinen M. Local binary features for texture classification: Taxonomy and experimental study. Pattern Recognition. 2017;**62**:135-160

[26] Liu L, Zhao L, Long Y, Kuang G, Fieguth P. Extended local binary patterns for texture classification. Image and Vision Computing. 2012;**30**(2):86-99

[27] Martínez AM, Kak AC. Pca versus lda. IEEE Transactions on Pattern Analysis and Machine Intelligence. 2001;**23**(2):228-233

[28] Hu X, Peng S, Wang L, Yang Z, Li Z. Surveillance video face recognition with single sample per person based on 3D modeling and blurring. Neurocomputing. 2017;**235**:46-58

[29] Mandal S, Thavalengal S, Sao AK. Explicit and implicit employment of edge-related information in super-resolving distant faces for recognition. Pattern Analysis and Applications. 2016;**19**(3):867-884

Chapter 8

Matrix Factorization on Complex Domain for Face Recognition

Viet-Hang Duong, Manh-Quan Bui and Jia-Ching Wang

Abstract

Matrix factorization on complex domain is a natural extension of nonnegative matrix factorization, but it is still a very new trend in face recognition. In this chapter, we present two complex matrix factorization-based models for face recognition, in which the objective functions are the real-valued functions of complex variables. Our first model aims to build a learned base, which is embedded within original space. The second model finds the base whose volume is maximized. Experimental results on datasets with and without outliers show that our proposed algorithms are more effective than competitive algorithms.

Keywords: complex matrix factorization, face recognition, nonnegative matrix factorization, projected gradient descent

1. Introduction

Face recognition is a central issue in computer vision and pattern recognition. The variations in lighting conditions, pose and viewpoint changes, facial expressions, makeup, aging, and occlusion are challenges that significantly affect recognition accuracy. Generally, the challenges in face recognition can be classified into four main categories as follows:

Illumination variations: The face of a person can appear dramatically different when illumination changes. This occurs because of spectra or source distribution and intensity changes. In practice, many two-dimensional (2D) methods show that recognition performance is notably decreased when illumination strongly occurs [1, 2]. Therefore, the problem of lighting variation is considered as one of the key challenges for face recognition system designer. Several methods have been proposed to handle variable illuminations such as extraction of illumination invariant features [3–7]; images with variable illuminations transformed to a canonical representation [8, 9]; modeling the illumination variations [10–11]; facial shapes and albedos are based on 3D face models [12].

Pose/viewpoint changes: Deformed face and self-occluded face usually occur by pose or viewpoint changes which affect the recognition process [13]. Generally, viewpoint face recognition approaches are divided into two categories: viewpoint-transformed and cross-pose based [14]. Viewpoint transformed recognition methods aim to transform the probe image to match the gallery image in the pose, whereas cross-pose-based approaches attempt to estimate the light field of the face [15, 16]. Besides, other approaches integrated 2D and 3D information [17, 18] in order to cope with pose and illumination variations.

Facial expression: Face recognition tasks are more challenging when dealing with emotional states of a person in an image. In addition, hairstyle or facial hair such as beard and mustache can change facial appearance. To handle with difficulties of expression, facial expression recognition (FER) systems, including static image FER [19–21], and dynamic sequence FER [22–24] are designed. In static-based methods, the spatial information from the current single image is extracted to obtain the feature representation. In contrary, the dynamic-based methods consider the temporal relation among adjacent frames in the sequence of input facial expression.

Occlusion: Faces may be partially occluded by other objects such as sunglasses, scarf [62], etc. Other situations of occlusion are some faces may be occluded by other faces of a group of people [25]. It is very difficult to be observed and recognized because the available part of the face is very small. Therefore, occlusion problems become harder and need to be solved in face recognition.

In face recognition, image representation (IR) techniques play an important role in improving the accuracy performance. Commonly, an IR system is to transform the input signal into a new representation which reduces its dimensionality and explicates its latent structures. Over the past decades, the subspace methods, such as principal component analysis (PCA) [26], linear discriminant analysis (LAD) [27, 28], and nonnegative matrix factorization (NMF) [29, 30] have been successfully used in feature extraction. In particularly, PCA is known as a powerful technique for dimensionality reduction and multivariate analysis. PCA seeks a linear combination of variables such that the maximum variance is extracted from the variables by projecting data onto an orthogonal base which is represented in the directions of largest variance. In image representation, eigenfaces (PCA) result in dense representations for facial images, which mainly applied the global structure of the whole facial image. Likewise, LAD finds a linear transformation that maximizes discrimination between classes.

NMF is known as an unsupervised data-driven approach in which all elements of the decomposed matrix and the obtained matrix factors are forced to be nonnegative. Furthermore, NMF is able to represent an object as various parts, for instance, a human face can be decomposed into eyes, lips, and other elements. In order to make NMF algorithms more efficient, one has proposed some constraints into the cost function such as sparsity [31, 32], orthogonally [33], discrimination [34], graph regularization [35, 36], and pixel dispersion penalty [37]. Additionally, proposing an appropriate distance metric for an NMF model plays an important role in enhancing the efficacy of the estimated linear subspace of the given data. NMF techniques commonly apply the squared Frobenius norm (Fr) or the generalized Kullback–Leibler (KL) divergence for the independent and identically distributed noise data. But in many cases, they produce an arbitrarily biased subspace when data is corrupted by outliers [38]. To overcome this drawback, L_2 and L_1 norms were proposed by Kong et al. [39] to obtain a robust NMF, in which the noise was assumed to follow the Laplacian distribution. Similarly, the earth mover's distance (EMD) and the Manhattan distance were also suggested in the work of Sandler et al. [40] and Guan et al. [41], respectively. A family of cost functions parameterized by a single shape parameter beta, called the beta-divergence [42], is commonly used on NMF approaches. Although NMFs are able to learn part-based representations and capture the Euclidean structure of high-dimensional data space, they are still limited to comprise the nonlinear sub-manifold structure behind the data.

Recently, matrix factorization techniques have been extended to complex matrix factorizations (CMFs) where the input data are complex matrices. These models have been obtaining promising results in facial expression recognition and data representation tasks [43–45]. The main idea of complex methods for face and facial expression recognition is that the original signal is projected on to the complex field by a mapping such that the distances of two data points in the original space and projection space are equivalent. Particularly, by transforming the real values of pixel intensive to complex domain, it is shown that the squared Frobenius norm of corresponding complex vectors and the cosine dissimilarity of real-valued vectors are equivalent. As a result, the real optimization problem with cosine divergence is replaced by optimizing a complex function with the Frobenius norm. Most of the mentioned CMF models were applied to facial expression and object recognition.

In this chapter, we present two complex matrix factorization-based models for face recognition. In the following sections, we denote M-dimensional column vector $\mathbf{y} = (y_1, \dots, y_M)^T \in \mathbb{R}_+^M$ to be an observed sample. Let $\mathbf{Y}$ be a dataset comprising of N-observations; $\mathbf{Y}$ is expressed in the matrix form as $\mathbf{Y} = (\mathbf{y}_1, \dots, \mathbf{y}_N) \in \mathbb{R}_+^{M \times N}$, where $\mathbb{R}_+$ denotes the set of nonnegative real numbers. In the proposed models, the real data set $\mathbf{Y}$ is transformed to the complex domain, and the complex data matrix $\mathbf{Z}$ is factorized under imitating NMF frameworks. The contributions of this chapter are summarized as follows:

1. The image analysis methods on the complex domain, which are called structured complex matrix factorization (StCMF) and constrained complex matrix factorization (CoCMF), are proposed.

2. In complex domain, the updating rule for StCMF and CoCMF is derived based on gradient descent method.

3. A thorough experimental study on face recognition is conducted, the results show that the proposed StCMF and CoCMF yield better performance compared to extensions of the real NMFs.

2. Background

2.1 Nonnegative matrix factorization

Assume that we are given an initial data matrix $\mathbf{Y} \in \mathbb{R}_+^{M \times N}$ and a positive integer $K \ll \min\{\mathbf{M}, \mathbf{N}\}$. NMF methods aim to find a basis matrix $\mathbf{U} \in \mathbb{R}_+^{M \times K}$ and a coding variable matrix $\mathbf{V} \in \mathbb{R}_+^{K \times N}$, such that $\mathbf{Y} \approx \mathbf{UV}$. The standard NMF is usually formulated as an optimization:

$$\min_{\mathbf{U},\,\mathbf{V}} D(\mathbf{Y} \| \mathbf{UV}) \text{ s.t.} \mathbf{U} \geq 0,\ \mathbf{V} \geq 0 \tag{1}$$

where $D(\mathbf{Y} \| \mathbf{UV})$ is a divergence function to measure the distance between $\mathbf{Y}$ and $\mathbf{UV}$.

Most NMF techniques estimate the linear subspace of the given data by the Frobenius norm (F) or the generalized Kullback–Leibler (KL) divergence which have the following forms:

$$D_F(\mathbf{A} \| \mathbf{B}) = \|\mathbf{A} - \mathbf{B}\|_F^2 = \sum_{i,j} \left(\mathbf{A}_{ij} - \mathbf{B}_{ij}\right)^2 \tag{2}$$

$$D_{KL}(\mathbf{A} \| \mathbf{B}) = \lim_{\beta \to 0} D_\beta(\mathbf{A} \| \mathbf{B}) = \sum_{i,j} \mathbf{A}_{ij} \log \frac{\mathbf{A}_{ij}}{\mathbf{B}_{ij}} - \mathbf{A}_{ij} + \mathbf{B}_{ij} \tag{3}$$

The problem (1) is non-convex; thus, it may result in several local minimal solutions. To find an optimization solution, the iterative methods are commonly used.

Generally, there are three classes of algorithms for solving this problem including multiplicative update, gradient descent, and alternating nonnegative least squares algorithms. The most popular approach to solve (1) is the multiplicative update rules proposed by Lee and Seung [30]. For example, the iteratively updating rules of a Frobenius NMF cost function are given by

$$\mathbf{V}_{ij}^{(t)} \leftarrow \mathbf{V}_{ij}^{(t-1)} \frac{\left(\mathbf{U}^{(t-1)T}\mathbf{Y}\right)_{ij}}{\mathbf{U}_{ij}^{(t-1)^T}\left(\mathbf{U}^{(t-1)}\mathbf{V}\right)_{ij}}; \tag{4}$$

$$\mathbf{U}_{ij}^{(t)} \leftarrow \mathbf{U}_{ij}^{(t-1)} \frac{\left(\mathbf{Y}\mathbf{V}^{(t-1)T}\right)_{ij}}{\left(\mathbf{U}^{(t-1)}\mathbf{V}\right)_{ij}\mathbf{V}_{ij}^{(t-1)^T}}; \tag{5}$$

2.2 The cosine divergence

Given the representations of two images, $\mathbf{I}_t$ and $\mathbf{I}_s$ are M-dimensional vectors $\mathbf{y}_t$, $\mathbf{y}_s$ in the lexicographic order, respectively. First, $\mathbf{y}_t, \mathbf{y}_s \in \mathbb{R}^M$ is normalized to get the values $\mathbf{y}_t(c), \mathbf{y}_s(c) \in [0, 1]$, where c is the element vector index or the vector spatial location. The correlation between images $\mathbf{I}_t$ and $\mathbf{I}_s$ through the cosine dissimilarity between $\mathbf{y}_t$ and $\mathbf{y}_s$, is introduced by

$$D_C(\mathbf{y}_t, \mathbf{y}_s) = \sum_{c=1}^{M} \{1\text{-}\cos\left(\alpha\pi\mathbf{y}_t(\mathrm{c})\text{-}\alpha\pi\mathbf{y}_s(\mathrm{c})\right)\} \tag{6}$$

One of interesting properties of the cosine distance measurement is suppression outlier which is proved in [46]. The comparison between Frobenius norm and cosine divergence is showed in **Figure 1**. Liwiki et al. [46] show that the Frobenius distance between the original and the same subject is smaller; in contrary, a large distance between the original image and the image of a different person or occlusion image results from the cosine-based measure.

2.3 Euler's formula and a space transformation

Let us consider two mappings:
$g : \mathbb{R}^M \to \mathbb{R}^{2M}$ such that

$$g(\mathbf{y}_t) = \frac{1}{\sqrt{N}}\left[\cos(\mathbf{y}_t)^T \ \sin\left(\mathbf{y}_t\right)^T\right]^T; \forall \mathbf{y}_t \in \mathbb{R}^N \tag{7}$$

where

$$\cos(\mathbf{y}_t) = \left[\cos(\mathbf{y}_t(1)), \cos(\mathbf{y}_t(2)), \ldots, \cos(\mathbf{y}_t(M))\right]^T \tag{8}$$

$$\sin\left(\mathbf{y}_t\right) = \left[\sin\left(\mathbf{y}_t(1)\right), \sin\left(\mathbf{y}_t(2)\right), \ldots, \sin\left(\mathbf{y}_t(M)\right)\right]^T \tag{9}$$

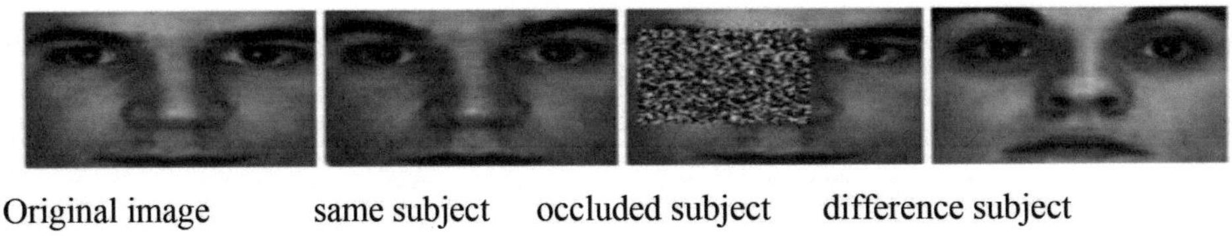

Figure 1.
Sample images for making comparison between dissimilarity measures.

$$\left\| g\left(\mathbf{y}_t\right)\right\| = 1 \tag{10}$$

and $h : \mathbb{R}^M \to \mathbb{C}^M$ is defined by

$$\mathbf{z}_t = h\left(\mathbf{y}_t\right) = \frac{1}{\sqrt{2}} e^{\,i\alpha\pi\mathbf{y}_t} = \frac{1}{\sqrt{2}} \begin{bmatrix} e^{i\alpha\pi\mathbf{y}_t(1)} \\ \vdots \\ e^{i\alpha\pi\mathbf{y}_t(M)} \end{bmatrix} \tag{11}$$

The nonlinear function h is to transform the real-valued features to complex feature space. In other words, a complex vector space with M-dimensions can be regarded as a 2 M-dimensional real vector space.

It is proven that the cosine dissimilarity distance of a pair of data in the input real space equals to the Frobenius distance of the corresponding data in complex domain [47]. This observation is the first motivation of StCMF and CoCMF by mapping the samples into the complex space with a nonlinear mapping function h and performing matrix factorization in this complex feature space.

2.4 Wirtinger calculus

Any function of a complex variable z can be defined as $f(z)|_{z=x+iy} = F(x,y) = U(x,y) + i\,V(x,y)$, where $i^2 = -1$ and x, $y \in \mathbb{R}$. Palka et al. [48] defined the complex differentiability as follows:

Definition 1. Let $A \subset \mathbb{C}$ be an open set. The function $f : A \to \mathbb{C}$ is said to be differentiable at $z_0 \in A$ if there is a limit $\lim_{z \to z_0} \frac{f(z)-f(z_0)}{z-z_0}$ which exists independently on the manner where $z \to z_0$.

A necessary condition for f being holomorphic is that the Cauchy-Riemann equations hold, that is, $\frac{\partial U}{\partial x} = \frac{\partial V}{\partial y}$ and $\frac{\partial U}{\partial y} = -\frac{\partial V}{\partial x}$; otherwise, it is nonholomorphic. In statistical signal processing, the functions of interest are real-valued and have complex arguments z and hence are not analytic on complex plane. In this case we can use Wirtinger calculus [49], which writes the expansions in conjugate coordinate system by considering the function $f(z)$ as a bivariate function $f(z, z^*)$ and treating z and z^* as independent arguments.

Definition 2. The pair of partial derivative operators for function $f(z) = f(z, z^*)$ referred to as the Wirtinger derivative [49] is defined by

$$\frac{\partial f}{\partial z} = \frac{1}{2}\left(\frac{\partial f}{\partial x} - i\frac{\partial f}{\partial y}\right), \frac{\partial f}{\partial z^*} = \frac{1}{2}\left(\frac{\partial f}{\partial x} + i\frac{\partial f}{\partial y}\right) \tag{12}$$

In case of real-valued function of complex variables, we also have one special property which is useful for optimization theory described later.

Lemma 1. The differential df of a real-valued function $f : A \to \mathbb{R}$ with complex valued $z \in A \subset \mathbb{C}$ can be expressed as

$$df = 2\,\mathrm{Re}\left(\frac{\partial f(z)}{\partial z^*} dz\right) \tag{13}$$

3. Complex matrix factorization

Let the input data matrix $\mathbf{Y} = (\mathbf{Y}_1, \mathbf{Y}_2, \ldots, \mathbf{Y}_N)$ contain N data vectors as columns. As described in previous sections, the elements of real matrix $\mathbf{Y}$ are normalized and transformed into a complex number field to yield the complex data matrix $\mathbf{Z}$. Two unconstraint and constrained optimization problems in an unordered complex field is introduced in the following sections, respectively.

3.1 Structured complex matrix factorization (StCMF)

The idea of structured complex matrix factorization (StCMF) is to build a learned base which is embedded within original space. The basis matrix in StCMF is constructed by the linear combination of the complex training examples. Given the complex data matrix $\mathbf{Z} \in \mathbb{C}^{M \times N}$, StCMF factorizes $\mathbf{Z}$ into the encoding matrix $\mathbf{V} \in \mathbb{C}^{K \times N}$ and the exemplar-embed basis matrix $\mathbf{U} = \mathbf{ZW}$ where $\mathbf{W} \in \mathbb{C}^{M \times K}$. Therefore, the objective function of StCMF problem can be formulated as follows:

$$\min_{\mathbf{W},\mathbf{V}} f_{StCMF}(\mathbf{W}, \mathbf{V}) = \min_{\mathbf{W},\mathbf{V}} \frac{1}{2} \|\mathbf{Z} - \mathbf{ZWV}\|_F^2 \tag{14}$$

where $\|.\|_F$ denotes the Frobenius norm and $K \ll \min\{N, M\}$

$$\begin{aligned} \text{and } \|\mathbf{Z} - \mathbf{ZWV}\|_F^2 &= Tr(\mathbf{Z} - \mathbf{ZWV})^H (\mathbf{Z} - \mathbf{ZWV}) \\ &= Tr\left(\mathbf{Z}^H\mathbf{Z} - \mathbf{V}^H\mathbf{W}^H\mathbf{Z}^H\mathbf{Z} - \mathbf{Z}^H\mathbf{ZWV} + \mathbf{V}^H\mathbf{W}^H\mathbf{Z}^H\mathbf{ZWV}\right) \end{aligned}$$

3.2 Constrained complex matrix factorization (CoCMF)

Considering a dataset of N complex vectors $\mathbf{Z} = [\mathbf{Z}_1, \mathbf{Z}_2, \ldots, \mathbf{Z}_N]$, each of $\mathbf{Z}_i$ represents a data instance. The proposed CoCMF model decomposes $\mathbf{Z}$ into a product of two matrices $\mathbf{W}$ and $\mathbf{V}$ such that each instance $\mathbf{Z}_i$ is a convex combination of latent components $\mathbf{W}$. We call $\mathbf{V}$ and $\mathbf{W}$ the encoding matrix and the basis matrix, respectively. Geometrically, the data points $\mathbf{Z}_i$, i = 1, 2, ..., N all lie in or on the surface of a simplicial cone $\mathbf{S}_\mathbf{W}$, whose vertices correspond to the columns of $\mathbf{W}$ and

$$\mathbf{S}_\mathbf{W} = \left\{ \mathbf{z} : \mathbf{z} = \sum_{i=1}^{K} \mathbf{W}_i \mathbf{v}_i; \mathbf{v}_i \in \mathbb{R}_+ \right\} \tag{15}$$

Note that $\mathbf{S}_\mathbf{W}$ lies in the positive orthant and the volume of $\mathbf{S}_\mathbf{W}$ (Vol ($\mathbf{S}_\mathbf{W}$)) is given by the following formula [48]:

$$Vol(S_\mathbf{W}) = \frac{|\det(\mathbf{W})|}{(K-1)!} \tag{16}$$

In [51], Zhou et al. illustrated that the small-cone constraint on the bases $\mathbf{W}$ will impose suitable sparseness on $\mathbf{V}$. Inversely, the large-cone penalty will result in sparseness on the bases of factorization and the reconstruction errors on the training data, and the test data will be simultaneously decreased [50, 52]. Therefore, all observed data can be reconstructed by linearly combining the bases of a dictionary. Combining the goals of enlarging the volume of the simplex base, the constrained complex matrix factorization (CoCMF) problem is formulated as follows:

$$\min_{\mathbf{W},\mathbf{V}} f_{CoCMF}(\mathbf{W},\mathbf{V}) = \min_{\mathbf{W},\mathbf{V}} \frac{1}{2}\|\mathbf{Z}-\mathbf{WV}\|_F^2 - \frac{|\det(\mathbf{W})|}{(K-1)!} \tag{17}$$

$$\text{s.t } \mathbf{W}\in\mathbb{C}^{M\times K},\ \mathbf{V}\in\mathbb{R}_+^{K\times N} \text{ and } \sum_{i=1}^{K}\mathbf{V}_{ij} = 1\ \forall j$$

Since $0 < \det(\mathbf{W}^T\mathbf{W}) \le 1$ holds under the assumptions $1^T\mathbf{W}_i = 1$. To simply the model, in this work, the log-determinant function is exploited to modify the volume penalty, and Eq. (17) can be written as the following form:

$$\min_{\mathbf{W},\mathbf{V}} f_{CoCMF}(\mathbf{W},\mathbf{V}) = \min_{\mathbf{W},\mathbf{V}} \frac{1}{2}\|\mathbf{Z}-\mathbf{WV}\|_F^2 - \log\left(\det\left(\mathbf{W}^T\mathbf{W}\right)\right) \tag{18}$$

$$\text{s.t } \mathbf{W}\in\mathbb{C}^{M\times K},\ \mathbf{V}\in\mathbb{R}_+^{K\times N}\ \sum_{i=1}^{K}\mathbf{V}_{ij} = 1, \text{ and } \sum_{i=1}^{K}\left|\mathbf{W}_{ij}\right| = 1\forall j$$

3.3 Complex matrix factorization via projected gradient descent

It can be seen that (12) and (16) are non-convex minimization problems with respect to both variables **W** and **V**, so they are impractical to obtain the optimal solution. These NP-hard problems can be tackled by applying the block coordinate descent (BCD) with two matrix blocks [53] to obtain a local solution. The specific problems (14) and (18) were solved by the following scheme:

Fixing **W** and solving the following one variable optimization problems

$$\min_{\mathbf{V}} f_{StCMF\_V}(\mathbf{V}) = \min_{\mathbf{V}} \frac{1}{2}\|\mathbf{Z}-\mathbf{ZWV}\|_F^2 \tag{19}$$

$$\min_{\mathbf{V}} f_{CoCMF\_V}(\mathbf{V}) = \min_{\mathbf{V}} \frac{1}{2}\|\mathbf{Z}-\mathbf{WV}\|_F^2 \tag{20}$$

$$\text{s.t } \mathbf{V}\in\mathbb{R}_+^{K\times N},\ \sum_{i=1}^{K}\mathbf{V}_{ij} = 1\ \forall j$$

Then, **W** is updated based on the Moore-Penrose pseudoinverse [54], which is dented by † and $\mathbf{W} = (\mathbf{Z}^\dagger\mathbf{Z})\mathbf{V}^\dagger$ for Eq. (14) and $\mathbf{W} = \mathbf{Z}\mathbf{V}^\dagger$ for Eq. (18) with fixed **V**.

Taking advanced of Wirtinger calculus, the gradient is evaluated in the forms

Algorithm 1: Complex projected gradient (CPG) with Armijo rule

Input: **Z**, **W**

Output: **v**

1. Initialize any feasible $\mathbf{V}_0$, $0<\beta<1$, $0<\sigma<1$

2. Iterations, for k = 1, 2, ...

$$\mathbf{V}_{k+1} = P[\mathbf{V}_k - \alpha_k \nabla_{\mathbf{V}^*} f(\mathbf{W},\mathbf{V}_k)]$$

where $\alpha_k = \mu^{t_k}$, t_k is the first nonnegative integer such that

$$f(\mathbf{W},\mathbf{V}_{k+1}) - f(\mathbf{W},\mathbf{V}_k) \le 2\sigma \mathrm{Re}\{\langle\nabla_{\mathbf{V}^*} f(\mathbf{W},\mathbf{V}_k), \mathbf{V}_{k+1}-\mathbf{V}_k\rangle\}$$

$$\nabla_{\mathbf{V}} f_{StCMF\_V}(\mathbf{V}) = -\mathbf{W}^H\mathbf{Z}^H\mathbf{Z} + \mathbf{W}^H\mathbf{Z}^H\mathbf{Z}\mathbf{W}\mathbf{V} \quad (21)$$

$$\nabla_{\mathbf{V}} f_{CoCMF\_V}(\overline{\mathbf{V}}) = \mathbf{W}^H\mathbf{W}\,\overline{\mathbf{V}} - \mathbf{W}^H\mathbf{Z} \quad (22)$$

$$\text{where } \overline{\mathbf{V}} = \left[\frac{\mathbf{V}_1}{\|\mathbf{V}_1\|_1}, \frac{\mathbf{V}_2}{\|\mathbf{V}_2\|_1}, \ldots, \frac{\mathbf{V}_N}{\|\mathbf{V}_N\|_1}\right]; \overline{\mathbf{V}} \geq 0 \quad (23)$$

We summarize the projected gradient method for optimizing (21) and (22) in **Algorithm 1**.

4. Experiments

To investigate the recognition performance of the proposed StCMF and CoCMF methods, we have conducted extensive experiments on the ORL dataset [55] and the Georgia Tech face dataset [56] in two scenarios for face recognitions including holistic face and key point occluded face.

First, we give brief description about the data collections and experiment setting. Second, the performance comparisons and corresponding results are shown.

4.1 Datasets and experiment setting

The ORL dataset contains 400 grayscale images corresponding to 40 people's face. The images were captured at different times, under different lighting conditions, with different facial expression (open or close eyes, smiling or non-smiling) and facial details (glasses or no glasses). All the face images are manually aligned and cropped. For the computational efficiency, each cropped image is resized to 28×23 for face recognition without occlusion and 32×32 pixels for face recognition with occlusion. **Figure 2** shows some instances of such random face on ORL dataset.

The Georgia Tech face dataset (GT) contains images of 50 people taken during 1999 and stored in JPEG format. For each individual, there are 15 color images captured at resolution of 640×480 pixels. Most of the images were taken in two different sessions to take into account the variations in illumination conditions, facial expression, and appearance. In our experiments, original images are normalized, cropped and scaled into 31×23 pixels, and finally converted into gray level images. Examples of GT dataset are shown in **Figure 3**.

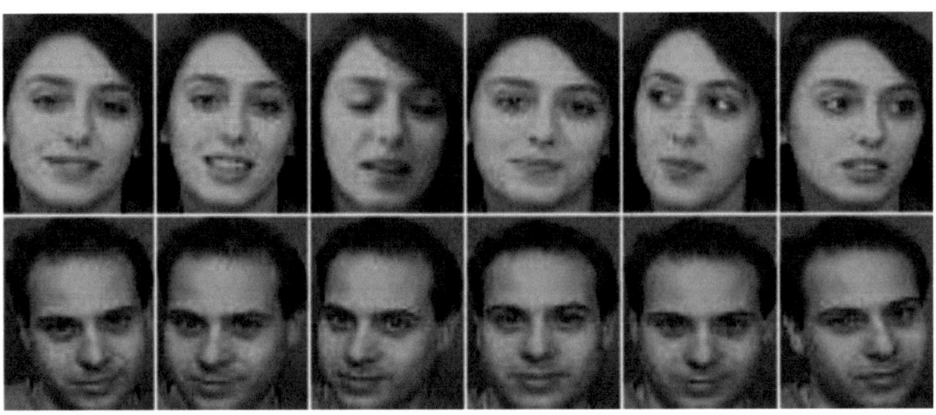

Figure 2.
Sample facial images from ORL dataset [55].

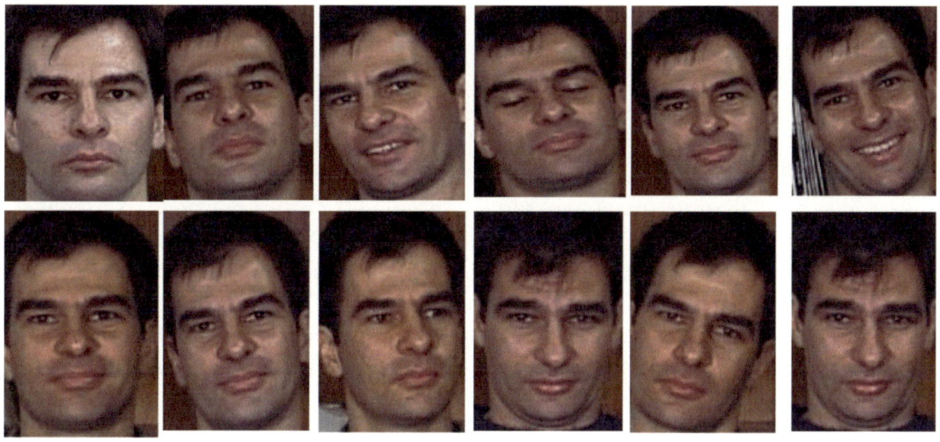

Figure 3.
Sample facial images from GT dataset [56].

We use the nearest neighbor (NN) classifier for all face recognition with/without occlusion experiments. The platform was a 3.0 GHz Pentium V with 1024 MB RAM running Windows. Code was written in MATLAB.

4.2 Performance and comparison

4.2.1 Face recognition on ORL dataset

For this case, in order to evaluate the performance of the proposed StCMF and CoCMF, we make the comparisons with seven representative algorithms, namely, NMF [29], P-NMF [57], P-NMF (Fr) [58], P-NMF (KL) [58], OPNMF (Fr) [59], OPNMF (KL) [59], NNDSVD-NMF [60], and GPNMF [60]. Different training numbers ranging from five to nine images were randomly chosen from each individual to construct the training set, and the rest images constitute the test set which was used to estimate the accuracy of face recognition [61]. The learning basic images in all selected algorithms are $K = 40$, and the mean recognition rate are described in **Table 1**.

Table 1 shows the detailed recognition accuracies of compared algorithms. As can be seen, our algorithms significantly outperform the other algorithms in all the cases. Almost algorithms achieve the best accuracy when the number of training face images per class is eight exceptionally our proposed methods and GPNMF. Besides, there is the same trend between the number of training images and accuracy rate; that is, the lower training numbers lead to a decreasing rate of

No. Trains	StCMF	CoCMF	GPNMF	NMF	PNMF	P-NMF (Fr)	P-NMF (KL)	OPNMF (Fr)	OPNMF (KL)	NNDSVD-NMF
5	**90.85**	**90.30**	86.5	84.5	82.4	83.7	85.0	80.0	79.0	43.0
6	**91.75**	**92.25**	87.5	84.4	85.81	85	84.4	83.0	82.0	39.3
7	**91.17**	**94.75**	87.5	83.3	87.33	85.6	85.9	84.4	80.0	36.8
8	**93.75**	**93.88**	88.75	88.75	88.5	88.8	88.0	84.3	83.0	40.8
9	**97.50**	**95.50**	92.5	85	90.75	87.25	87.5	84.0	83.0	42.3
Avg.	**93.00**	**93.34**	88.55	85.19	86.96	86.07	86.16	83.14	81.4	40.44

Table 1.
Face recognition accuracy on the ORL dataset with different train numbers.

recognition. StCMF achieves the best performance (97.50%) when the number of training samples is chosen largest. However, CoCMF achieves higher improvement in general.

It is observed that the above-selected algorithms employ a different kind of measurements such as Frobenius (Fr) and Kullback–Leibler (KL) and add more graph to regularize as well as adjust basic NMF to projective NMF. In a reprocessing image, centered aligning image technique is applied for other methods to enhance effective recognition rate that cannot be focused on our StCMF and CoCMF models. However, the best recognition rate of all obtained by our proposed CoCMF method which has extra regularizes term.

One of the difficulties in NMF is the estimation of the number of components or K. The choice of K results in a compromise between data fitting and model complexity; that is, a greater K leads to a better data approximation, but a smaller K makes a model being easier to estimate and fewer parameters to transmit. In almost NMFs, K is typically chosen such that it is larger than the estimated number of sources and follows the constraint $(N + M)K \ll NM$. This limit of NMFs illustrated by the observation that among all results, the lowest rate belongs to NNDSVD-NMF, one NMF method utilizes SVD to get initialization which results from significant independency of NNDSVD-NMF on the number of bases K.

4.2.2 Face recognition on GT dataset

Table 2 shows the recognition rates versus feature dimension by the competing methods on GT dataset. GT dataset exists with many challenging samples that are harder to recognize. Thus, the performance of all methods is lower than those of ORL dataset. In this dataset, the implement was done similarly as those in the previous section in choosing algorithms to compare as well as dividing randomly into two different sets, each containing a different number of testing and training images. In our experiments, we set $K = 50$ and range the number training being five odd numbers as {5, 7, 9, 11, 13}. The experimental results show that as the number of training images increases, the efficiency of the recognition system also increases. We can see that CoCMF method achieves the best performance and StCMF holds the second place in overall. All the methods obtain their best results when 13 training samples are used (the largest number of training sample in our experiment). In this case, the highest recognition rate belongs to the StCMF method again.

4.2.3 Face recognition on occluded ORL images

For a more convincing experimental assessment of the power of our proposed models in occlusion processing, we test the performance on occluded images of

No. Trains	StCMF	CoCMF	GPNMF	NMF	PNMF	P-NMF (Fr)	P-NMF (KL)	OPNMF (Fr)	OPNMF (KL)	NNDSVD-NMF
5	**39.64**	**59.40**	59.14	54.70	46.84	58.90	57.97	57.89	48.08	23.80
7	**54.80**	**62.25**	60.96	59.38	52.50	60.20	60.88	60.44	48.68	23.83
9	**75.20**	**69.67**	62.5	62.40	54.93	64.03	63.35	62.48	48.84	24.30
11	**69.50**	**70.50**	65.37	65.20	57.25	63.75	63.38	63.17	49.36	27.35
13	**77.60**	**73.00**	69.00	67.40	61.60	65.60	64.05	63.50	49.50	30.20
Avg.	**63.35**	**66.96**	63.39	61.82	54.63	62.50	61.93	61.50	48.90	25.90

Table 2.
Face recognition accuracy on the GT dataset with different train numbers.

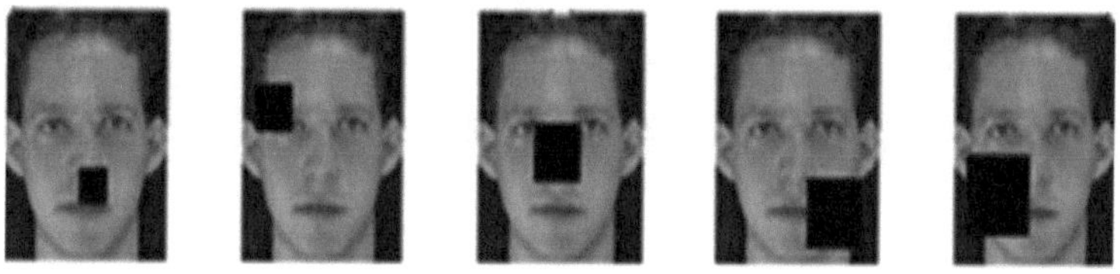

Figure 4.
Occluded face samples from ORL dataset with patch sizes of 15 × 15, 20 × 20, 25 × 25, 30 × 30, and 35 × 35.

Occluded Size	StCMF	CoCMF	GPNMF	NMF	PNMF	P-NMF (Fr)	P-NMF (KL)	OPNMF (Fr)	OPNMF (KL)	NNDSVD-NMF
15×15	**79.58**	**80.21**	75.16	74.32	72.55	69.16	71.25	74.18	45.16	54.46
20×20	**72.08**	**73.79**	64.52	65.45	62.15	67.52	71.23	65.00	41.52	25.62
25×25	**70.00**	**71.17**	65.54	55.18	52.38	65.54	62.19	55.00	35.54	19.83
30×30	**52.08**	**61.54**	54.53	45.62	43.87	48.53	55.21	45.89	28.53	13.22
35×35	**39.17**	**41.00**	43.25	33.63	31.06	43.25	38.79	33.39	23.25	16.13
Avg.	**62.58**	**65.54**	60.60	54.84	52.40	58.80	59.73	54.69	34.80	25.85

Table 3.
Face recognition accuracy on the occluded ORL image with different occlusion sizes.

ORL database. In cropped 112 × 92 dimension test image gallery, occlusion was simulated by using a sheltering patch with different size ranges in set {10 × 10, 15 × 15, 20 × 20, 25 × 25, 30 × 30} and placed at random locations before resized in 28 × 21. **Figure 4** shows examples of occluded ORL images.

In this experiment, we take randomly the training images with the ratio 4:6 for training/testing and test several times on each sort of percent of randomly occluded test image. **Table 3** shows the detailed recognition accuracy on all selected algorithms and our proposed methods. It can be seen that the recognition rate of all methods is increased when the size of occlusion batch is decreased. Obviously, StCMF and CoCMF outperform other tested approaches even if occlusion. This reveals that StCMF and CoCMF are more robust outlier than the other.

5. Summary and discussion

In this paper, we have proposed a new approach to complex matrix factorization to face recognition. Preliminary experimental results show that StCMF and CoCMF achieve promising results for face recognition by utilizing the robustness of cosine-based dissimilarity and extend the main spirits of NMF from real number field to complex field which adds flexible constraints for the real-valued function of complex variables. We have also noted how strong is the proficiency of StCMF as well as CoCMF on face recognition task. Our proposed methods are simple frameworks which do not need more complicated regularizes like NMFs in the real domain. We believe that this capability of proposed methods will be stable in other application tasks. In future work, three aspects of the proposed system will be centered on. First, we add more regularized rules into objective function to a range of further application such as speech and sound processing. Second, we employ other classifiers such as complex neural network or complex SVM to treat well the complex-valued feature. Last, kernel methods will be exploited in both feature extraction and classification of StCMF and CoCMF constructed paradigm to develop the performance of nonlinear contexts.

Acknowledgements

This research is partially supported by the Ministry of Science and Technology under Grant Number 108-2634-F-008-004 through Pervasive Artificial Intelligence Research (PAIR) Labs, Taiwan.

Author details

Viet-Hang Duong[1], Manh-Quan Bui[2] and Jia-Ching Wang[2,3]*

1 Faculty of Information Technology, BacLieu University, VietNam

2 Department of Computer Science Information Engineering, National Central University, Taiwan

3 Pervasive Artificial Intelligence Research (PAIR) Labs, Taiwan

*Address all correspondence to: jcw@csie.ncu.edu.tw

References

[1] Batur AU, Hayes MH. Segmented linear subspaces for illumination robust face recognition. International Journal of Computer Vision. 2004;**57**(1):49-66

[2] Chen T, Yin W, Zhou X, Comaniciu D, Huang T. Total variation models for variable lighting face recognition. IEEE Transactions on Pattern Analysis and Machine Intelligence. 2006;**28**(9): 1519-1524

[3] Gao XY, Maylor KHL. Face recognition using line edge map. IEEE Transactions on Pattern Analysis and Machine Intelligence. 2002;**24**(6): 764-779

[4] Guo B, Lam KM, Lin KH, Siu WC. Human face recognition based on spatially weighted Hausdorff distance. Pattern Recognition Letters. 2003;**24**: 499-507

[5] Adini Y, Moses Y, Ullman S. Face recognition: The problem of compensating for changes in illumination direction. IEEE Transactions on Pattern Analysis and Machine Intelligence. 2001;**19**(7): 721-732

[6] Lee KC, Ho J, Kriegman D. Acquiring linear subspaces for face recognition under variable lighting. IEEE Transactions on Pattern Analysis and Machine Intelligence. 2005;**27**(5): 684-698

[7] Han H, Shan S, Chen X, Gao W. A comparative study on illumination preprocessing in face recognition. Pattern Recognition. 2013;**46**(6): 1691-1699

[8] Zhao W, Chellappa R. SFS based view synthesis for robust face recognition. In: Proc. the 4th Conference on Automatic Face and Gesture Recognition. 2000

[9] Shashua A, Tammy RR. The quotient image: Class-based rerendering and recognition with varying illuminations. IEEE Transactions on Pattern Analysis and Machine Intelligence. 2001;**23**(2): 129-139

[10] Georghiades AS, Belhumeur PN, Kriegman DJ. From few to many: Illumination cone models for face recognition under variable lighting and pose. IEEE Transactions on Pattern Analysis and Machine Intelligence. 2001;**23**(2):643-660

[11] Ishiyama R, Sakamoto S. Geodesic illumination basis: compensating for illumination variations in any pose for face recognition. In: Proc. the 16th International Conference on Pattern Recognition. Vol. 4. 2002. pp. 297-301

[12] Gao W, Shan SG, Chai XJ, Fu XW. Virtual face generation for illumination and pose intensitive face recognition. In: IEEE International Conference on Acoustics, Speech, and Signal Processing. Vol. 4. pp. 776-779

[13] Ho H, Chellappa R. Pose-invariant face recognition using Markov random fields. IEEE Transactions on Image Processing. 2013;**22**(4):1573-1584

[14] Blanz V, Grother P, Phillips PJ, Vetter T. Face recognition based on frontal views generated from non-frontal images. In: IEEE Conf. Computer Vision and Pattern Recognition. 2005. pp. 454-461

[15] Gross R, Matthews I, Baker S. Appearance-based face recognition and light-fields. IEEE Transactions on Pattern Analysis and Machine Intelligence. 2004;**26**(4):449-465

[16] Wu G, Masia B, Jarabo A, Zhang Y, Wang L, Dai Q, et al. Light field image processing: An overview. IEEE Journal

of Selected Topics in Signal Processing. Special Issue on Light Field Image Processing. 2017

[17] Malassiotis S, Strintzis M. Robust face recognition using 2D and 3D data: Pose and illumination compensation. Pattern Recognition. 2005;**38**(12): 2537-2548

[18] Asthana A, Marks T, Jones M, Tieu K, Rohith M. Fully automatic pose-invariant face recognition via 3D pose normalization. IEEE International Conference on Computer Vision (ICCV 2011). 2011:937-944

[19] Shan C, Gong S, McOwan PW. Facial expression recognition based on local binary patterns: A comprehensive study. Image and Vision Computing. 2009;**27**(6):803-816

[20] Liu P, Han S, Meng Z, Tong Y. Facial expression recognition via a boosted deep belief network. In: Proc. the IEEE Conference on Computer Vision and Pattern Recognition. 2014. pp. 1805-1812

[21] Mollahosseini A, Chan D, Mahoor MH. Going deeper in facial expression recognition using deep neural networks. In: Proc. IEEE Winter Conference on Applications of Computer Vision. 2016. pp. 1-10

[22] Zhao G, Pietikainen M. Dynamic texture recognition using local binary patterns with an application to facial expressions. IEEE Transactions on Pattern Analysis and Machine Intelligence. 2007;**29**(6):915-928

[23] Jung H, Lee S, Yim J, Park S, Kim J. Joint fine-tuning in deep neural networks for facial expression recognition. In: Proc. IEEE International Conference on Computer Vision (ICCV). 2015. pp. 2983-2991

[24] Zhao X, Liang X, Liu L, Li T, Han Y, Vasconcelos N, et al. Peak-piloted deep network for facial expression recognition. In: European Conference on Computer Vision. Springer; 2016. pp. 425-442

[25] Aleix MM. Recognizing imprecisely localized, partially occluded, and expression variant faces from a single sample per class. IEEE Transactions on Pattern Analysis and Machine Intelligence. 2002;**24**(6):748-763

[26] Fukunaga K. Statistical Pattern Recognition. Acadamic; 1990

[27] Hyvarinen A, Karhunen J, Oja E. Independent Component Analysis. Wiley Interscience; 2001

[28] Belhumeur PN, Hespanha JP, Kriegman DJ. Eigenfaces vs. Fisherfaces: Recognition using class specific linear projection. IEEE Transactions on Pattern Analysis and Machine Intelligence. 1997;**19**(7):711-720

[29] Lee DD, Seung HS. Learning the parts of objects by non-negative matrix factorization. Nature. 1999;**401**(6755): 755-791

[30] Lee DD, Seung HS. Algorithms for non-negative matrix factorization. In: Proc. NIPS. 2000. pp. 556-562

[31] Hoyer P. Non-negative sparse coding. In: Proc. IEEE Neural Networks for Signal Processing. 2002. pp. 557-565

[32] Hoyer P. Non-negative matrix factorization with sparseness constraints. Journal of Machine Learning Research. 2004;**5**:1457-1469

[33] Li H, Adal T, Wang W, Emge D, Cichocki A. NMF with orthogonality constraints and its application to Raman spectroscopy. VLSI. 2007;**48**:83-97

[34] Guan N, Tao D, Luo Z, Yuan B. Manifold regularized discriminative nonnegative matrix factorization with fast gradient descent. IEEE Transactions on Image Processing. 2011;**20**(7): 2030-2048

[35] Cai D, He XF, Wu X, Han JW. Non-negative matrix factorization on manifold. In: Proc. IEEE Int'l Data Mining (ICDM '08). 2008. pp. 63-72

[36] Cai D, He XF, Wu X, Han JW, Huang TS. Graph regularized non-negative matrix factorization for data representation. IEEE Transactions on Pattern Analysis and Machine Intelligence. 2011;**33**(8):1548-1560

[37] Duong VH, Lee YS, Pham BT, Mathulaprangsan S, Bao PT, Wang JC. Spatial dispersion constrained nmf for monaural source separation. In: Proc. the 10th International Symposium on Chinese Spoken Language Processing (ICSLP). 2016

[38] Cichocki A, Zdunek R, Amari S. Csisz'ar's divergences for non-negative matrix factorization: Family of new algorithms. In: Proc. Int. Conf. Independent Component Analysis and Signal Separation. 2006. pp. 32-39

[39] Kong D, Ding C, Huang H. Robust nonnegative matrix factorization using $L_{2,1}$ norm. In: Proc. ACM Int. Conf. Information and Knowledge Management. 2011. pp. 673-682

[40] Sandler R, Lindenbaum M. Nonnegative matrix factorization with earth mover's distance metric for image analysis. IEEE Transactions on Pattern Analysis and Machine Intelligence. 2011;**33**(8):1590-1602

[41] Guan N, Tao D, Luo Z, Shawe-Taylor J. MahNMF: Manhattan non-negative matrix factorization [Online]. 2012. Available from: http://arxiv.org/abs/1207.3438

[42] Cichocki A, Cruces S, Amari S. Generalized alpha-beta divergences and their application to robust nonnegative matrix factorization. Entropy. 2011; **13**(1):134-170

[43] Duong VH, Lee YS, Pham BT, Mathulaprangsan S, Bao PT, Wang JC. Complex matrix factorization for face recognition [Online]. 2016. Available from: https://arxiv.org/ftp/arxiv/papers/1612/1612.02513.pdf

[44] Duong VH, Lee YS, Pham Ding JJ, Pham BT, Bui MQ, Bao PT, et al. Exemplar-embed complex matrix factorization for facial expression recognition. In: Proc the 42nd International Conference on Acoustics, Speech and Signal Processing (ICASSP 2017). 2017

[45] Duong VH, Bui MQ, Ding JJ, Lee YS, Pham BT, Bao PT, et al. A new approach of matrix factorization on complex domain for data representation. IEICE Transactions on Information and Systems. 2017;**E100-D** (12):3059-3063

[46] Liwicki S, Tzimiropoulos G, Zafeiriou S, Pantic M. Euler principal component analysis. International Journal of Computer Vision. 2013;**1**: 498-518

[47] Duong VH, Lee YS, Ding JJ, Pham BT, Bui MQ, Bao PT, et al. Projective complex matrix factorization for facial expression recognition. EURASIP Journal on Advances in Signal Processing. 2018;**10**

[48] Palka BP. An Introduction to complex function theory. Springer; 1991

[49] Wirtinger. Wirtinger Zur formalin Theorie de Funktionen von mehr komplexen Ver anderlichen. Mathematische Annalen. 1927;**97**:357-375

[50] Strang G. Linear Algebra and Its Applications. 4th ed. Belmont, Ca: Thomson, Brooks/Cole; 2006

[51] Zhou G, Xie S, Yang Z, Yang JM, He Z. Minimum volume constrained nonnegative matrix factorization: enhanced ability of learning parts. IEEE Transactions on Neural Networks. 2011; **22**(10):1626-1637

[52] Liu T, Gong M, Tao D. Large-cone nonnegative matrix factorization. IEEE Transactions on Neural Networks and Learning Systems. 2016. DOI: 10.1109/TNNLS.2016.2574748

[53] Kim J, He Y, Park H. Algorithms for nonnegative matrix and tensor factorizations: A unified view based on block coordinate descent framework. Global Optimization. 2013;**58**:285-319

[54] Barata JCA, Hussein MS. The Moore-Penrose pseudoinverse: A tutorial review of the theory. Brazilian Journal of Physics. 2012;**42**:146-165

[55] The ORL Dataset of Face. Website: http://www.cl.cam.ac.uk/research/dtg/attarchive/facedataset.html

[56] Dataset by Georgia Institute of Technology. Website: http://www.anefian.com/research/facereco.html

[57] Lin CJ. Projected gradient methods for non-negative matrix factorization. Neural Computation. 2007;**19**:2756-2779

[58] Yang Z, Yuan Z, Laaksonen J. Projective non-negative matrix factorization with applications to facial image processing. International Journal of Pattern Recognition and Artificial Intelligence. 2007;**21**(8):1353-1362

[59] Yang Z, Oja E. Linear and nonlinear projective non-negative matrix factorization. IEEE Transactions on Neural Networks and Learning Systems. 2010;**21**(5):734-749

[60] Boutsidis C, Gallopoulos E. SVD based initialization: A head start for nonnegative matrix factorization. Pattern Recognition. 2008;**41**(4):1350-1362

[61] Liu Y, Jia C, Li B, Pang S, Yu Z. Graph regularized projective non-negative matrix factorization for face recognition. Journal of Computer Information Systems. 2013;**9**(5):2047-2055

[62] Sharif M, Sajjad M, Jawad JM, Younas JM, Mudassar R. Face recognition for disguised variations using gabor feature extraction. Australian Journal of Basic and Applied Sciences. 2011;**5**(6):1648-1656

Chapter 9

Granular Approach for Recognizing Surgically Altered Face Images Using Keypoint Descriptors and Artificial Neural Network

Archana Harsing Sable and Haricharan A. Dhirbasi

Abstract

This chapter presents a new technique called entropy volume-based scale-invariant feature transform for correct face recognition post cosmetic surgery. The comparable features taken are the key points and volume of the Difference of Gaussian (DOG) structure for those points the information rate is confirmed. The information extracted has a minimum effect on uncertain changes in the face since the entropy is the higher-order statistical feature. Then the extracted corresponding entropy volume-based scale-invariant feature transform features are applied and provided to the support vector machine for classification. The normal scale-invariant feature transform feature extracts the key points based on dissimilarity which is also known as the contrast of the image, and the volume-based scale-invariant feature transform (V-SIFT) feature extracts the key points based on the volume of the structure. However, the EV-SIFT method provides both the contrast and volume information. Thus, EV-SIFT provides better performance when compared with principal component analysis (PCA), normal scale-invariant feature transform (SIFT), and V-SIFT-based feature extraction. Since it is well known that the artificial neural network (ANN) with Levenberg-Marquardt (LM) is a powerful computation tool for accurate classification, it is further used in this technique for better classification results.

Keywords: face recognition, plastic surgery, scale-invariant feature transform, (SIFT) feature, EV-SIFT feature, Levenberg-Marquardt-based neural network classifier (LM-NN)

1. Introduction

Human faces are multidimensional and complex visual stimuli, which contain useful information about the uniqueness of a person. Recognizing their faces used for security and authentication purposes has taken a new turn in the current era of computer image and vision analysis, for example, in monitoring applications, image recovery, man-machine interaction, and biometric authentication. Normally, the facial recognition system does not have the sense of touch or human interaction to complete the recognition process. This is one of the benefits of face recognition in relation to other recognition methods. Facial recognition can designate the verification phase [1] or the identification phase [2]. In the verification phase, the correspondence between two faces is resolved. There are many methods available to achieve facial recognition [3–8]. But the accuracy of recognition is not always high. This is due to variations in lighting levels, facial expressions, poses, aging, low-resolution input images, or facial markings [9, 10]. Several investigators have implemented several methods of face recognition to treat the effects of imposition [11] of illumination [12], low resolution [13], aging [14], or a combination thereof [15]. However, these uncertainties could be overcome, and, in the face of plastic surgery, recognition will intensify with the identification of the person. The fact that face recognition in plastic surgery is due to the lack or variation of facial components, the texture of the skin, the general appearance of the face, and the geometric relationship between facial features or variation of the facial components [16–18]. Plastic surgery, both economic and sophisticated, has attracted people from all over the world. However, only a few contributions or research methodologies have been reported in the literature to address the problem of face recognition of plastic surgery. Few of them include recognition by local region analysis [19], a local form of cascade texture function (SLBT) with periocular features [20]. A review was also carried out in [21] to illustrate the use of multimodal features in the recognition of plastic surgery on the basis of contributions.

1.1 Related works

De Marsico et al. [22] have made perfect recognition of the face, undergone cosmetic surgery, with region-based approach on a multimodal supervised architecture, also named as Split Face Architecture (SFA). Author proved dominance of their method by the application of supervised SFA to conventional PCA as well as FDA, toward LBP in the multiscale, rotation-invariant version with uniform patterns, face analysis for commercial entities (FACE), as well as face recognition against occlusions and expression variations (FARO).

Kohli et al. [23] enclose layout of multiple projective dictionary learning framework (MPDL) that never needs to figure norms to recognize usual faces, which have undergone modification via cosmetic surgery. Several projective dictionaries as well as compact binary face descriptors have been used to understand local and global plastic surgery face representations, in order to facilitate the distinction between plastic surgery faces and their original faces. The tests performed on the plastic surgery database resulted in an accuracy of about 97.96%.

Chude-Olisah et al. [24] has overcome the degradation of facial recognition performance; they have found that the approach had gone beyond the facial recognition approaches of cosmetic surgery before accessible, regardless of changes in lighting, facial expressions, and other changes resulting from cosmetic surgery. Ouanan [25] has introduced HOG feature-based facial recognition approach, which uses HOG as a substitute of DOG in the scale-invariant feature transform. Ouloul [26] introduces a perfect recognition approach for face using SIFT feature in RGBD images which depend on RGBD images produced by Kinect; this kind of cameras are low price, as well as it can be utilized in every setting and in several situations. Bhatt et al. [27] have proposed a multi-objective granular evolutionary method, which provides the pairing of images taken before and after in cosmetic surgery. Primarily, the algorithm generates superimposed face granules in three levels of granularity. Facial recognition in plastic surgery has undergone several developments in recent years. Contributions to the research were reported in the literature, either in the feature extraction phase, in the classification phase, or in both phases.

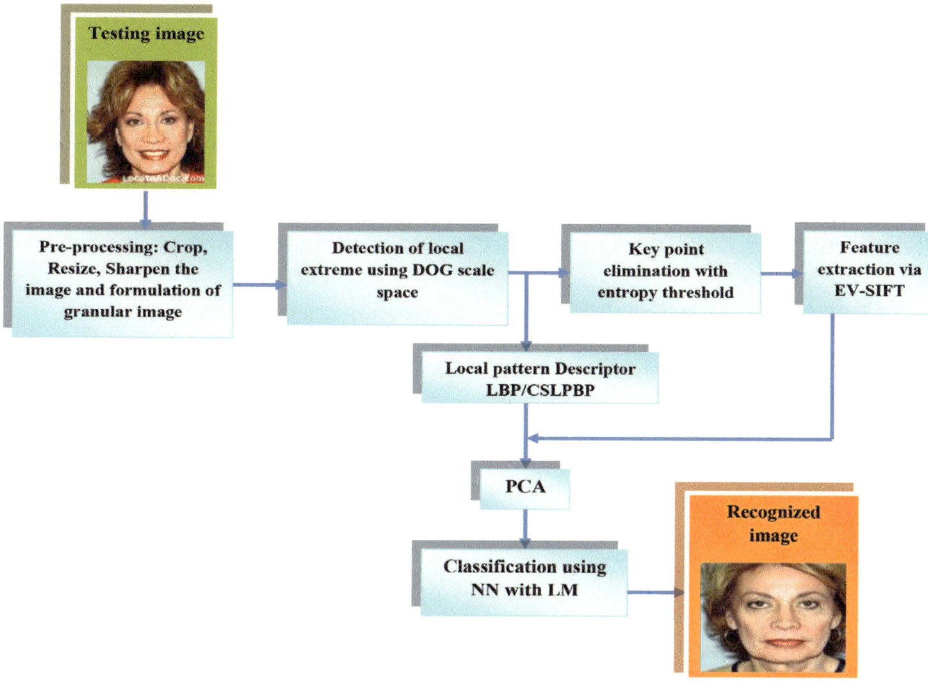

Figure 1.
Block diagram of the proposed granular approach for recognizing plastic surgery faces.

2. Granular approach for recognizing surgically altered face images using EV-SIFT and LM trained NN

The surgical face recognition is developed, which is based on the granular approach and Laplacian sharpening since it is identified that the sharpening of images will automatically enhance the cornerness and contrast of the image granules. Further, the key point elimination is done in this technique with entropy threshold, because entropy is the effective selection criterion that is used to eliminate the unreliable interest points. Since it is well known that the artificial neural network (ANN) with Levenberg-Marquardt (LM) is a powerful computation tool for accurate classification, it is further used in this technique for better classification results. The architecture diagram of the proposed face recognition technique is diagrammatically illustrated in **Figure 1**.

The testing image I^T is initially preprocessed, in such a way that the image I^T gets cropped, resized, and formulated granularly. Then the local extrema of the preprocessed image I_p^T is detected using DOG scale space. Moreover, in this proposed recognition technique, EV-SIFT descriptor is used to extract the features. The NN classifier with LM is also adopted for better classification.

3. Preprocessing: granular and Laplacian sharpening

This is the initial process with the input image I^T, where the image gets resized, cropped, and formulated. Two types of preprocessing are carried out, namely, Laplacian sharpening and granular processing.

3.1 Preprocessing-I

The image I^T from database is cropped and resized to 150 × 150.

Laplacian operator: This operator is also called derivative operator that is used to identify the edges in an image. The foremost difference among Laplacian and other operators such as Sobel, Prewitt, Kirsch, and Robinson is that all the mentioned operators are first-order derivative masks, whereas the Laplacian is the second-order derivative mask. Further, two classifications are there in this mask:

- Positive Laplacian operator
- Negative Laplacian operator

Moreover, one of the differences among the operators is that Laplacian will not use any corresponding direction. However, it uses edges in two classifications:

- Inward edges
- Outward edges

Positive Laplacian operator: This category has the standard mask, the center element of the mask is the negative element, and the elements that present in the corner of the mask must be zero, which is utilized to take the outward edges in the image, which is illustrated in **Figure 2**.

Negative Laplacian operator: This operator also has a standard mask, in which the center element must be positive; all the elements that exist in the corner must be zero, and the remaining mask elements must be −1. This operator is utilized to take the inward edges in the image, which is illustrated in **Figure 2**.

Working strategy of Laplacian: This operator deemphasizes the region in image by using gray-level discontinuities, and it is happened by slowly varying gray levels. The operation results in the image that has grayish edge line with dark background, which grants both the inward and outward edges in image. The filter application basically emphasizes two major strategies: it is impossible to apply both the operators (positive and negative); rather only one operator can be applied. If the positive operator is applied to the image, then the resultant image is subtracted from the original image to get the sharpened image. Same as this, if the negative

0	1	0
1	-4	1
0	1	0

(a)

0	-1	0
-1	4	-1
0	-1	0

(b)

Figure 2.
Standard mask of (a) positive Laplacian operator and (b) negative Laplacian operator.

Laplacian operator is applied to the image, then the resultant image is added to the original image for the sharpened image.

3.2 Preprocessing II

This is the foremost process of the developed model. Consider I as the nominated plastic surgery face image of $n \times m$ size. The face granules are formed with the consideration of three levels of granularity. The initial level outputs the information, namely, global information at multiple determinations. The inner and outer information from the face are resulted from the second level of granularity. Normally, features termed "local facial features" play a leading role in the recognition of face and therefore in the third-level extracts of the local facial features. The brief explanation of the three granularities is explained below:

First level of granularity: In this level, the face granules are generated by applying the Gaussian and Laplacian operators. In accordance with this, Gaussian operator gives the series of low-pass filtered image along 2D Gaussian kernel, whereas the Laplacian operator gives the sequence of band-pass images. Consider I_g^G as the granules that are resultant from Gaussian as well as Laplacian operators, where g denotes the granule number. If the face image is of size 196×224, the output image might be in the pyramid view with six granules I_{g1}^G to I_{g6}^G, and it may be either higher or lower determination. From the generated six granules, the facial features are separated at varied determination for providing blurriness, smoothness, edge information, and noise, which presents in I. Hence, the variations are compensated in this level with the alteration of face textures like skin resurfacing, dermabrasion, and facelift.

Second level of granularity: In this level, the face image I is divided into varied regions to get the horizontal granules I_{g7}^G to I_{g15}^G and the vertical granules I_{g16}^G to I_{g24}^G. The size of the first three granules is $n \times m/3$. From the size of the next three granules, the size of I_{g10}^G and I_{g12}^G is $n \times (m/3 - \in)$, and the size of I_{g11}^G is $n \times (m/3 + 2\in)$. Further, $n \times (m/3 + \in)$ is the size of I_{g13}^G and I_{g15}^G, and $n \times (m/3 - 2\in)$ is the size of I_{g16}^G. In the same manner, it generates the vertical granules. In this way, the second level grants the variations in both the inner and the outer facial regions. The variations that are present in the chin, cheek, ears, and forehead are denoted with the aid of relations among vertical and horizontal granules.

Third level of granularity: In general, humans classify individuals by identifying their local face regions like the eyes, mouth, and nose. This property is accomplished in this level, which extracts the local facial regions and is used as the granules. In eye coordinate, with the use of golden ratio face template, it is probable to extract 16 local facial regions. Every region is determined as the local information, in which it denotes the deviations due to the plastic surgery. This granularity preprocessing grants flexibility to deviations in both the inner and outer facial sections. It uses the relation among horizontal and vertical granules to view the deviations in the cheeks, chins, forehead, and ears that changed due to plastic surgery processes.

4. EV-SIFT, local binary pattern (LBP), and center-symmetric local binary pattern (CSLBP)

4.1 EV-SIFT

Consider the face image F_j and database I_i^D, where $i = 1, 2.......N_D$, which must satisfy the condition $F_j \subset I_i^D$ and $j = 1, 2.....N_S$, and the database size is given as

$(M \times N)$. The preprocessing phase initiates with resizing of image. The resizing model of the image is defined in Eq. (1), where S_M and S_N denote the scaled number of columns and rows:

$$I(x,y) = I_i(m_r, n_r) = \frac{1}{S_M * S_N} \sum_{u=(m_r-1)S_M}^{m_r S_M} \sum_{v=(n_r-1)S_N}^{n_r S_N} I_i(u,v) \quad (1)$$

In Eq. (1), $u \in [1, M]$ and $v \in [1, N]$, $0 \le m_r \le M_r - 1$ and $0 \le n_r \le N_r - 1$, $(M_r \times N_r)$ is the size of the resized image, and $[\cdot]$ denotes the round-off function of the nearest integer:

$$S_M = \left[\frac{M}{M_r}\right] \quad (2)$$

$$S_N = \left[\frac{N}{N_r}\right] \quad (3)$$

4.1.1 Acquisition of the EV-SIFT key points

Choosing the key points in the variation of the Gaussian function is the vital role to be considered. The parameters of the key point are purely depending on distribution property of the gradient operation of the image. Thus, the formulation of both the orientation and gradient modules is done, which registers the invariance toward the rotation of the image. The computation of orientation and gradient module is defined in Eqs. (4) and (5), where $\theta(x,y)$ denotes the orientation of key points and the gradient magnitude and $L(x,y)$ refers to the image sample:

$$\theta(x,y) = \tan^{-1}\left(\frac{(L(x,y+1) - L(x,y-1))^2}{(L(x+1,y) - L(x-1,y))^2}\right) \quad (4)$$

$$m(x,y) = \left(\sqrt{\begin{array}{l}(L(x+1,y) - L(x-1,y))^2 \\ +(L(x,y+1) - L(x-1,y-1))^2\end{array}}\right) \quad (5)$$

The scales used by L are the respective scale for each key point. Further, an orientation histogram is achieved as a result of gradient operation of sample points.

4.1.2 Entropy-based feature descriptor

The Changeable information is measured using entropy. It basically defines the statistical measure of randomness, which determines the texture of the input image. Only the least effect remains in the higher-order statistical feature due to the entropy on uncertain deviations in the face. The following steps show the entropy-based feature descriptor:

Step 1: The volume of the image is evaluated with the aid of V-SIFT formulation, which is determined in the matrix form as defined in Eq. (6):

$$V(i,j) = \begin{bmatrix} v(i_1,j_1) & v(i_1,j_2) & . & v(i_1,j_n) \\ v(i_2,j_1) & v(i_2,j_2) & . & v(i_2,j_n) \\ . & . & . & . \\ v(i_m,j_1) & v(i_m,j_2) & . & v(i_m,j_n) \end{bmatrix} \quad (6)$$

Step 2: The information basis is both memory less and static. The volume of the structure in EV-SIFT analysis is defined in Eq. (7), which is the probability function:

$$V_p(i,j) = \frac{V(i,j)}{\sum_i \sum_j V(i,j)} \quad (7)$$

Step 3: The computation of entropy is done from the volume of the structure. The entropy calculation for EV-SIFT process is determined in Eq. (8), which states that if $E(V)$ is high entropy, then the volume is from the unvarying direction, and if it is low entropy, then it means that the volume is a varied distribution. Thus, F_i^D describes the entire database that achieved the final EV-SIFT descriptor:

$$E(V) = -V_p(i,j) \log V_p(i,j) \quad (8)$$

The level of Gaussian blur of the image is selected by orientation and gradient magnitude with entropy, and also the volume of the image is also sampled in terms of scale of key points at particular key point location. The sample is an 8×8 neighbor window, which is centered on the key point and splits the neighbor into 4×4 child window. Hence, the formulation of gradient orientation histogram is done along with eight bins with the aid of each child window. In such a way that within each key point, each descriptor intends the 4×4 array of histograms that comprises eight bins. The feature vector attained is the size of $4 \times 4 \times 8$ = 128 dimension.

4.2 Local binary pattern (LBP)

LBP [1] operator is designed for texture description. It encodes the pixel-wise data in texture images, in such a way that a label is assigned to every pixel of the image. This is done by thresholding the 3×3 neighborhood of all pixel value with the center pixel, and the result must be a binary number. The basic LBP thresholding function $f^T(.,.)$ is defined as given in Eq. (9), where Y_i, $i = 1, \ldots 8$ is the eight neighborhood point around Y_0, which is shown in **Figure 3**. LBP in other words is termed as the concatenation of binary gradient direction, which is also known as "micro pattern":

$$f^T\left(I^T(Y_0), I^T(Y_i)\right) = \begin{cases} 0, & \textit{if } I^T(Y_i) - I^T(Y_0) \leq \textit{threshold} \\ 1, & \textit{if } I^T(Y_i) - I^T(Y_0) > \textit{threshold} \end{cases}, i = 1, 2, 3\ldots\ldots, 8 \quad (9)$$

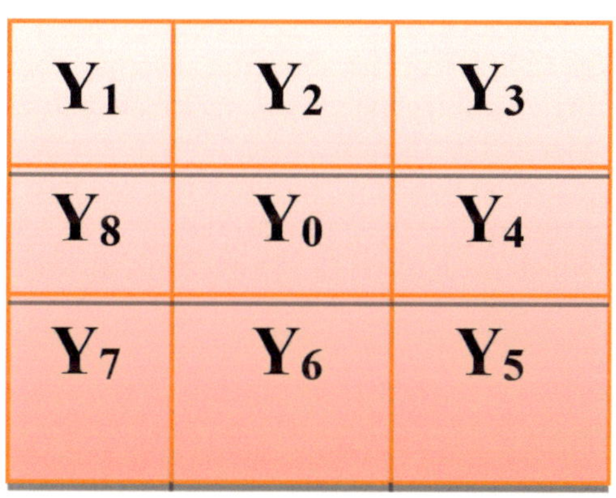

Figure 3.
Example of eight neighborhoods around Y_0.

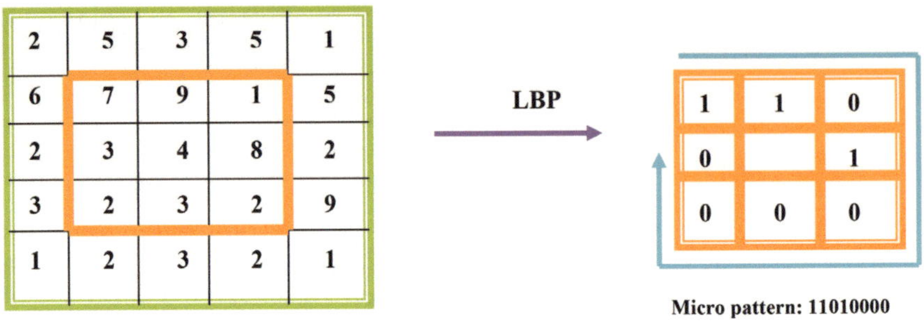

Figure 4.
An example for LBP micro pattern for a given region.

Figure 4 illustrates the sample of attaining an LBP micro pattern when the threshold is set to 0. Further, the resultant histogram of the micro pattern presents the data related to the distribution of edges, spots, and more local features that present in the image. It is observed that the LBP is a great tool for face recognition. Despite a number of static learning approaches that tune with more parameters, LBP is more effective since it has an "easy-to-formulate" feature extraction process, and also the matching strategy is also very simple.

4.3 Center-symmetric local binary pattern (CSLBP)

CSLBP [1] is established for interest region description. It purposes for least LBP labels to generate smaller histograms, which are well suited to utilize in region descriptors. Moreover, it is designed for better stability, especially in regions that include the face image. Here, the comparison of pixel values are not done between the pixels and center pixels; rather the opposing pixels are symmetrically compared in correspondence to the center pixel, which is defined in Eq. (10):

$$CSLBP_{S,T}(u,v) = \sum_{i=0}^{(S/2)-1} t\left(s_i - s_{i+(S/2)}\right), t(u) = \begin{cases} 1, & u > T \\ 0, & otherwise \end{cases} \tag{10}$$

where s_i and $s_{i+(S/2)}$ refer to the gray values of center-symmetric pairs of S similarly space out pixels.

In this work, the value of T threshold is 1% of pixel value. T is set to 0.01 since the data lies among 0 and 1. The size of the neighborhood is eight as illustrated in **Figure 5**. From the CSLBP formulation, it is evident that CSLBP is related to gradient operator, and also it considers the gray level G differences among pairs of contrary pixels in neighborhood. Thus, the CSLBP features show the advantage of both the LBP parameters and gradient features. CSLBP generates 16 varied binary patterns. Feature vector of every key point is generated by concatenating 128-dimensional descriptor as well as LBP [256-dimensional descriptor]/CSLBP [16-dimensional descriptor]. The feature vectors' dimensions are diminished to 25 dimensions by evaluating the covariance matrix for PCA, from which the highest 25 eigenvectors are chosen for description.

5. Recognition system: Levenberg-Marquardt-based neural network classifier (LM-NN)

In this work, LM-NN classifier is used for recognition purpose. The NN model is represented in Eqs. (11)–(13), where n denotes the hidden neurons, $w_{(bn)}^{(h)}$ refers to

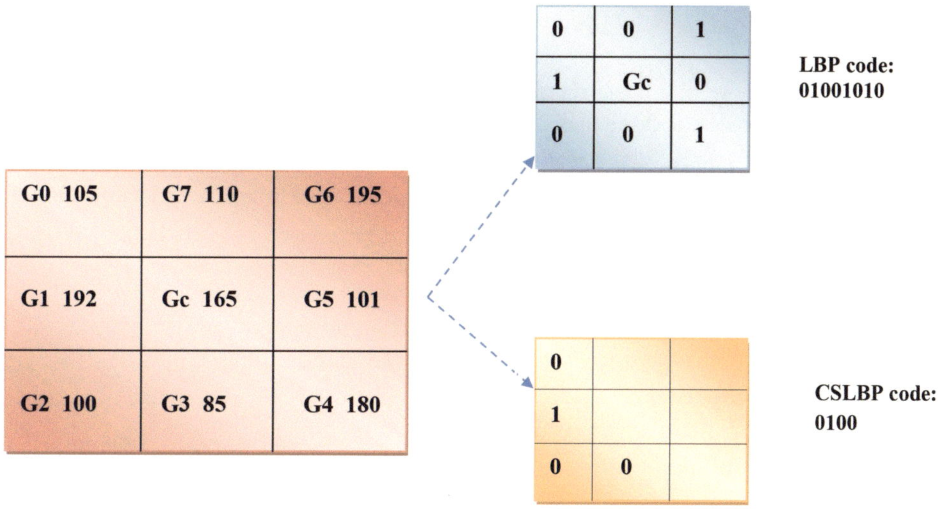

Figure 5.
CSLBP establishment.

the bias weight to n^{th} hidden neurons, and $w_{jn}^{(h)}$ represents the hidden neuron's weight. The input is the dimensional reduced features from PCA, which is denoted as f, $A^{(h)}$ is the output of the hidden layer that is defined in Eq. (11), and the nonlinear function is represented as $F(\bullet)$:

$$A^{(h)} = F\left(w_{(bn)}^{(h)} + \sum_{j=1}^{N^{(I)}} w_{jn}^{(h)} f\right) \tag{11}$$

where $N^{(I)}$ denotes the count of input neurons. $\hat{B}$ is the output of the network model that is defined in Eq. (12), where $w_{bk}^{(o)}$ is the weight of the output bias to k^{th} layer, $w_{ik}^{(o)}$ is the output weight from i^{th} hidden neuron to k^{th} layer, and $N^{(h)}$ is the count of hidden neurons. The weight w^* is optimally chosen by reducing the objective function, which is defined in Eq. (13), where B denotes the actual output and $N^{(o)}$ is the number of output neurons:

$$\hat{B} = F\left(w_{bk}^{(o)} + \sum_{i=1}^{N^{(h)}} w_{ik}^{(o)} A_i^{(h)}\right) \tag{12}$$

$$w^* = \underset{\left[w_{(bi)}^{(h)}, w_{ji}^{(h)}, w_{bk}^{(o)}, w_{ik}^{o}\right]}{\arg\min} \sum_{k=1}^{N^{(o)}} \|B - \hat{B}\| \tag{13}$$

Here, the LM algorithm is used for training the NN model. The error function$EF^{(w)}$ to be reduced is represented as the sum of squared errors among the target output B^T and the network model output $\hat{B}$, which is defined in Eq. (14):

$$EF^{(W)} = v^T v \tag{14}$$

where $W = W_1, W_2, \ldots\ldots\ldots W_N$, which presents all the weights of the network and v is the error vector which includes the error of all the training samples. While training with LM model, the growth of weight ΔW is obtained, and it is defined in Eq. (15):

$$\Delta W = \left(M^T M + \eta\right)^{-1} M^T v \tag{15}$$

where M is the Jacobian matrix and the learning rate to be updated is represented as η. The updation of η is done using α, which depends to the outcome. Particularly, η is multiplied by α, $(0 < \alpha < 1)$ decay rate when $EF^{(W)}$ minimizes, whereas when $EF^{(W)}$ increases, η is divided by α. The given pseudo-code shows the training process of LM.

Step 1 Initializing the weights W and parameter η (η=.01 (approx.))
Step 2 Sum of the squared errors is formulated on the entire $EF^{(W)}$ inputs.
Step 3 Increment of weights ΔW is computed using Eq. (14)
Step 4 Recomputing $EF^{(W)}$
Step 5 Use $W + \Delta W$ as the trail $W$and evaluate

```
If trail EF^(W) < EF^(W) in step 2 then
        W = W + ΔW
        η = η · α (α = 0.01)
        Back to step 2
else
        η = η/α
        Back to step 4
End if
```

6. Results and discussion

6.1 Experimental setup

The cosmetic surgery face recognition experimentation is conducted in MATLAB 2015a. The database including presurgery faces and postsurgery faces are downloaded from http://www.locateadoc.com/pictures/. The experimentation is performed for different plastic surgery faces. The total number of plastic surgery faces in the database is 460, where it comprises 68 images from blepharoplasty (eyelid surgery), 51 images from brow lift (forehead surgery), 51 images from liposhaving (facial sculpturing), 17 images from malar augmentation (cheek implant), 18 images from mentoplasty (chin surgery), 54 images from otoplasty (ear surgery), 75 images from rhinoplasty (nose surgery), 74 images from rhytidectomy (facelift), and 52 images from skin peeling (skin resurfacing).

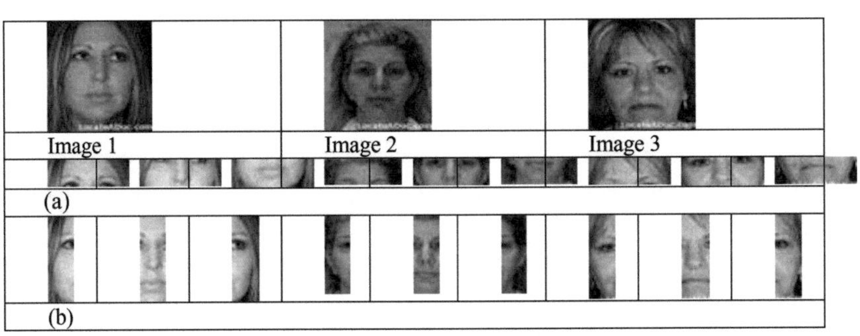

Figure 6.
Computation of granular images 1, 2, and 3. (a) Horizontal granules and (b) vertical granules.

6.2 Granularity preprocessing

By dividing the face image into varied regions, we get the vertical as well as horizontal face granules as illustrated in **Figure 6**. The horizontal granules are represented as R1, R2, and R3, and the size is 150 × 150/3. Similarly, the vertical granules are denoted as R4, R5, and R6, which is of 150/3 × 150 size.

6.3 Analysis on EV-SIFT

In this work, EV-SIFT descriptor is used for the feature extraction. **Figure 7** illustrates the original images. For each original image, the corresponding vertical edge and horizontal edge of the image were evaluated, and it is illustrated in **Figures 8** and **9**. The gradient magnitude of the images is also shown in **Figure 10**. Similarly, the theta images of the given input images are illustrated in **Figure 11**.

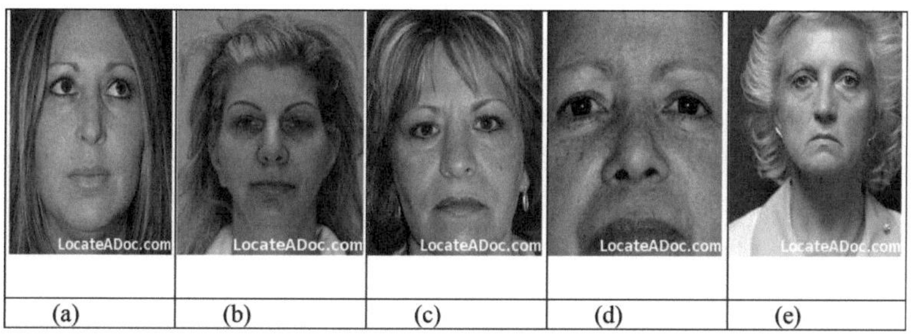

Figure 7.
Original images: (a) image 1, (b) image 2, (c) image 3, (d) image 4, and (e) image 5.

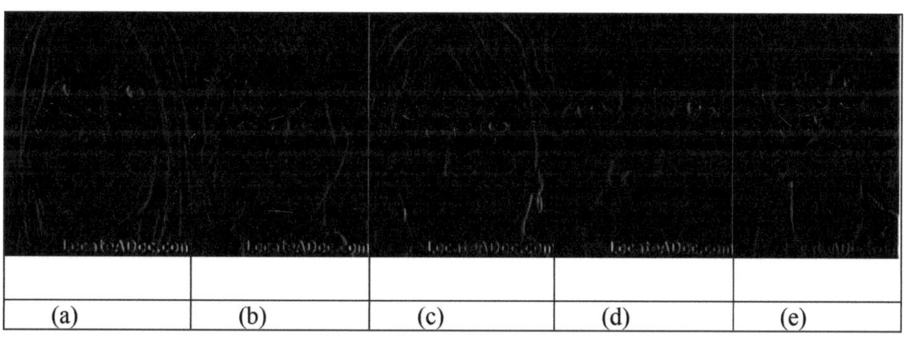

Figure 8.
Vertical edge of the given images: (a) image 1, (b) image 2, (c) image 3, (d) image 4, and (e) image 5.

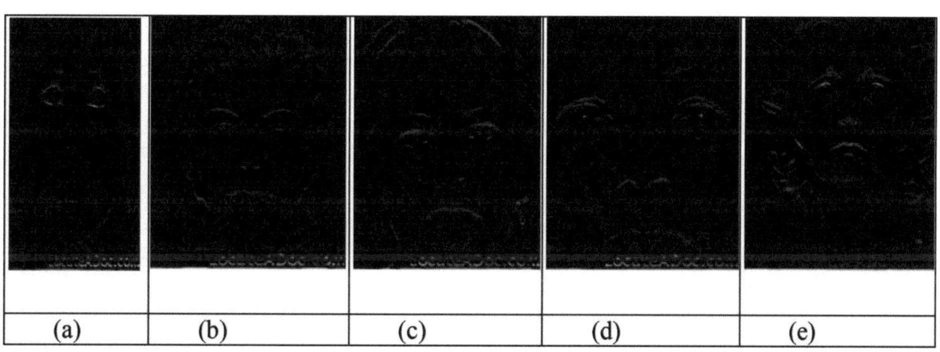

Figure 9.
Horizontal edge of the given images: (a) image 1, (b) image 2, (c) image 3, (d) image 4, and (e) image 5.

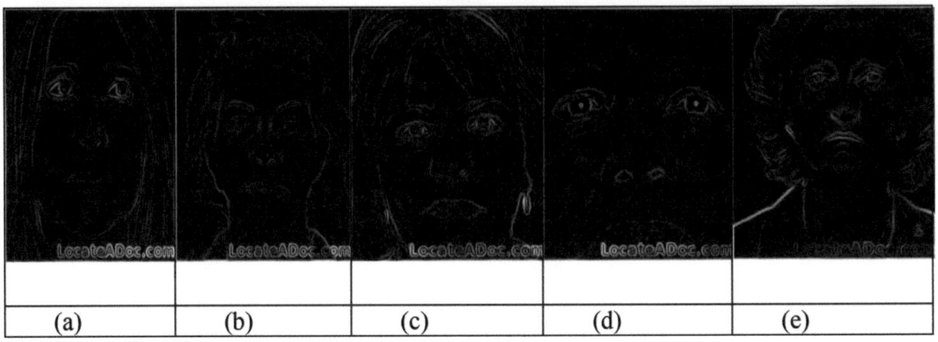

Figure 10.
Gradient magnitude of the images: (a) image 1, (b) image 2, (c) image 3, (d) image 4, and (e) image 5.

(a) (b) (c) (d) (e)

Figure 11.
Theta representation of the images: (a) image 1, (b) image 2, (c) image 3, (d) image 4, and (e) image 5.

One of the important processes is the evaluation of image orientation of the eight angles such as 0, 45, 90, 135, 180, 225, 270, and 315° in each image, which is shown in **Figures 12–16**. The resultant EV-SIFT contour of the input images is illustrated in **Figure 17**.

6.4 Learning performance of LM-NN

The performance of the LM-NN classifier is illustrated in **Figure 18**. It is observed that the best performance of the classifier is attained at the epoch 7, where the training performance is 0.00022204, gradient is 7.0363e-08, Mu is 1e-10, and the validation fail is 0 since there is no validation attained.

6.5 Comparative performance analysis of best-performing methods of proposed approaches

While analyzing the first research technique, in the evaluation on LM-NN, it is observed that the EV-SIFT proposed technique attained better results in all the measures like accuracy, sensitivity, specificity, precision, false-positive rate (FPR), false-negative rate (FNR), net present value (NPV), false discovery rate (FDR), and F1score (also F-score or F-measure) which is a measure of a test's accuracy and Matthews correlation coefficient (MCC), respectively. The evaluation is summarized in **Tables 1–3**.

It is observed that the proposed V-SIFT with LM-NN has achieved more over the conventional methods for various plastic surgeries, which is summarized in

DOI: http://dx.doi.org/10.5772/intechopen.85550

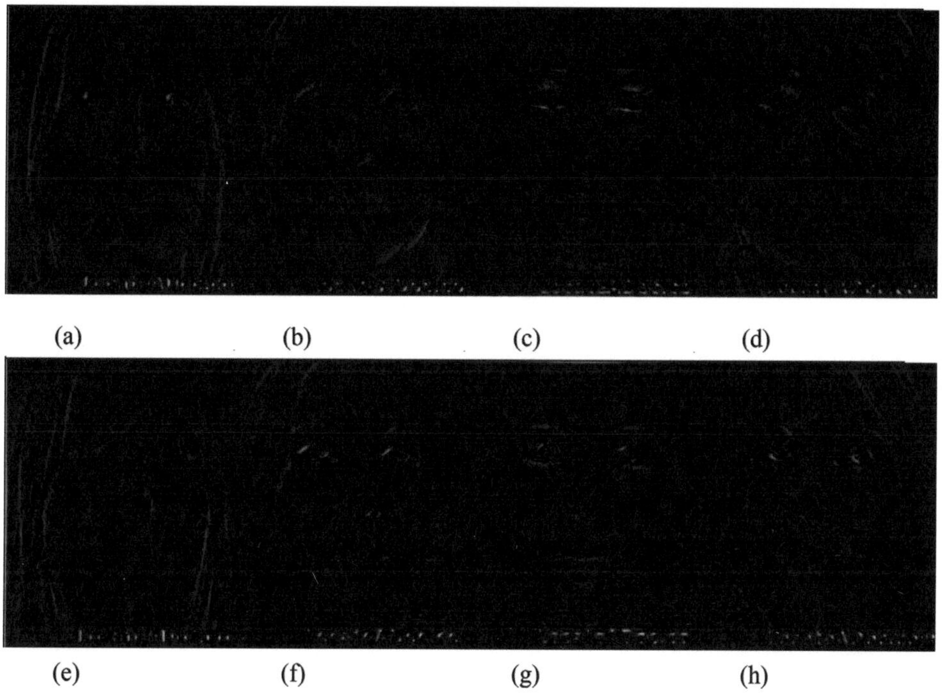

Figure 12.
Image orientation of eight angles (image 1): (a) 0°*, (b)* 45°*, (c)* 90°*, (d)* 135°*, (e)* 180°*, (f)* 225°*, (g)* 270°*, and (h)* 315°.

Figure 13.
Image orientation of eight angles (image 2): (a) 0°*, (b)* 45°*, (c)* 90°*, (d)* 135°*, (e)* 180°*, (f)* 225°*, (g)* 270°*, and (h)* 315°.

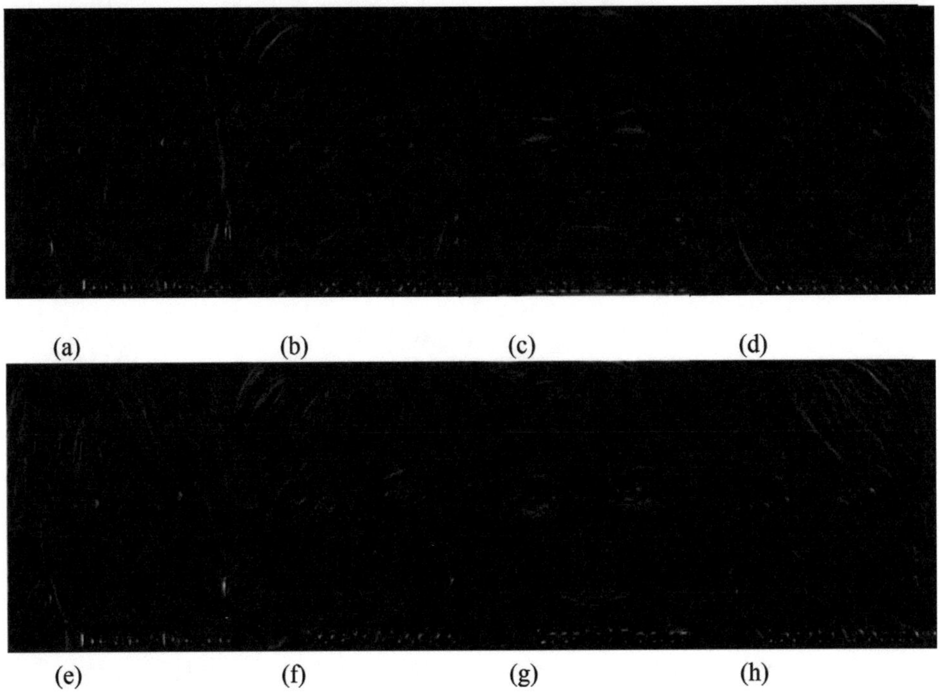

Figure 14.
Image orientation of eight angles (image 3): (a) 0°, *(b)* 45°, *(c)* 90°, *(d)* 135°, *(e)* 180°, *(f)* 225°, *(g)* 270°, *and (h)* 315°.

Figure 15.
Image orientation of eight angles (image 4): (a) 0°, *(b)* 45°, *(c)* 90°, *(d)* 135°, *(e)* 180°, *(f)* 225°, *(g)* 270°, *and (h)* 315°.

DOI: http://dx.doi.org/10.5772/intechopen.85550

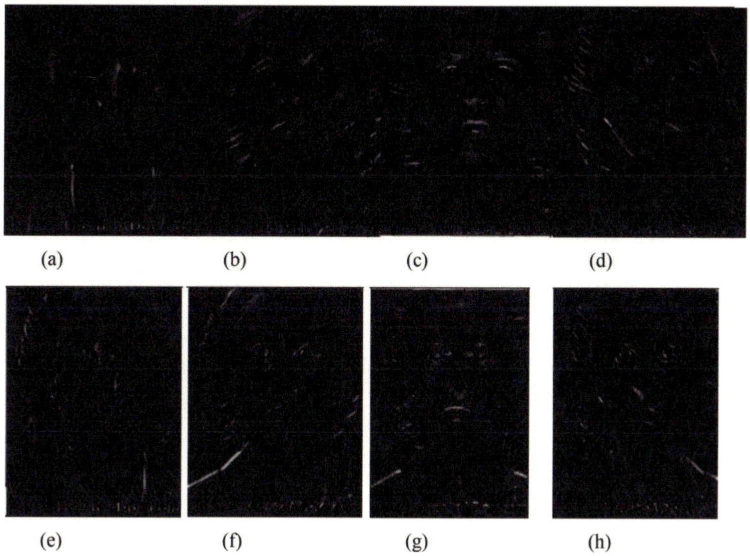

Figure 16.
Image orientation of eight angles (image 5): (a) 0°, (b) 45°, (c) 90°, (d) 135°, (e) 180°, (f) 225°, (g) 270°, and (h) 315°.

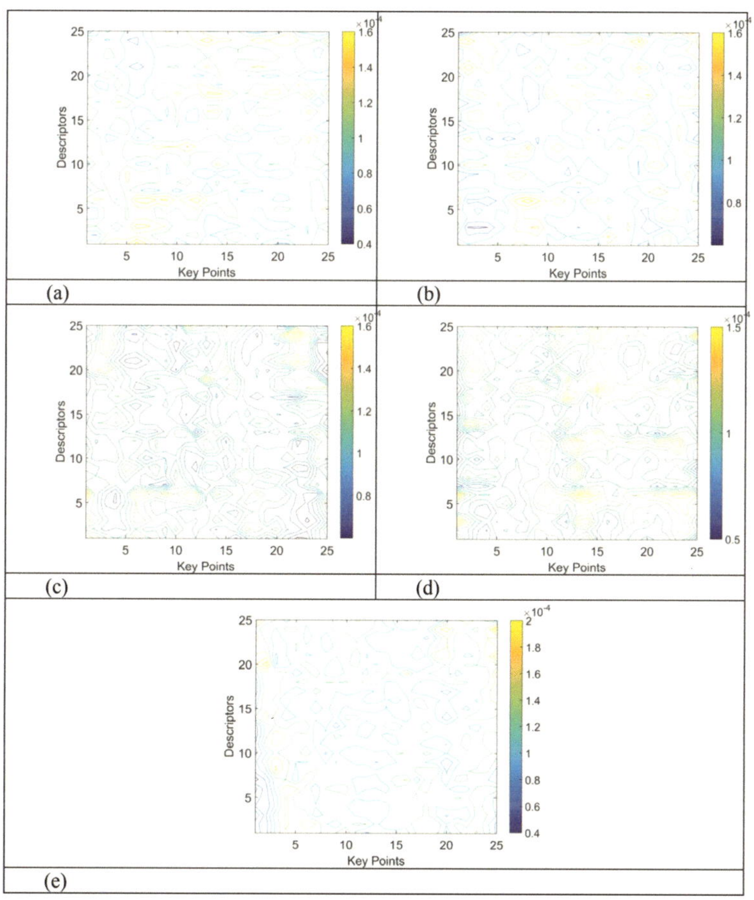

Figure 17.
EV-SIFT contour of images: (a) image 1, (b) image 2, (c) image 3, (d) image 4, and (e) image 5.

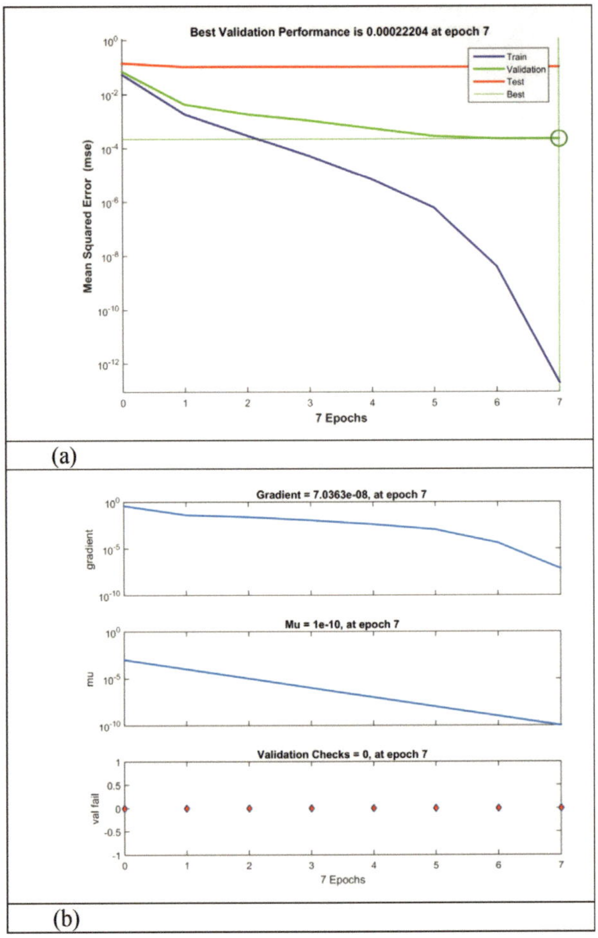

Figure 18.
Performance of LM-NN classifier in correspondence with (a) validation performance and (b) gradient, Mu, and validation fails.

	LM-NN	
Accuracy	Rhinoplasty	0.92
Sensitivity	Malar augmentation	0.24
Specificity	Rhinoplasty	0.97
Precision	Skin peeling	0.04
FPR	Rhinoplasty	0.03
FNR	Malar augmentation	0.76
NPV	Rhinoplasty	0.97
FDR	Skin peeling	0.96
F1score	Skin peeling	0.06
MCC	Skin peeling	0.04

Table 1.
Proposed SIFT with LM-NN of different plastic surgery faces.

	LM-NN	
Measures	**Surgery**	**Attained result**
Accuracy	Rhytidectomy	0.93
Sensitivity	Mentoplasty	0.19
Specificity	Rhytidectomy	0.97
Precision	Skin peeling	0.03
FPR	Rhytidectomy	0.03
FNR	Mentoplasty	0.81
NPV	Rhytidectomy	0.97
FDR	Skin peeling	0.97
F1score	Skin peeling	0.05
MCC	Skin peeling	0.03

Table 2.
Proposed V-SIFT with LM-NN of different plastic surgery faces.

	LM-NN	
Accuracy	Rhinoplasty	0.984
Sensitivity	Brow lift	0.17
Specificity	Rhinoplasty	0.97
Precision	Skin peeling	0.04
FPR	Rhinoplasty	0.03
FNR	Malar augmentation	0.83
NPV	Rhinoplasty	0.97
FDR	Skin peeling	0.96
F1score	Skin peeling	0.06
MCC	Skin peeling	0.04

Table 3.
Proposed EV-SIFT with LM-NN of different plastic surgery faces.

Table 2. It is observed that for all the measures, the method has attained better results, which also leads to the other types of plastic surgery.

From the second technique, it is observed that the proposed EV-SIFT with LM-NN are achieved more over the conventional methods for various plastic surgeries, which is summarized in **Table 3**. It is observed that for all the measures, the method has attained better results.

7. Conclusions

This chapter gives the detailed description of the second research technique. The feature descriptor EV-SIFT that is used for feature extraction is well explained. Further, the LM-based NN classifier is defined in this chapter, and the performance of both the EV-SIFT and LM-NN classifiers is shown in the Result section. The better work of EV-SIFT is effectively demonstrated in this section, which shows how the images are distinguished between them. The analysis of the LM-NN classifier is also more satisfactory with better performance.

Acknowledgements

To begin with, I express gratitude to God Shri Gajanan Maharaj, who provided me the potency as well as the ability to bring out this research. Additionally, I express my gratefulness to supervisor, Prof. S.N. Talbar, for his inspiration, priceless suggestion, and support along with concentration during exploration of research. I express thanks to every friend for giving out their experience and information. I also want to give an exceptional thanks to my companion for his honest advice and steady support to do a high-quality research.

Author details

Archana Harsing Sable[1]* and Haricharan A. Dhirbasi[2]

1 School of Computational Sciences, Swami Ramanand Teerth Marathwada University, Nanded, Maharashtra, India

2 Department of Mathematics, N.E.S. Science College, S.R.T.M. University, Nanded, Maharashtra, India

*Address all correspondence to: helloarchu27@gmail.com

References

[1] Sao AK, Yegnanarayana B. Face verification using template matching. IEEE Transactions on Information Forensics and Security. 2007;**2**(3):636-641

[2] Schwartz WR, Guo H, Choi J, Davis LS. Face identification using large feature sets. IEEE Transactions on Image Processing. 2012;**21**(4):2245-2255

[3] Turk MA, Pentland AP. Face recognition using eigenfaces. In: Proceedings of the IEEE Computer Society Conference on Computer Vision and Pattern Recognition; Maui, HI; 1991. pp. 586-591

[4] Ruiz-del-Solar J, Navarrete P. Eigenspace-based face recognition: A comparative study of different approaches. IEEE Transactions on Systems, Man, and Cybernetics, Part C (Applications and Reviews). 2005;**35**(3): 315-325

[5] Lawrence S, Giles CL, Chung Tsoi A, Back AD. Face recognition: A convolutional neural-network approach. IEEE Transactions on Neural Networks. 1997;**8**(1):98-113

[6] He X, Yan S, Yuxiao H, Niyogi P, Zhang H-J. Face recognition using Laplacianfaces. IEEE Transactions on Pattern Analysis and Machine Intelligence. 2005;**27**(3):328-340

[7] Inan T, Halici U. 3-D face recognition with local shape descriptors. IEEE Transactions on Information Forensics and Security. 2012;**7**(2):577-587

[8] Lu Z, Jiang X, Kot AC. A color channel fusion approach for face recognition. IEEE Signal Processing Letters. 2015;**22**(11):1839-1843

[9] Xu Y, Fang X, Li X, Yang J, You J, Liu H, et al. Data uncertainty in face recognition. IEEE Transactions on Cybernetics. 2014;**44**(10):1950-1961

[10] Jain AK, Klare B, Park U. Face recognition: Some challenges in forensics. In: 2011 IEEE International Conference on Automatic Face & Gesture Recognition and Workshops (FG 2011); Santa Barbara; 2011. pp. 726-733

[11] Sharma P, Yadav RN, Arya KV. Pose-invariant face recognition using curvelet neural network. IET Biometrics. 2014;**3**(3):128-138

[12] Lee S-H, Kim D-J, Cho J-H. Illumination-robust face recognition system based on differential components. IEEE Transactions on Consumer Electronics. 2012;**58**(3): 963-970

[13] Zou WWW, Yuen PC. Very low resolution face recognition problem. IEEE Transactions on Image Processing. 2012;**21**(1):327-340

[14] Park U, Tong Y, Jain AK. Age-invariant face recognition. IEEE Transactions on Pattern Analysis and Machine Intelligence. 2010;**32**(5): 947-954

[15] Mudunuri SP, Biswas S. Low resolution face recognition across variations in pose and illumination. IEEE Transactions on Pattern Analysis and Machine Intelligence. 2016;**38**(5): 1034-1040

[16] Singh R, Vatsa M, Noore A. Effect of plastic surgery on face recognition: A preliminary study. In: 2009 IEEE Computer Society Conference on Computer Vision and Pattern Recognition Workshops; Miami, FL; 2009. pp. 72-77

[17] Singh R, Vatsa M, Bhatt HS, Bharadwaj S, Noore A, Nooreyezdan SS. Plastic surgery: A new dimension to face recognition. IEEE Transactions on

Information Forensics and Security. 2010;**5**(3):441-448

[18] Liu X, Shan S, Chen X. Face recognition after plastic surgery: A comprehensive study. In: Computer Vision – ACCV 2012, Lecture Notes in Computer Science. Vol. 7725. Springer. pp. 565-576

[19] De Marsico M, Nappi M, Riccio D, Wechsler H. Robust face recognition after plastic surgery using local region analysis. In: Image Analysis and Recognition, Lecture Notes in Computer Science. Vol. 6754. Springer. pp. 191-200

[20] Lakshmiprabha NS, Majumder S. Face recognition system invariant to plastic surgery. In: 2012 12th International Conference on Intelligent Systems Design and Applications (ISDA); Kochi; 2012. pp. 258-263

[21] Gulhane AR, Ladhake SA, Kasturiwala SB. A review on surgically altered face images recognition using multimodal bio-metric features. In: Proceedings of the 2015 2nd International Conference on Electronics and Communication Systems (ICECS); Coimbatore; 2015. pp. 1168-1171

[22] De Marsico M, Nappi M, Riccio D, Wechsler H. Robust face recognition after plastic surgery using region-based approaches. Pattern Recognition. 2015; **48**(4):1261-1276

[23] Kohli N, Yadav D, Noore A. Multiple projective dictionary learning to detect plastic surgery for face verification. IEEE Access. 2015;**3**: 2572-2580

[24] Chude-Olisah CC, Sulong GB, Chude-Okonkwo UAK, Hashim SZM. Edge-based representation and recognition for surgically altered face images. In: Proceedings of the 2013 7th International Conference on Signal Processing and Communication Systems (ICSPCS); Carrara, VIC; 2013. pp. 1-7

[25] Ouanan H, Ouanan M. GaborHOG features based face recognition scheme. TELKOMNIKA Indonesian Journal of Electrical Engineering. 2015;**15**(2): 331-335

[26] Ouloul MI, Moutakki Z, Afdel K, Amghar A. An Efficient Face Recognition using SIFT Descriptor in RGBD Images. International Journal of Electrical and Computer Engineering (IJECE). 2015;**5**(6)

[27] Bhatt HS, Bharadwaj S, Singh R, Vatsa M. Recognizing surgically altered face images using multiobjective evolutionary algorithm. IEEE Transactions on Information Forensics and Security. 2013;**8**(1):89-100